*Victor Berger
and the Promise
of Constructive
Socialism,
1910 – 1920*

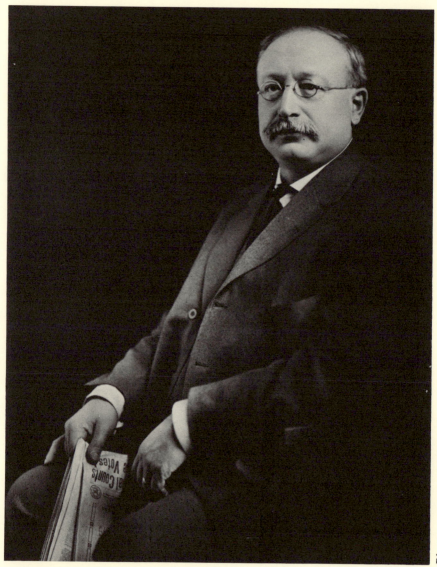

Victor Berger

"It is not always a disgrace to be
arrested. Sometimes it is an honor
to be arrested."

Victor Berger and the Promise of Constructive Socialism, 1910—1920

SALLY M. MILLER

Contributions in American History,
Number 24

GREENWOOD PRESS, INC.
WESTPORT, CONNECTICUT
LONDON, ENGLAND

Library of Congress Cataloging in Publication Data

Miller, Sally M   1937—
   Victor Berger and the promise of constructive
socialism, 1910-1029.

   (Contributions in American history, no. 24)
   Bibliography: p.
   1. Berger, Victor L., 1860-1929.   2. Socialist
Party (U. S.) I. Title.
HX86.M493   335′0092′4 [B]   72-175609
ISBN 0-8371-6264-5

Copyright © 1973 by Sally M. Miller

Library of Congress Catalog Card Number: 72-175609

ISBN: 0-8371-6264-5

First published in 1973

Greenwood Press, Inc. Publishing Division

51 Riverside Avenue, Westport, Connecticut 06880

Printed in the United States of America

To my parents, Clara and Robert Miller,
Whose generosity, adaptability, and strength
remain a tribute to the human spirit

Contents

Preface

A popular view holds that morality and politics are nonintersecting, or as more often expressed, that all politicians are unprincipled self-seekers. That this has been true of all too many may be granted easily, but nevertheless there have been men in political life who have attempted to walk the narrow line of principle in the larger world of compromise. Those who have chosen this difficult path are embodiments of Max Weber's teaching that a moral man can participate in an immoral world and yet retain his own soul.

In the Socialist party of America during the years in which it exerted some impact on American politics, one wing of the party attempted to translate hallowed principles into meaningful political action. Its conservative or reformist wing confronted the revolutionists of the party and believed that principled actions could create a more acceptable life within the existing American framework while simultaneously seeking to transform that system; it did not assume, then, that the only acceptable course was the realization of the world of tomorrow at one abrupt stroke. The reformist leader who bore greatest responsibility for shaping this Weber-like view and for emancipating the faction from traditional socialist dogmatism and immobility was Victor L. Berger of Milwaukee. He was the guide and mentor who sought to make his party relevant to the United States.

Berger and his wing dominated party machinery and policy in the movement's vibrant years, but surprisingly there has not yet appeared a study of this faction. Interpretations—valid or not—of the inevitability of socialist failure in the United States and analyses of the party's internal shortcomings do exist. But none examine the functioning of this dominant group and of Berger, a major influence on the party's evolution. Berger is of vital significance in tracing the rise and fall of the faction and the party; in many ways his own experiences paralleled those of the party's. This study attempts to fill the existing gap, following Berger and his wing in the most significant years in the lives of the man and the party.

A secondary but important role—and one which Berger played in the eyes of the public—was that of symbol of the right to dissent in wartime. As we in our own generation witness the conflict between individual rights and government imperatives, so an earlier act of this persistent drama occurred during World War I. Berger's publicized opposition to a national war brought him many of the ordeals familiar to the current period of social tension. He found himself subject to a trial for conspiracy and denied a congressional seat to which he had been elected. Such issues, while not the main thrust of his career, give Berger a contemporary and perennial significance.

All the major archives have been exploited in this study: the Socialist Party Collection at Duke University, the various collections housing the available papers of Victor Berger, and the Rand School Collection at the Tamiment Institute. The relevant documents of the period, published and otherwise, have been consulted. And finally, the various histories, which began to appear after World War II, have been examined. All of these stress the question of the time limits of party vitality. The early studies tend to terminate the growth of the Socialist party prematurely at 1912. This is true of the surveys by Daniel Bell and David A. Shannon and the monograph by Ira Kipnis. Recent publications, such as those of James Weinstein, have demonstrated convincingly that it was World War I and its aftermath which broke the party. That interpretation is developed further here, as accompaniment to the central theme.

Stockton, California
April 6, 1971

It should be added that the manuscript was completed in the winter of 1970-1971.

Acknowledgments

I wish to express grateful appreciation to Professor Kenneth W. McNaught of the Department of History of the University of Toronto who was consistently helpful in the preparation of this work and generous of his time. Gratitude is extended to: Mrs. Louise Heinze of the Tamiment Institute, whose library offers the most congenial atmosphere for research which I have encountered; Mrs. Virginia R. Gray of the Duke University Library; Director Harry H. Anderson of the Milwaukee County Historical Society; Mr. Paul G. Sotirin of the Milwaukee Public Library; and Dr. Josephine L. Harper, Manuscripts Curator of the State Historical Society of Wisconsin. Gratitude must also be expressed for a Province of Ontario Graduate Fellowship through which the original research was supported some years ago and for a University of the Pacific Research Grant, which eased the burden of the final manuscript preparation costs. Thanks also to three former students, Terry Smith Milne, Charlotte Nelson, and Sherry Holm, who typed the manuscript in its various drafts and who demonstrated varying degrees of enthusiasm and patience as the project continued.

I would like to give grateful thanks to the following for permission to reprint material which has appeared elsewhere: the Milwaukee County Historical Society for my "A Socialist Represents Milwaukee," *Historical Messenger* 22 (December 1966): 132-138; Frederick I. Olson for his "The Milwaukee Socialists, 1897-1941" (Ph.D. diss., Harvard University, 1952); and to the editors of *Science and Society* for my "Socialist Party Decline and World War One: Bibliography and Interpretation" (Winter 1970): 398-411.

Finally, warmest thanks must be expressed to Dr. Joseph Levitt of the Department of History of the University of Ottawa for thoughtful suggestions, expressions of confidence, and perceptive insights and criticisms over several years of discussions of our mutual research interests. Also to Dr. Mary E. Tomkins of the Department of American Thought and Language of Michigan State University for substantive and editorial suggestions during the particularly harried days of last-minute editing. And, especially, to Margaret J. Keranen for invaluable assistance in meticulous attention to detail and in extensive revisions and rewritings along the way: thanks unbounded.

Victor Berger and the Promise of Constructive Socialism, 1910 – 1920

1

Introduction

Fifty years ago, Max Weber explored the relationship between ethics and politics. In a lecture entitled "Politics as a Vocation" he confronted his students with the ethical paradox of politics based on principle and outlined the dilemma inherent in the life of any responsible politician in modern society.

In simpler societies than our own, the dilemma was not absolute. If a public figure had serious criticisms of the existing procedures, he could effect desired changes relatively swiftly via a new edict or a sudden forced alteration in power relationships. Weber pointed out, however, that the complex societies of modern times have greatly magnified the problems involved in effecting change. A great gulf exists between the struggle over means and the achievement of the end, with many shifts required to produce essential change which previously one blow might accomplish. Thus, the issue posed for a modern politician having a commitment to change in the status quo becomes that of cooperation with the existing system.

The politician may function within the system while simultaneously attempting certain modifications aimed at molding the society in accord with his own perspective. If he follows this path, the inherent danger is that of circumscribing his own goals; his reforms of the system which he ultimately wishes to reject may prolong the life of the system.

3

The opposite alternative is to refuse entirely to work within the system of which he disapproves. In this instance, he may live outside the political process, either as an outlaw attempting to undermine the system through illegal means or as an uninvolved propagandist attempting to impose a new order. While this choice may enable him, unlike the participating reformer, to maintain his own integrity, the cost is aloofness from society and reality.

Weber argued that in the extreme, the choice before a conscientious political dissenter becomes either the ethic of responsibility or the ethic of ultimate ends. While denying that the former inevitably means opportunism and the latter irresponsibility, Weber cited these as possible pitfalls. To follow the ethic of responsibility means participation in the public process in order to achieve that which is possible. To adhere to the ethic of ultimate ends is to ignore the daily processes and concentrate on the final goal, unconcerned with immediate needs and problems. In the first instance, the hope for eventual achievement of a long-range goal may be irretrievably lost, while in the second, the ultimate ends may be discredited because the spokesmen have been totally unconcerned about the immediate.[1]

For any individual or organization tied to certain prescribed principles, the dilemma as to whether or not to participate in the existing situation is crucial. A pacifist is faced with a quandary when his own nation goes to war. He must first determine whether the particular war does in fact merit his support in a noncombatant role or whether he must reject the war *in toto*, and accept the penalties. The royalist living in a republic is confronted with the dilemma of accepting the undesirable form of government while meantime supporting the cause of the pretender to the throne, or refusing entirely to recognize the existing system. Similarly, a theist is faced with a difficult choice when a government based on an atheistic posture triumphs. Should he attempt to mold and reform the new government or should he follow the dictates of his own conscience and refuse a relationship to it? Should he risk violation of his own principles for the sake of participation in a world not of his own choosing? Should he, in short, merely live in the world or should he be of the world as well?

While Weber gave this dilemma its classical delineation, he has not been the only one to deal with it. Others, both before and after his analysis, have considered the problem of a moral man attempting to make a series of choices in what is to him an immoral, or less than perfect, society. The general conception of the ethical paradox has been that the individual makes his choice between the two contrasting positions; he either follows the ethic of responsibility at the cost of his own soul, or he follows the ethic of ultimate ends at the price of immobilizing himself from immediate action.[2]

Weber, however, did not believe that the two ethics were invariably contrasts. He argued that a mature politician was able to adhere to both ethics as supplementary to one another. A mature, and thus responsible, individual seeking alterations in the status quo will attempt to act within the existing framework of his society while working toward his eventual goal. He will play an active role which takes into consideration the consequences of his choices and relates them to the principles upon which he stands. His is then a life of involvement and participation. His actions, however, are based upon his precepts, and when further participation in the political order would violate his basic principles, he withdraws. At that point he separates himself from politics as the art of the possible, and, in so doing, he becomes what Weber describes as "a genuine man—a man who *can* have the 'calling for politics.' "[3]

Weber's belief that the dilemma of the relationship between ethics and politics is soluble can be explored through the various socialist parties of the western world. These political parties, far more than others, represented an effort to adhere to basic principles in opposition to the existing framework while at the same time working for change in the system. The inherent paradox has been evaluated by different writers who have not explicitly set out to relate their analyses to Weber's thesis. They tend implicitly to accept the view of the basic contrast but never reach Weber's conclusion on the possibility of drawing the two ethics into a symbiotic relationship.

It would be instructive to investigate the dilemma of a socialist party in its attempt to work within the status quo in order to alter it in accord with party principle, and to determine whether or not the two ethics have been brought together. Before dealing with the Socialist party of America, the position of the Social Democratic party of Weber's Germany will be examined briefly since that party was the first to grapple with the dilemma on a wide scale.

The SPD was the first socialist party to win mass acceptance leading to electoral success; such success caused the party to confront its own theoretical foundations which appeared to proscribe its political posture. While Weber himself was not intimately concerned with the SPD, he noted the party's effort to avoid staining itself by participating fully in the parliamentary system.[4]

In 1890, the German socialists won full recognition as a political party, as the Anti-Socialist laws were allowed to lapse. Thereafter the party expanded in membership, votes, and deputies elected to the Reichstag. These advances within the Second Reich forced some in the party to reevaluate their theoretical assumptions and to construct a new theory of the road to socialism.

Marxist doctrine upon which the party stood taught that material progress resulted from tensions between opposing forces. These constructive tensions were seen as a creative way to achieve sudden change. Marxism denied any intrinsic value in gradualism, for its reduction of social and especially economic tensions would minimize opportunities for real progress. To the Marxists the ultimate goal of economic emancipation loomed significantly close, and its proximity reinforced aversion to gradualism. Political compromises were rejected in favor of promoting the collapse of the capitalist system as a whole.

As clearly as capitalism had emerged from feudalism, so socialism was seen to be the next stage of civilization. Through the growth of trusts and cartels, capitalism was itself producing the conditions of socialism. Simultaneously, industrialization had created a propertyless, alienated urban class whose ranks were continuously expanded by the depression of the middle class at the hands of the capitalists. Thus, the time would soon be ripe for creative tensions to cause the final eruption. That inevitable moment was to be encouraged, according to theory, by socialist leadership of the unenlightened proletariat. Once the revolution was achieved successfully, a dictatorship of the proletariat would construct the new order.

It was on such a platform that the German Social Democratic party stood in the 1890s when some of its membership began to question if in fact Marxist theory was in accord with existing conditions. Both precepts and predictions were challenged and the result was a schism within the party. The polarization meant that thereafter two ideologies and two factions existed side by side.

The position of the party in the nineties created the revisionists. As a rapidly growing legal political organization, the party had reason to believe that it soon would assume sufficient strength to influence, if not formulate, policy. If the party managed to obtain a majority within the Reichstag, it might be able to begin the transformation of the system. Thus, perhaps it was neither logical nor necessary to wait for tensions of opposing forces to cause a bloody upheaval which would lead to the millennium.

Revisionist theory, formulated in the main by Edward Bernstein, stressed the gradual achievement of socialism. Its adherents emphasized that due to its own growth, capitalism was experiencing daily modifications toward socialism. At the same time, social evolution was not further impoverishing the propertyless workers and depressing the bourgeoisie according to Marx's expectations. Instead, the workers and the middle class were coming to enjoy a bit of the cut of the pie, and their share ought logically to continue to increase. Thus, the tensions leading to the violent cataclysm were absent. Rather than violent change, peaceful realization of socialism was to be expected and encouraged.

The goal of the revisionists remained that of the orthodox Marxists—the collective ownership within the context of democratic control of the main instruments of production and distribution. The revisionists stressed the continuous process of economic concentration, but also noted that small businesses clung to life. Shopkeepers were not disappearing, nor were all small landowners. These groups continued to remain as part of the class structure but found that the gap between themselves and the workers, who were not totally shut out from the fruits of their labor by the end of the century, was lessening. Hence, it would strengthen each of these classes if they chose to coalesce against the forces of capital and together vote the socialist ticket, which indeed, the worker had already done.

In this manner, the revisionists elected to substitute evolution for the dialectic. Time was on the side of change; it favored the forces seeking to open society to an egalitarian orientation. Thus, it would be illogical to concentrate only on the distant achievement of the ultimate end, but logical to work toward immediate goals en route to the long-range goal. It was always possible, some of the revisionists came to believe, that the millennium would not arrive. This admitted, it appeared that stress must be on the here and now. Once the coming of the new order was recognized as uncertain, the movement itself toward the goal took on new importance. To obtain needed reforms, to exploit universal suffrage, and to use the parliamentary framework in order to accomplish as expansive a transformation as possible became perhaps of greater significance than the faraway day of cooperative control of the economic system.

By the end of the century, the German socialists were active in the Reichstag and in the trade unions. Instead of following an obstructionist path, they sought reforms for the masses, and they cooperated with non-proletarian parties and attempted to appeal to and win the support of middle-class elements, including the German peasant. The party had become parliamentary rather than revolutionary, and yet it hedged. While its actions were reformist due to its revisionism, it could not publicly proclaim that orthodoxy and revolutionism had been abandoned. In fact Bernstein himself was censured by the party and his program voted down, while the Social Democrats nevertheless continued moving toward full embrace of revisionism. The party had clung to its old label even though many privately thought it worn.

The reformist faction refrained from accepting responsible positions within the Reichstag, and because of its commanding numbers in that body, it handicapped the parliamentary system. Yet the reformists maintained that theirs was the responsible and constructive path toward socialism. They were responsible, they argued, because they concerned themselves with contemporary conditions and sought to alleviate the baser ills of society. They were at the same time constructive because their policies involved neither blood nor violence, but the building of a better society through creative and gradual steps. Their opponents, they said, were impossible and even irresponsible for ignoring the immediate.

The orthodox Marxists rejected the revisionist arguments. They refused to believe that history since Marx had negated or distorted his logic and thus they preferred to seize the moment of revolution when the contradictions of society would create sufficient tension. Reform of the existing system remained basically inconsequential and most probably harmful. Direct action at the ripe moment was preferable to wasting effort on meaningless parliamentary change in a system which was soon to disappear. The Marxists dismissed their opponents as dreamers. Their own response to criticism was that they themselves were the constructive socialists, for out of the holocaust they awaited would come the new order.

The argument between the self-styled constructive wing (the reformists) and the direct actionist, purist wing (the revolutionists) was never really settled but rather ended by the schism which occurred during World War I. While they remained tied together, however, one called the other "impossibilist" and the other replied with the invective, "utopian." The revisionists followed the path of reformism while seeking to cloud it with occasional revolutionary rhetoric, as the orthodox Marxists ineffectively restrained the opposing faction while witnessing the dilution of revolutionary idiom.

In the summer of 1914, the German Social Democratic party was forced to take a position on World War I. Most of the party, after excruciating self-examination, chose to support the national effort, while some of the orthodox faction elected the lonely path of opposition to the war. Those who supported the war rationalized their position by maintaining that the German worker had developed a stake in his society and that the Social Democratic party bore the responsibility of continuing to represent the worker within the system. The framework itself was still objectionable, but the society had become less closed, and to challenge the whole on the basis of a war possibly waged for the protection of the German capitalist would represent an irresponsible act that at least the revisionists of the party could not embrace.

Thus, in terms of Weber's thesis, the revisionists of the German Social Democratic party had forced the party as a whole into a policy which they believed brought together the ethic of responsibility and the ethic of ultimate ends into a symbiotic relationship. The party would argue, in the face of heavy criticism, that it had acted on the basis of its principles. If the revisionists had been correct in their belief that conditions were new and required a modification of ideology, they could well defend themselves with a similar argument in 1914. If the party had up to that time acted on the basis of its belief that the worker was entering more and more into society, that he indeed had a country, it might now with consistency maintain that he was no longer homeless and he could in fact support with logic a national war effort. At the moment of crisis, self-delusion may have been employed to obscure war causes and aims, but for the party to reason and act otherwise would mean that it had abandoned its ethic of responsibility for the ethic of ultimate ends. This then was the outline of the revisionist defense as seen against the framework of Weber's thesis.

The orthodox, on the other hand, who never had accepted the foundation of the revisionist argument, would quickly reject this further explanation, by arguing that the crisis of capitalism had peaked. The tensions of the system were about to bring on the great explosion that had all along been their aim. With the capitalist giants of the world confronting one another in battle, the revolutionists could only encourage the revolution.

Whether the party's official policy of war support was justifiable is beside the point here. The majority itself, midway through the war, repudiated its earlier position by supporting a Peace Resolution which implicitly challenged the existing German government. What is important is that the ideological and factional polarization was a cancer within the body of this and every other socialist party of the time, with each side viewing itself as following the principled path. To understand the struggle in any individual party, it must be seen in the context of the general conflict within the international socialist movement.

In the United States, the Socialist party of America was characterized by the same basic divisions. The members, as in the European parties, operated within distinctive frames of reference, and as a result found themselves in perpetual disagreement.

The two main factions of the party agreed on the inadequacy and injustice of capitalism and desired to replace it with a socialist regime. They also shared the belief that socialism was the wave of the future and that the day of collective ownership of the means of production and distribution could not be far off. Both factions expected that the next and ultimate stage of civilization would be socialism; like the German Social Democrats, they believed that it would follow capitalism as surely as capitalism had followed feudalism. It is noteworthy that the members of the American Socialist party saw no need to modify this determinist vision to allow for the fact that the United States had not experienced a feudal period. More than most Americans, the majority of socialists thought of the United States as an extension of Europe rather than an isolated whole.

There was little else that the American socialists agreed upon other than their commitment to the goal of collectivism. The individual within the party looked upon the path toward that future as reformist or revolutionist, depending as much upon his own temperament as upon his own perspective of the American present.

Revolutionary socialists stressed the continuing state of misery in which they saw the American workingman living out his span of years. The worker's life followed a road from crisis to crisis; and while his own mode of existence changed little, the American capitalist grew richer. Such an analysis of the situation of the American "slave" and "plutocrat" was common currency among some party members.

This faction believed that Marx had been proven correct by the American experience. While the industrial revolution had resulted in impressive economic developments, the struggles between capital and labor waged on American shores were the fiercest that the Western world had viewed. Labor struggles were far bloodier than those in Europe. Thus, it was clear to these orthodox Marxists that the tensions between the opposing forces were certain to lead shortly to the moment of revolution. And it was as obviously the party's responsibility to hold itself ready for that moment. It must offer to the workers propaganda and enlightenment to prevent them from following some misguided progressive or reformer, whose suggestions would only offer them a change far short of the ultimate end. It must encourage appropriate direct actions by the workers. Above all it must itself not be enticed into initiating palliatives that might improve the level of existence for the masses in what was, after all, only a passing phase of civilization. Such a position, the embodiment of the ethic of ultimate ends, invited the epithet of "impossibilism," but the party, this faction believed, bore no relationship to the present or responsibility for the consequences stemming from its own posture. The only responsibility for the party was that of bringing on the millennium as soon as possible.

Others in the Socialist party viewed the American present in different colors. To these party members the life of the working man seemed improved in recent years. The achievement of a shorter working day and of wage increases had inevitably meant that the worker was emerging from his destitution. Clearly, he was not yet enjoying the fair share of the pie that was his; he was still little more than a wage slave. However, his life was less often crisis-ridden and consequently it was not clear that only a socialist revolution could improve his position.

The fact that he could be described as less impoverished than formerly meant that social tensions were not as fierce as they had been. Thus, to view the situation in terms of the past was self-deluding and a disservice to the cause of socialism.

This faction, then, emphasized the importance of bringing Marx up to date, and became known, like its German counterpart, as revisionist in ideology and reformist in strategy. The faction stressed immediate demands; the daily aspects of the movement could not be neglected. Efforts should be exerted to move gradually, even a step at a time, toward the alleviation of the burdens of working-class life, so that eventually the workers might gain control of the system and of their own destinies.

The logic of this analysis impelled the revisionists toward reformism in the concrete, and toward the ethic of responsibility in the abstract. The duty of the party was to secure a place in the structure of American society where it would be able to work for reform of the capitalist system. Instead of confining itself to propaganda, the party must win the active support not only of the workers but also of farmers and even the middle class in order to be in a position with some leverage. Once an adequate degree of support was obtained, the party could function as a legislative pressure group and, through the exploitation of universal suffrage, as a political party seeking election.

The revisionists, stressing the process to the ultimate goal, left themselves open to the charge of opportunism, but they believed that they were acting with a sense of responsibility to the present on the basis of principles tied to the future.

The disparity of these views which divided the party into right and left factions was intensified by the composition of the membership itself. Unlike the various European socialist parties, the American party, as a reflection of American society, was a heterogeneous body. The Socialist party was composed of foreign-born members in eastern and midwestern cities who were quick to impose European experience upon an American situation. In the mountain states and far west, the membership lists were dominated by former populists who had turned to a new protest organization after the collapse of the People's party in the nineties. The urban socialists tended generally to get bogged down in political machines as a result of the need for organization in the metropolises, and each of these machines developed the usual bureaucracy with vested interests and the political participation that invited opportunism. On the other hand, the rural and western socialists felt no need of political organization to compromise their purity and thus they were free to remain uninvolved impossibilists. Therefore, the size of the country as well as the variety in the population added new dimensions to the typical Socialist party divisions.

The reformist faction managed to dominate the founding sessions of the party at the Unity Convention of 1901, and a plank favoring immediate demands was included in the party platform. This plank set the pattern, and thereafter the gradualist ethos of the party was never upset.

Because of the distinctive frames of reference from which they operated, the two factions found themselves in perpetual disagreement and antagonism over basic issues. Each problem involved a polarization resulting in a consistent division between reformist and revolutionist elements. One such divisive issue was the relationship of the Socialist party to the union movement.

The Marxist faction treated the American labor movement contemptuously because of organized labor's pure-and-simple unionism which eschewed radicalism and even political commitment. To the chagrin of the Marxists, the Unity Convention passed a resolution favoring support for all unions, radical and conservative. The second convention three years later witnessed an intricate debate on unionism which resulted once more in a positive plank. The Marxists were angry about tying the party to a labor movement which they believed to be working against the proletariat's interests, while the reformists felt that it was illogical to avoid involvement with a movement which clearly touched the lives of American workers—as the Socialist party did not. The Marxists preferred at best an aloof position while the reformists wanted to exploit the unions as an economic weapon.

The two factions of the party also quarreled at their early conventions over a policy toward the American farmer. The reformists favored inviting agrarian support, arguing that the farmer was essentially a working man, rather than a property owner, who was not being depressed out of existence as Marx had predicted. The orthodox position, however, disdained involvement with the capitalist American farmer who, it held, had no fundamental interest in the class struggle. The difference of opinion over the farmer's role in the proletarian struggle surfaced whenever party platforms were discussed. Consistently, the reformists stressed the farmer's inherent radicalism as evidenced by his participation in nineteenth-century protest movements; the exploited farmer was a logical adjunct to the movement. The Marxists countered with emphasis on the pace of agricultural concentration; since under such conditions, most farmers would eventually become propertyless, it was best to ignore consideration of what was only a passing phenomenon. It was not until the party's fourth convention that an agricultural plank entered the party program.

A third issue that always invited lengthy debate was the party's policy toward immigration. This issue was particularly emotional, for many in the party were themselves of alien background and thus had foreign-born constituents whom they were representing at the socialist conventions. A further complication was the party's relationship with the organized labor movement. The reformists who valued that tie felt the need to consider labor's hostility to the government's open door policy on immigration. The orthodox Marxists, however, stressed the unity of workers everywhere, and dismissed issues of immigration quotas and subsidized immigration as unimportant and transitory in the larger struggle.

In each of these divisive issues the line was clearly drawn between those who thought it necessary to take a position on issues of contemporary America, and those who dismissed the contemporary as meaningless. The orthodox pointed out that the party need only be concerned with issues which transcended the current transitionary period of civilization, and which were of essential concern to the working class. To some extent, the reformists agreed and they avoided stances on items commanding public attention which they considered illusory, such as the gold standard and the tariff. But in general, the determination of which matters were vital proved elusive to the party. Never was there basic agreement on which subjects transcended the system of capitalism.

Instead of that agreement, then, the Socialist party of America followed two separate paths, and its unity lay in name only. One was wedded to the ethic of responsibility while the other followed only the ethic of ultimate aims.

Among the leadership of the party's factions, one individual clearly was in a position to bring together the two ethics as supplementary to one another rather than oppositional. Victor L. Berger as a national leader of the controlling reformist faction wished to direct the party out of its dilemma. He wanted the party to stand on a platform of updated Marxism from which it could wage a struggle against the status quo. He did not believe that the Socialist party must either sell its own soul in political action or remain immobilized until the historic revolution arrived. Rather than opt for either choice, he argued that it was possible to act on the basis of relevant socialist principles within the American political system. Waiting for the ultimate moment of revolution through direct action seemed both irresponsible and impossible to him. His willingness to act as a moral man in an immoral society invited taunts of opportunism, but in his attempt to solve the ethical paradox inherent in political action he was striving to become Max Weber's "genuine man" with a "calling for politics."

The way in which the reformist Berger attempted to realize Weber's thesis is the subject of this study.

At the outset, it must be stated that the Socialist party of America did not succeed in the eyes of either of its factions. Whether or not it was inevitable that it would not fulfill the promise of its early growth cannot be answered. The matter of inevitability has been argued back and forth ever since the party's war-induced decline and schism, and no consensus is likely. However, it should be readily acknowledged that a reformist party would have had a better chance of continued growth and successes in American politics than either a revolutionary party or a disunited party.

While there are always external environmental factors that complicate and doom the efforts of third parties in the United States, this inquiry will limit itself to the exploration of the internal reasons for the lack of a united, reformist party, and hence the party's ultimate decline. Unlike others, this study concentrates on the dominant right wing of the party and on its potentially most effective leader, Berger, in the important years of both man and party. Berger's role will be examined in the preponderance and subsequent decline of that wing and the concurrent collapse into ineffectiveness of the Socialist party of America.

NOTES

1. Max Weber, *From Max Weber: Essays in Sociology*, ed. H. H. Gerth and C. Wright Hills (New York: Oxford University Press, 1946), pp. 120-125.

2. The analysis that most closely attempts to relate the dilemma of the moral man in an imperfect society in terms of the subject pertinent here is found in Daniel Bell, *Marxian Socialism in the United States* (Princeton: Princeton University Press, 1967); it is addressed to the problem of being in, but not of, the world. Bell borrowed this phrase from Martin Luther's view of the church and applied it to American radicalism, and it subsequently has been used freely by other writers dealing with this issue. But Bell, by ignoring the full

development of Weber's view, arbitrarily rejects his solution. Moreover, by neglecting to distinguish among American socialists in a meaningful way, he fails to note the exceptions who sought to solve the dilemma. The examination of such exceptions forms the burden of this analysis. Bell, *Marxian Socialism*, pp. viii-ix, 5-6.

3. Weber, *From Max Weber*, p. 127.

4. Ibid., pp. 111-112.

2

Berger and the Promise of Constructive Socialism

Victor L. Berger was born in the Austrian empire on 28 February 1860. At this time the empire was only beginning to experience the heat of the nationalist enthusiasms of its component peoples, but the Ignatz Berger household in the Nieder-Rehbach region of Austria was untouched by contemporary currents. While others participated in the movement which ultimately culminated in the destruction of the Austrian empire, the Berger family remained royalist in its tastes. The parents operated the village inn and enjoyed relative prosperity. Young Victor, the oldest of four children, initially studied with tutors at home and later attended private schools. During his adolescence, the family business declined and the boy found himself in public schools.

Following the European tradition of exposure to various major universities, Victor Berger attended the University of Vienna and the University of Budapest. During his two years of higher education, he was a serious student whose interests lay in politics. He studied history and political economy and, although not a political activist, he encountered scientific socialism in these years. His formal education terminated without the completion of his degree, however, with the family's decision to emigrate in 1878.[1]

The Berger family settled in Bridgeport, Connecticut. The oldest son, Victor, wandered westward, moving from one job to another as did so many immigrants who lacked a particular trade and familiarity with English. But Berger studied the language of his adopted country diligently and by 1881 he had settled permanently in Milwaukee and had become a German teacher in the public school system.

That Berger chose to live in Milwaukee is not surprising, for the city was more German than American in this period. The census of 1890 indicated that Milwaukee was the most foreign in population of the 28 largest cities in the United States, with 39 percent of her residents born abroad. At century's end, more than 150,000 of Milwaukee's population of 285,315 were German by birth or parentage, with the rest of the populace divided among native Americans and several other nationality groups.[2] The German vote prevailed in local politics and German newspapers enjoyed twice as much circulation as did English papers. The German theater dominated the entertainment and cultural scene, and "the German spirit had penetrated the life of the whole city. . . ."[3]

The various newcomers to the emerging urban and industrial culture of Milwaukee in the last decades of the nineteenth century were faced with a series of adjustments. The necessity for adjustment was not limited to the recent immigrants, for the native-born too were first-generation migrants to industrial society "even if they never actually moved from the place in which they had been born."[4] Indeed, in many instances it is probable that German immigrants assimilated more easily into the bustling life of Milwaukee factories, shops, and flats than did some of the native Americans. Many of the Germans arrived fresh from an industrial background in the Old Country. The natural result was that these Germans were imbued with a sense of survival, based on their knowledge of the urban-industrial complex which they had confronted previously. They knew how to cope with the modern environment, or at least, where help might be found and how to obtain it.

The second great wave of German immigration to Wisconsin came a generation after the forty-eighters. In the 1870s and 1880s a new inundation occurred, and its character contrasted with that of the earlier immigration. While the antebellum German-speaking immigrants had tended to be economically driven peasants or politically harassed intellectuals, those who emigrated after the completion of German unification in 1871 were apt to be industrial workers. Workers left the Second Reich in flight from heavier taxes, compulsory military service, and the pressures of rapid industrialization. The necessity of coping with the industrial environment, however, fostered acclimatization to the new order. By the time the decade ended, Bismarck's paternal and socialist-inspired policy of social legislation had served to cushion the adjustment process and, indeed, to diminish the flow of emigration. But for those immigrants who had lived through the crucial years of Germany's industrialization, the means of self-protection in such an environment were clear: worker organization and government responsibility. Thus, in addition to the usual baggage immigrants took with them to their new homes, the German immigrants of the latter part of the nineteenth century carried the ideas of labor unions, socialist parties, and social legislation.[5]

These years are marked off in the history of Milwaukee as its period of most significant industrial growth, with the value of manufactured products increasing sharply each decade. In the early 1870s a lack of banking capital and a sufficient supply of skilled labor served to brake the industrial pace, but by the 1880s the revolutionary dimensions of the city's industrial expansion were established sharply enough to inspire editorial predictions of Milwaukee's future as the industrial center of the mid-continent. Advances in meat packing, tanning, iron and steel, and in the city's most famous industry, brewing, resulted in an output of manufactured products in 1899 valued at $123,786,449, compared with $18,798,122 in 1869.[6] Such impressive economic growth bore a price tag in human costs which any perceptive visitor observed with only a glance at the end-of-the-century slum housing of the immigrant factory workers. Expansion and rationalization of industrial processes had occurred in a vacuum, unrelated and unresponsive to social effects.[7]

Those workers who lived the industrial revolution might readily have reflected on their unprotected state to one another as they gathered together at their local Turnverein. This fraternal organization existed in every German community in the United States after 1848. Originally a gymnastic society, the turner movement served as a focus of community life. Some of the societies were mainly social centers, while others were devoted to cultural and intellectual affairs, often with a radical or socialist accent. After 1865 the movement officially divested itself of any radical ideology but it remained the bastion of German-American life and the clubhouse of the workers well after its overt receptiveness to socialist currents was muted.[8]

The expanding economy of Milwaukee experienced a cycle of booms and depressions after the Civil War, as did the rest of the country. Against this background, the labor movement grew, and its agitation was marked by socialist participation. While the Knights of Labor enjoyed support among Milwaukee workers up to the mid-1880s, as early as the 1870s the Knights found themselves in competition with socialist spokesmen. Some of the German immigrants of a socialist persuasion stressed the worker's need for trade unions while others emphasized the necessity of forming a labor party. These various Marxists and Lassalleans alternately succeeded in organizing economic and political workers' actions in Milwaukee, until May 1886, when the issue of the eight-hour day culminated in national agitation and class conflict. In Milwaukee, during the same month as the Haymarket Affair in Chicago, a series of strikes disintegrated in the face of police anti-labor activity. As a result of their role in the labor conflict the Knights declined and, while the German socialists moved to ballot box action later that year, the most significant event was the formation of the Federated Trades Council of Milwaukee. The cigar makers', typographical, and molders' unions formed a central labor organization and affiliated with the newly organized American Federation of Labor. The FTC grew rapidly until, at the start of the twentieth century, sixty locals were affiliated to it, claiming the allegiance of the bulk of skilled labor in Milwaukee. By that date, the Social Democratic party had emerged "to weld together effectively the predominantly German adherents of socialistic thought and the advocates of trade unionism who had . . . developed the movement independently of socialist ideology."[9]

As these two strains of German labor in Milwaukee coalesced, it ought to be noted that the opportunities and roles of German-Americans were by then diversified. They lived everywhere in the city and suburbs and were influential in the economic, political, religious, and social life of the area. Class stratification divided Germans from one another as some experienced mobility into the middle class and beyond. A conservative orientation characterized the community as a whole, and the middle class as well as the non-union German workers voted for the Democrats or Republicans, with neither party able to take their vote for granted. Certainly the vociferous socialist movement never claimed the allegiance of the majority of the Germans in Milwaukee.[10]

For the "new immigrants" (that arbitrary descriptive term imposed upon those who came to the United States in great numbers from eastern and southern Europe after the mid-1880s), life's choices were narrower and more structured than for their German predecessors. The various waves of Slavs, Hungarians, Greeks, and Italians were "broken" into modern society, in the expression of Eric Hobsbawm, rather than allowed to grow into it, and the disorientation they experienced knew many dimensions.[11] These people were almost entirely products of village backgrounds thrust into a factory economy which openly barred their full participation in the new culture. Handicapped by residential segregation, family upheaval, and economic marginality, their survival in Milwaukee depended on self-help. Thus, the inability to disperse among the greater population was transformed into an instrument of survival. They erected their own institutions which served to counter the danger of individual and family breakdown. Their churches, newspapers, and fraternal societies allowed them to cope with the urban-industrial complex, as a sense of solidarity overcame helplessness and weakness became strength.

The new immigrants trod a path somewhere between the culture of poverty and social integration. Their own institutions counteracted potential community disorganization, disintegration of traditions, and personal hopelessness, in the process of staving off formation of a subculture of poverty.[12] On the other hand, the viability of those institutions served to reinforce the isolation imposed upon them, for their survival and even influence in the outer society depended on the maintenance of cohesiveness. As an example, the Polish population of Milwaukee, the second largest ethnic group, was segregated in the southwestern corner of the city. That section early in the twentieth century suggested Warsaw in Wisconsin, and the self-interest of the Poles dictated its permanency. Their Catholicism, nationalist organizations, and solid Democratic commitment all served as a means to the end of Polish influence within city affairs. Polish power in the urban culture became an acknowledged fact, recognized by Milwaukee politicians who came to regard the Poles as holding the balance in local politics. Indeed, when the Milwaukee socialists first captured City Hall in 1910, one significant factor was their breakthrough in the Polish community. That year their campaigning in the Polish language had undercut clerical admonitions against socialism, and they were able to win the solidly Polish and Democratic fourteenth ward. Normally, however, the Poles remained aloof from external appeals and clung to their separatist institutions.[13]

A distinct pecking order existed, as discussed by Gerd Korman, in which ethnic stereotypes pervasive in Milwaukee determined occupational as well as other opportunities. As Bayrd Still writes, small ghettoized population groups, such as the Czechs on the south side and the Hungarians on the east side, were suspended in the urban culture rather than integrated into it. They brought with them psychological perspectives which had been honed in their peasant societies in isolation from other ethnic groups. Lacking technical skill, education, and capital, they substituted muscle, tenacity, and willingness to work hard. Life for them was shaped not by the city's diversity but by its structured insistence upon residential segregation and occupational limitation. Political power was slow in coming to the dozen or so nationalities whose numbers were few compared to Germans and Poles. Life's amenities stemmed from primary relationships within the ethnic community, and for some, the focus was always upon the mother country to which one might return with his fortune, send for a bride, or spend one's old age. The dreams of many of the new immigrants, at least, involved looking eastward to the Old Country.[14]

It was in this atmosphere that Victor L. Berger grew to maturity. In 1897 he married a former pupil, Meta Schlichting, and became a devoted family man. Mrs. Berger frequently assisted him with party and newspaper work and held party responsibilities of her own. In 1909, for example, she was elected on the socialist ticket to the Milwaukee school board, on which her father had served. The marriage was a partnership with its dimensions governed by the demands and crises of the movement. Even in times of severe political pressure, they would find moments in their separations to exchange letters of affection and devotion to one another. But when Berger was home, his book-lined study claimed most of his time, although even that luxury might be sacrificed to the party, since the Berger home was often a center for socialist gatherings. The atmosphere in the home was heavily Old World and the two Berger daughters, Doris and Elsa, at first spoke only German, indicative of their parents' cultural allegiance.[15]

In appearance Berger was short and stocky, and in expression studious and somber. His mustache and steel-rimmed glasses enhanced the impression of a Viennese academic, as a friend once noted.[16]

Berger early demonstrated the personality traits that would prevail throughout his life. He had a sense of humor with the gift of poking fun at himself, his accent, and his peculiar constituency. Even his bossism could be joked about, but only to a point. He also had a temper which might flare easily in an argument, and at times cost him support. With his associates he was congenial, loyal, and forthright. When he did not want a non-German socialist speaker in Milwaukee, he would good-naturedly but firmly bar the would-be campaigner. He was known to have told one party member that while he enjoyed hearing him speak, he was not wanted in Milwaukee. Somehow Berger's *gemütlichkeit* precluded serious rancor in such instances. His was a very human mixture of bombast, affability, confidence, and generosity.[17]

His dominant characteristic was ambition. Energy, drive, and aggressiveness were the offshoots of this quality, and even friendly commentators considered Berger capable of ruthlessness. To one, he explained that it was always necessary "to hit hard" in order to impress the popular mind. The associate who probably knew him best, Morris Hillquit, described Berger as a man with strong convictions on every subject: "He was inclined to be self-assertive and domineering and utterly intolerant of dissenting views. He was sublimely egotistic, but somehow his egotism did not smack of conceit and was not offensive. It was the expression of deep and naive faith in himself, and this unshakable faith was one of the mainsprings of his power over men." Another associate, John Spargo, with whom he eventually broke, remembered Berger for his integrity, honesty, and intellectual gifts, but he stressed his bossism. Berger made an unusual number of enemies but it has been observed that "The violence of the attacks made on Berger personally throughout his career testify to the conviction of his opponents that he was an effective political leader."[18]

He was a skilled political negotiator and seldom lost an opportunity to advance his cause, but he could be ponderous and redundant. Nevertheless his ability to handle men and situations was consistently evident and was best illustrated in the Milwaukee socialist organization. He preferred dealing with individuals rather than with groups, and his campaigning sometimes betrayed reluctance to mix with a crowd. One of his assistants in Milwaukee, Oscar Ameringer, recorded that he often had to drag Berger into saloons for the purpose of electioneering. Ameringer thought of Berger as an "intellectual aristocrat" whose dignity and even elitism prevented backslapping.[19]

Berger was never more than a fair speaker, certainly no orator. Indeed, complaints were recorded from dissatisfied members of the audiences after particularly fumbling addresses. Hampered by a voice that did not carry, he would not accept outdoor speaking engagements and therefore seldom gave lectures in summer. He was a competent writer in both English and German, and tended to compose his speeches in full detail, especially when he was in Congress. His phrasing was seldom elegant, and he was capable of awkward metaphors and incongruous figurative expressions. But his pen was a potent weapon, as his writings were punctuated with the fruits of constant reading and studying. His strength lay in editing, where he had no peer.[20]

In both politics and daily relationships he was unusually honest and straightforward. He had no interest in money and was vulnerable for handouts and never-to-be-repaid loans. Although always occupied in either party or newspaper work, Berger was never without a moment for questions on socialism from students or other interested persons. Despite his mercurial temperament, he was likeable and enjoyed pleasant relations with non-radicals.

As a young man in Milwaukee, Berger demonstrated an innate curiosity and sensitivity to the urban, industrial world about him. Perhaps because of his family's loss of wealth and his own experiences with poverty, he was sensitive to the plight of the unemployed and the poor. Had he not known the contrasts of relative security and dismal anxiety, he might not have been so observant and empathetic.

Along with his teaching, Berger immersed himself in the community affairs of German Milwaukee. He became active in the local Turnverein, and quickly assumed leadership of it. Through this community institution, he made contacts among working people and cast aside his conservative and religious family traditions. Thus out of both his observations of political and industrial conditions and his own associations was welded a commitment to socialism. The transformation of a personally ambitious young man into a dedicated idealist cannot be followed minutely, for the result was the sum of his experiences.[21]

Victor Berger, the socialist, never worshipped at the shrine of doctrine. He was a revisionist thoroughly grounded in Marxist study and the European socialist movement, and was as willing to exploit Bernstein's revisionism as Marxist orthodoxy. His familiarity with the European experience endowed him with a perspective that many of his reformist colleagues lacked, but it did not serve to cloud his vision of the United States. He chose to follow socialist theories as amended to American conditions and, when necessary, to look beyond orthodoxy and revisionism for the resolution of a problem. In his utilization of theory, he was strikingly autonomous.[22]

He prided himself on a scientific approach and for that reason insisted on the freedom to choose among different means to the end. His pragmatic emphasis caused some to minimize his genuine commitment to the socialist movement, but his life's work was the advancement of that cause.

Berger's rhetoric and tone generally recalled the Marxist because of his familiarity with doctrine, but the authorities he used varied with each particular problem. Berger's own contributions to socialist theory were nil, but his use of doctrinal views was the foundation on which his practical efforts were based. Loose criticism has been leveled at him for a readiness to compromise and accept political realities, but his entire outlook demanded that existing situations be confronted and then remolded as far as possible.

His definition of socialism as collective ownership and management of the means of production and distribution was not unique to him. He preferred such sweeping definitions, for a wide scope permitted him to explain particulars according to specific situations.[23]

Berger never tired of explaining that the achievement of the collectivist state would be both gradual, as the revisionists maintained, and inevitable, as the Marxists held. Since the future was assuredly to be socialist, no violence need be exerted to guarantee the coming of the millennium. He eschewed the use of force in general, and was particularly opposed to its advocacy in the United States, although he could see that it might be necessary in a society wholly closed to the possibility of legal change, one in which the channels to exert pressures for alterations in the status quo simply were unavailable. Such a position could well be maintained in regard to countries in Eastern Europe, Berger would admit, where the working masses were so far from exercising any influence that only direct action of a forceful nature could begin to open the society to them. However, because the worker had the ballot in the United States and politicians were required to display at least a façade of commitment to the interests of the voters, there was in fact a real alternative to force-induced change. Thus, Berger had no patience with the argument that a violent revolution was needed to allow the masses to play a role in society. They already held some leverage and his preference was to exploit that position.

Not only was violence unnecessary, it was undesirable. Berger rejected the idea that "a certain 'catastrophy' [*sic*] can change very much in the social system *per se*, unless economic conditions . . . are favorable" to complete change. He wrote that without a basically positive situation and an enlightened proletariat as well, a violent conquest of power would simply mean a change in masters. A new ruling class would exploit the same system that the old leaders had controlled and the people would still remain the servants of the few.[24]

But Berger by no means felt pessimistic as a result of this analysis. He believed that a complete change was in fact evolving and that inevitably the socialist future would materialize. The trend toward monopoly in the United States in the decades after the Civil War was inherently altering the economic system of the country. He interpreted the movement toward monopoly and trust as a gradual transformation of capitalism toward state control which could easily be turned into democratic collectivism.

Thus, Berger never denigrated the trusts as did nineteenth-century-oriented progressive reformers such as Woodrow Wilson and Robert M. La Follette. Instead of decrying the increasing size of business, Berger welcomed the trend. He expounded on the inability of the private individual and small business to defend themselves against the growing powers of the trusts. There was, however, no need to destroy the trusts since modern industrial conditions fostered monopoly as the most efficient means of production and distribution. But streamlined monopoly was not acceptable to him within the framework of private power and private profit, as it was to twentieth-century progressive reformers such as Theodore Roosevelt. The reformist socialist Berger said, "Monopoly is here, whether we wish it or not. The question, therefore, is only whether it shall be a private or a public monopoly. . . . The *nation* must get *possession* of the *trusts*."[25] He wished, then, to encourage monopolization to the point where large-scale production and distribution existed in all fields which best accommodated them. Once such conditions were attained and the enlightenment of the people accomplished, then the propitious moment for the transformation to public monopoly through nationalization would be at hand. The achievement of the collectivist state was essentially a matter of timing.

But because he was an activist, he could not sit with hands folded. He chose to encourage the inevitable and perhaps speed the whole procedure through various beneficial reforms within the existing capitalist framework. Thus, he opposed the obstructionism that other socialists espoused. While German Social Democrats chose to reject positions of responsibility once they were elected to the Reichstag, Berger favored effective policy-making following elections to city councils, state legislatures, or the Congress of the United States. He believed it illogical to assume halfway responsibility, and thus chose to exercise as much influence as was possible en route to the transformation of the system. Similarly, while many American socialists participated in campaign procedures merely for propaganda purposes, Berger ran to win election. It appeared to him nonsense to refrain from exploiting the political process to the utmost. Whenever he was confronted with a choice, he elected political action over direct action and participation over obstruction.

Berger always took pains to distinguish between socialism and communism, both within the party and to the general public. His emphasis on the need to separate the two was clear from the time of the founding of the Socialist party and increased as a communist movement grew and overwhelmed the socialists. Berger explained that communism would be a step backward for a society, a step toward a primitive stage of social relationships in which individual ownership of all property was prohibited in favor of collective ownership and consumption. Socialism, on the other hand, meant common ownership of capital but not nationalization of all property. In a socialist society the individual need not fear the loss of his personal effects and small holdings. Socialist collectivism was not communism, he wrote, and "Karl Marx and Frederick Engels . . . later on in life became collectivists and Social Democrats."[26]

Berger believed that the trade unions were to play an important role in the advancement of society. They served to complement the party's effort, for the trade unions organized workers in their economic capacities, while the Socialist party organized them politically. Through such a partnership, with each guiding its own sphere, the trade unions and the party together would strengthen the workers in the struggle against capitalism. Berger often referred to the organized labor movement and the socialist movement as two arms of the same body, with neither controlled by the other.[27] This view pitted Berger against socialists who envisioned the labor movement as subordinate to the party, but he never endorsed such emphasis since much of his home support came from unionists. However, while he refrained from assigning the unions a minor role in the class struggle, his own career focus on party work over union activities showed that he himself had made a choice between the two. As one is either right-handed or left-handed, an exact balance between the two arms could not be maintained.

Berger's involvement in trade unionism determined his attitude toward industrial unionism and the Industrial Workers of the World. The Wobblies with their freewheeling life styles and contempt for conventional political practices were easy to smear, and so Berger denounced the IWW as reviving the anarchy of the nineteenth-century labor movement. Genuinely fearful that the atmosphere of implicit violence surrounding the IWW would harm the entire labor-socialist movement and revive public memories of bloody labor battles, Berger was anxious to disassociate the "anarchical" Wobblies from the "peace-loving" socialists. He wrote of the Wobblies as "anarchy champions" who were following their doctrine into chaos. To his home audience he described their movement as one where "the individual is everything, and the state is nothing. . . . [T]he trouble begins in deciding where the rights of one man end, and where the rights of the other fellow begin."[28]

Berger's connection with organized labor influenced his attitude toward another issue, that of the party's position on immigration to the United States. Berger never favored an open door policy on immigration because that would alienate the organized unionists among the party supporters. Of greater significance in his attitude was his own racist vision. He held the pyramidal view common to most types of reformers in the Progressive Era and, in his case, reflective of a Milwaukee-style segregationist view: that is, there were definite ethnic lines dividing superior and inferior peoples. Whites were at the top of the color pyramid, yellow below, and black at the bottom. Distinguishing even further, Berger was convinced that among the whites, Teutons and Anglo-Saxons had greater potential than did Latins and Slavs.[29] The former were far more educable than the latter.

Even given the fact that Berger belonged to a movement which proclaimed the unity of workers of the world, this view was not remarkable since it was a product of an overtly imperialist era. His immediate interest lay in strengthening organized labor, and to this end he favored the exclusion of the Oriental and the neglect of the black American. He justified his un-Marxist position by pointing out, first, that Marx had not known twentieth-century America, and second, that the socialists who did know it had best deal with its realities. If the party were to assist the worker in his historic mission of collectivist control of society, it had better avoid flooding the American job market with men who could not understand the issues of the class struggle.

The broad basis of Berger's position was that the worker indeed did have a country. Again, times had moved beyond Karl Marx. While in 1848 in Europe it was manifest that the worker was not a part of the state, by the twentieth century most western countries had become nation-states with which the worker had begun to identify. To a degree, he felt he had a stake in his society and his immediate goal was to continue enlarging his role within it.[30] Hence, the clear task for the socialist was to work within national lines toward collectivism and avoid creating worker resistance through an anti-national posture. It made no sense to Berger to welcome from abroad workers unwanted by American labor who might better stay home and strive for their own new order.

Internationalism, then, had to be de-emphasized at this stage of society's evolution and of the worker's class consciousness. But Berger envisioned that as democratic collectivism developed in the various countries, an international community founded on the brotherhood of socialism would replace nationalism and war. He emphasized that the socialist movement could advance only from local to state, to national, and then international success. If the foundation were not solid, an apparent conquest on a national level would prove to be temporary. Thus, local autonomy within the Socialist party was the starting point of ultimate triumph. The party had to allow self-rule to locals since only individuals at the scene could be aware of the type of policy or action which would fit their particular context. Berger frequently stated that any socialist party that refused autonomy to its locals could not progress.[31] Underlying this principle was his interest in maintaining the Milwaukee organization as his personal fief against possible interference by the national officials of the party.

One of the points on which Berger differed from the Marxists was in his evaluation of the farmer's role. Recognizing that the United States of the early twentieth century still had an agricultural base, he dismissed the Marxist belief that agriculture would soon emulate industrial concentration. At every party convention, he stressed the point that the farmer must be recognized by the Socialist party as a self-employed laborer who was as much subject to external conditions as the urban worker.[32] Through such an analysis, Berger tried to expand the party's concept of the class struggle and force it to confront reality. The national party had only to look to its western, rural locals, he pointed out, to recognize the validity of his argument. If some farmers joined the Socialist party because they recognized their own participation in the class struggle, how irrelevant to them the party would become if it did not recognize that salient point.

Another aspect of Berger's effort to relate the party to the American situation was his approval of cooperation with non-socialist reforming elements. He favored such joint endeavors in order to attain the social legislation that would pave the road to the new regime—a policy European revisionists supported. In Wisconsin especially, socialist reformists and progressives could join hands in support of factory inspection legislation or the recall and referendum, but each partner in this alliance maintained his own identity. In both cases philosophical assumptions and constituent needs demanded separatism. La Follette's (and the early Wilson's) Jeffersonian commitment to limited government was castigated by Berger as retrogressive and superficial. On the other hand, socialist promotion of an increased role for the government meant regimentation to the progressives. The small capitalist in Oshkosh or Sheboygan over whom La Follette worried bore scant resemblance in his overt concerns to the German trade unionist in Milwaukee whom Berger primarily represented. The former emphasized legislation restrictive to big business to allow him to pursue his own commercial livelihood, while the latter wanted self-determination in the factory. Or so a La Follette and a Berger maintained.

Each side believed it must remain essentially aloof from the other, and each was jealous of its own identity and independence. "Under these circumstances, the growing prospects for reform served only to intensify the rivalry. . . ,"[33] and the progressives played out their role as a dominant force in the state of Wisconsin while the socialists played out theirs in the largest city of the state. Since the essence of Berger's thought was a commitment to democratic collectivism, fusion was out of the question, although cooperation was possible. Cooperation with reformers could strengthen the forces for change, but could be risked only if principles of socialization and of the class struggle remained the substance of the party's thrust. In campaigns a variety of demands might be focal points, but always against a background of socialist ideology; his own version of Marxism prohibited compromise on essentials. Outside Wisconsin, even the idea of cooperation with progressives was anathema to the national Socialist party and often Berger's position was attacked; once it even cost him his seat on the party's National Executive Committee. It was not until the 1924 election that Berger convinced the then broken Socialist party to follow his course.

Berger never clearly sketched the socialist regime which would follow capitalism. Since he was so preoccupied with guiding party policy while locked in frequent confrontations with the Marxist faction, there was little time left to engage in specifics of the coming order. However, through his general positions and various editorials and statements, Berger did leave behind a picture of what his Great Society might be.

His goal of a collectivist state in which the means of production and distribution would be subject to democratic management distinguished his future society from that of the American progressives. The fact that he often endorsed the same immediate demands as the progressives tended to obscure his differences with the reformers, but his goal remained the fashioning of the framework of a new society, whereas theirs was the reordering of the traditional system. The progressives' aim of a streamlined and efficient capitalism was unacceptable to this socialist who found the profit motive sordid and the system leveling men and denying their individuality.

At the same time, while he shared the basic Marxist vision of the future, his new society was distinct from that of the orthodox Marxists. His devotion to socialism was as firm as that of any member of the party; but his belief that the exact moment in which the socialist system triumphed would color the new society prevented his acceptance of several orthodox points. The traditional version of the forceful conquest followed by a dictatorship in the name of the masses was reprehensible to him, both because of his views of tactics and of priorities.

Berger rejected any means except persuasion because he believed that the majority must favor socialism before it could be effective. If a socialist order were imposed on a society which remained unreceptive to it, the new system would be opposed and the cost would be tallied in lives and bloodshed. Berger did not want to lose the positive characteristics of the old order as the new one replaced it. "We are the inheritors of a civilization . . . and all that is good in it—art, music, institutions, buildings, public works . . . the sense of right and wrong—not one of these shall be lost." While he wanted to build anew, he was determined to retain what was valuable in the old structure and would not risk sacrificing essentials. Tactics required preparing a people for the socialist future. They would not see the system imposed upon them before they were ready. Moreover, they would not find themselves denied of their property without compensation. Berger insured that the socialist platform included compensation rather than confiscation, for when the moment of transition was completed, he did not want to have on his hands a group of former property-owners set on revenge. "We will offer compensation. . . ," he said, "because it seems just to present-day thought and will prove the easiest, cheapest way in the end."[34]

Thus there were two cornerstones of his Great Society: socialism and democracy. And when the Socialist party floundered after World War I and disintegrated over the issue of Bolshevism, Berger stood for democratic values. If the cost of the new order was that of democracy in the guise of a dictatorship of the proletariat, that new order was not Berger's. At that moment, he left center stage. His choice was social democracy.

In Berger's future society, individuals would enjoy challenging and meaningful work as well as leisure time. Art and culture would be available to the newly enlightened and educated populace. And, in completing his description of the future, Berger responded to a question as to who would handle the drudgery in his future order by stating "Machines . . . which clean my house now."[35] The better life meant a society with opportunities open to all its members equally.

Berger joined the Socialist Labor party in 1889, but found himself in opposition to many of its policies. In general, he rejected the absolute reliance on Marxist ideology and the subserviance of the party to its leader, Daniel De Leon. The extreme centralization of the SLP, with what might be termed its cult of personality, caused him to resign after several months. His resignation coincided with his expulsion.

Berger had become convinced of the real necessity of building a constructive socialist party that would immerse itself in the problems of the here and now instead of the fine points of ideology. A few years later he turned from his schoolteaching and threw himself into the needs of a practical socialist movement. Convinced of the value of propaganda, Berger took the savings from eleven years of teaching and after the negotiation of more than one loan, he purchased a daily called the *Arbeiter Zeitung*. He changed its name to the *Wisconsin Vorwaerts* and, retaining German as the language of the paper, in January 1893, he became editor and publisher.[36]

In his paper's first issue Berger tried to mark a path that would appeal both to the older, still radical, local socialists and to the younger laboring men of the trade union movement. He emphasized immediate interests and demands and initiated the American stage of Milwaukee socialism. It was clearly the aim of Victor Berger and those who gathered around him and his newspaper to adapt scientific socialism to the American situation.

Berger later developed an English-language weekly, the *Social-Democratic Herald*, and, in 1913, supplanted it with a daily called the Milwaukee *Leader*. However, editing his newspaper remained a means of propaganda rather than a goal in itself. In 1893, his involvement in radical politics on the national scene began. He attended the Populist and American Federation of Labor conventions, opposed utopian colonization as a member of the short-lived Social Democracy, and with others, fostered the birth of the Social Democratic party in 1898 and then the united Socialist party in 1901.[37]

The founding of the party in the summer of 1901 officially ended a generation of factionalization that had plagued socialists. Henceforth most American socialists, with the exception of the small number composing the SLP, would be locked within one party where they could settle their differences privately. Or so it was envisioned when the Social Democratic party joined forces with a contingent of the SLP.

The party grew in numbers throughout the next decade, reaching the high point of its political strength in the 1910-1912 period:

SOCIALIST PARTY MEMBERSHIP[38]
1903-1920

1903	15,975	1912	118,045
1904	20,763	1913	95,957
1905	23,327	1914	93,579
1906	26,784	1915	79,274
1907	29,270	1916	83,284
1908	41,751	1917	80,279
1909	41,479	1918	82,344
1910	58,011	1919	104,822
1911	84,716	1920	26,766

In those years, the party showed encouraging growth in locals as well as in membership. In that two-year period itself, membership more than doubled and the socialists elected their first congressman. They also elected their greatest number of local officials, while achieving their largest vote for the Presidency.[39] Socialist campaigns throughout the country became a familiar phenomenon, and a socialist on the ballot in Oklahoma or Massachusetts was not cause for eyebrow-lifting among the voters.

The growth of the movement manifested itself in other and perhaps more meaningful and tangible ways. The socialist press experienced significant gains at this time, both in numbers of papers and in subscription rolls. Moreover, a variety of socialist institutions flourished both within and without the party. In 1906, the Rand School of Social Science was founded as a socialist educational center for workers. The Intercollegiate Socialist Society, born the previous year, saw its chapters on university campuses multiply rapidly, with its quarterly becoming fashionable reading for the young avant-garde.

The party itself spawned a number of subsidiary institutions. A Lyceum Department was established in the National Office in 1911 as a kind of socialist Chatauqua which supplied organizations with speakers. An Information Department was created the following year as a clearing house for socialist legislative activity.[40]

The reformist wing of the party generally monopolized the party offices and its subordinate organizations. The same people enjoyed successive election to party offices because their names were familiar to the membership. The Marxist wing could not reverse this trend. It lacked more than a few well-known names, and also it was nearly schizophrenic about political participation. The strength of the right wing can be seen, in fact, by the very existence of a Lyceum Department, as the left unalterably opposed all such institutions as irrelevant to the class struggle.

However, among famous socialist names, the most renowned nominally belonged to the Marxist wing. That faction claimed Eugene V. Debs, the perennial Socialist candidate for president and the man who personified the party to the United States. But in cold fact, during every crisis requiring a choice between reform and revolution, Debs did not stand with the revolutionists. While he opposed those who became enmeshed in reform platforms and machine methods, he also resisted the extremism of those who ignored immediate issues. He did not fit in either slot. He was untutored in Marxist scholarship and therefore not limited in his choices. Debs was not so much an American Marxist as a representative of the American radical tradition. He was a radical instinctively reacting to unjust conditions, a leader free of factions, politicking and conventions. And therefore his seeming identification with the revolutionists did not help them in their struggle against the reformists.

A second reason for Debs's failure to remain with one camp was that he closely related policies and individuals. Loyalty prevented him from turning permanently on old comrades. As his definitive biographer has written, "Debs, unable to join either . . . faction, was forced to hold an anomalous center position and fire blasts at both sides. He hoped for the impossible—that the two factions would neutralize each other without immobilizing the Party."[41]

The leader of the eastern, foreign-born wing of the party was Morris Hillquit, who had emigrated to the United States from Russia in 1866 and had become a successful New York labor lawyer and socialist leader. He had led a sizable contingent out of the SLP and become one of the founders of the Socialist party.[42] Hillquit was the leading theoretician of the party until his death in 1933, and in spite of his thorough Marxist grounding he favored immediate demands and political action.

By 1908-1909, Hillquit and his followers had cemented an alliance with the midwestern reformists whose leader was Berger.[43] Their collaboration was a major staple in the reformists' domination of policy which the revolutionists could not overcome but only affect by destroying the party. Further, it gave Berger the activist a strong position from which to exercise his qualities of leadership.

Berger's national role can only be understood after his Milwaukee power base has been explored, since the latter was the essential ingredient necessary to his other activities.

The Milwaukee Social Democrats first entered municipal elections in the spring of 1898. The platform they offered the Milwaukee voters was one of detailed reformism, including municipally owned utilities, public work projects for the unemployed, free medical services and textbooks, and urban renewal through substitution of recreation areas for slums. Their state platform that autumn included some of the same planks, as well as a graduated income tax and property tax to replace existing taxes, universal suffrage for literate adults, direct legislation, abolition of the governor's veto, proportional representation, abolition of the State Senate, state farm insurance, the prohibition of labor for those under the age of sixteen and of night work for women in factories.

Gradually the Social Democrats learned that the longer a platform, the fewer its readers. The programs grew shorter and the stress on minute details disappeared but immediate demands remained paramount. By 1906, the important plank forbidding the granting of franchises to private utility corporations was deleted. These and other modifications were effected in accordance with Berger's interest in courting the support of the small businessman. The party ought not alienate the middle class which often was subject to as many external pressures and manipulations as was the proletariat; neither controlled its own destiny.

The possibility of socialist inroads into the native middle class depended on external developments. While the socialists seemed to recognize that their base in the shrinking German community and their hold on skilled labor required supplementation, their ability to reach successfully outside their own foundation was related to issues in the greater community and the middle-class Yankee response to those issues. In the first decade of the twentieth century, Milwaukee politics gave the socialists their chance to embrace the middle class. The corruption and incompetence of the local Democratic and Republican parties became blatantly clear to the voters at a time of national emphasis on municipal reform. With muckraking articles omnipresent and state legislation in Wisconsin stressing honesty and efficiency in government, it was logical for the Milwaukee voter to turn toward the third party as his only alternative. The socialists' increasing emphasis on local corruption and graft opened the way for a coalition, however ephemeral, with clean government partisans.[44]

A consistent underlying cause in the Milwaukee movement's growing success was its alliance with the Federated Trades Council, involving strength in the Wisconsin State Federation of Labor. There was an overlapping of personnel, with the socialists within the FTC directing its political activities—cautiously, to be sure, to avoid annoying rank-and-file unionists. Berger headed his local of the Typographical Union, and his various newspapers became the voice of organized labor in Milwaukee. The planks of the Council's platform often matched those of the Social Democrats. After 1900, the close entente which had grown between the two organizations was cemented into a permanent alliance.[45]

Of the various factors in the strength of the socialist movement in Milwaukee—the experiences of its German population, the receptiveness of local organized labor, the occasional attention of non-German ethnic working men, and the anti-graft middle-class voter—only the first two components could be considered more than fleeting. The convergence of all four was brief and, indeed, even the first two phenomena were susceptible to dissipation in time. The very fact that the German population was not replenishing itself through additional immigration while simultaneously the industrial adjustments of the late nineteenth century were being completed meant that potential recruits for the Milwaukee socialists were not available. Moreover, the second and third generation German-Americans then maturing were exposed to the processes of assimilation which led them away from their fathers and grandfathers.

The Milwaukee labor movement too was experiencing assimilation that in turn implied a threat to its support for a radical minor party. The process, noted by John Laslett in his observations on the German brewery workers of the midwest, meant that a narrowing base of radical commitment within the union, coupled with the conservative influence and supportive role of the American Federation of Labor on its affiliates, might serve to deflect labor in Milwaukee from its original posture. While more than the ethnic factor was involved, the ethnicity of the commitment in itself meant impermanence.[46]

While the party had started slowly at the polls, by 1902 it gained confidence and the 1904 totals, aided by Berger's race for mayor and influenced by the external issue of local graft, showed nearly a 100 percent improvement over the previous election.

MUNICIPAL RETURNS FOR THE SOCIALIST MAYORALTY CANDIDATE[47]
1898-1908

1898	2,430
1900	2,585
1902	8,453
1904	15,343
1906	16,837
1908	20,887

Berger sensed the proximity of victory at the polls and the chance to initiate the first reforms toward socialism. At the same time, he already faced criticism for vote-chasing and so he cautioned against campaigning for non-class-conscious votes. Realizing the threat of party disruption, he declared in his *Social-Democratic Herald* on 22 August 1903, that the education of the voter was more important than the premature capture of his ballot.

Despite the possibility of division, the socialists elected several of their candidates—nine aldermen and eight other officials. Later, in the November election of 1904, Berger for the first time was a candidate for Congress from the Fifth Congressional District of Wisconsin (Milwaukee), and although he lost, the party elected five members to the Wisconsin State Assembly and one to the State Senate.[48]

A factor in the growing vote was the Social Democrats' campaign technique. Great stress was laid on the organization of districts for the dissemination of campaign literature. That the socialists must reach every Milwaukee household prior to an election was party dogma. Distribution was systematically managed block by block and the party boasted that it was able to saturate the city with 100,000 circulars in a twenty-four-hour period and never miss a household. Each of the four Sundays preceding an election, teams of men and boys would canvass the entire city. They would work from six to nine in the morning and as each voter arose he was greeted with a circular from the Social Democratic party. Because Milwaukee was a multilingual municipality, care had to be taken to insure that the right piece of literature got into each household. The material was printed in English, German, and Polish, while sometimes different pages of the same circular were in several languages. It was the burden of the campaign workers to know the language of every household.[49] Berger's pragmatic and tactical skills were responsible for the success of the "bundle brigade."

Thus, the painstaking organization of the Social Democratic party under Victor Berger, as well as the support of the trade unions and Milwaukee's peculiar background, led to the party's triumphs. Berger, because of his knowledge of socialism, his boldness and ability to envision realistic goals and determine appropriate means, won the respect of his comrades and the right to "boss" them. He met no real challenge to his leadership in this period.

The Milwaukee socialists, with the most politically successful organization in the Socialist party, argued that local autonomy was of absolute necessity in the movement, for only that could lead to the municipal success which inevitably must precede greater triumphs. The insistence on local autonomy was a tenet the Milwaukee socialists never modified. Any challenge to that autonomy was deeply resented.[50]

Berger's virtually unquestioned rule in Milwaukee can perhaps be explained by the local party's homogeneity and cohesiveness, which could account for its willingness to accept his idiosyncrasies. The national Socialist party, however, with its extreme diversity was not so eager to succumb to his egocentric personality.

Although his position was always open to challenge, Berger can nevertheless be considered the central figure in the national party by virtue of his Milwaukee power base, his activity in the party's internal politics, and his personal fame.[51] Debs, although better known to the general public, refused to participate in party politics. Hillquit, while active in party politics, divided his time between the party and his busy law practice, devoted to labor and socialist issues. Berger, on the other hand, was both a major leader within the party and a well-known political personality. Although he lacked Debs' ethereal and self-sacrificing qualities, and was without Hillquit's tact and ability to compromise, his ambition and dedication enabled him to become one of the most famous and influential socialists in the United States. His own experience paralleled the rise and fall of the party. He reached an apex with his election to Congress in 1910 when party strength was at its summit, and he experienced the agony of no other socialist in the 1918-1920 *götterdämmerung*.

Berger and his followers had satisfactorily resolved the conflict of working within existing conditions without fear of loss of socialist purity. If the Socialist party had been able to submit to his theories and leadership, it might have made a more permanent mark on American politics than it actually did. Victor Berger, except for his dilemma-induced war stand, tried to be both in and of the world; assuming responsibility while nevertheless aiming for fundamental change, he sought to lead the party beyond its contempt for American political issues. That he and his followers did not succeed is an important aspect of the decline of the Socialist party as a potential force in the United States.

NOTES

1. Edward J. Muzik, "Victor Berger's Early Career," *Historical Messenger* (Milwaukee) 17 (March 1961): 15-16; Max Lerner, "Victor Berger," *Dictionary of American Biography* II, Supp. 1 (1944): 72.

2. U.S., Bureau of the Census, *Eleventh Census of the United States: 1890, Vital and Social Statistics*, IV, 346, *Twelfth Census . . .* , I, 884-894; Bayrd Still, *Milwaukee: the History of a City* (Madison: State Historical Society, 1940), pp. 574-575.

3. Still, *Milwaukee*, p. 267.

4. Eric J. Hobsbawm, *Primitive Rebels* (New York: W. W. Norton and Co., Inc., 1959), p. 108.

5. Carl Wittke, *We Who Built America*, rev. ed. (Cleveland: Case Western Reserve Press, 1964), pp. 198, 205.

6. Still, *Milwaukee*, pp. 321-323, 329-337.

7. Gerd Korman, *Industrialization, Immigrants and Americanizers: The View from Milwaukee, 1886-1921* (Madison: State Historical Society, 1967), p. 3.

8. Wittke, *We Who Built America*, pp. 213-214.

9. Still, *Milwaukee*, pp. 289-295, 303.

10. Ibid., pp. 265-266; Korman, *Industrialization*, p. 42.

11. Hobsbawm, *Primitive Rebels*, p. 3.

12. Oscar Lewis, *La Vida: A Puerto Rican Family in the Culture of Poverty* (New York: Random House, 1965), p. xliii.

13. Marvin Wachman, *The History of the Social-Democratic Party of Milwaukee, 1897-1910* (Urbana: University of Illinois Press, 1945), p. 70; Still, *Milwaukee*, pp. 268-272.

14. Korman, *Industrialization*, pp. 41-42; Still, *Milwaukee*, p. 278; Theodore Saloutos, "The Greeks of Milwaukee," *Wisconsin Magazine of History* 53 (Spring 1970): 177, 181.

15. John M. Work, "Autobiography," II, Chapter 4, p. 1, typescript, John M. Work Collection, SHSW. No concurrent pagination; each chapter separately numbered.

16. Frederick I. Olson, "The Milwaukee Socialists, 1897-1941" (Ph.D. diss., Harvard University, 1952), p. 337.

17. John Spargo, "Memoir," Oral History Research Office, Columbia University, 1950, pp. 198-199.
18. William G. Bruce, "Memories of William G. Bruce," *Wisconsin Magazine of History* 18 (September 1934): 47; Morris Hillquit, *Loose Leaves from a Busy Life* (New York: Rand School of Social Science, 1933), p. 53; Olson, "Milwaukee Socialists," p. 20; Spargo, "Memoir," pp. 198-199.
19. Oscar Ameringer, *If You Don't Weaken* (New York: Henry Holt and Co., 1940), p. 296.
20. R. S. Campbell to Coit Lyceum Bureau, 25 March 1911, Berger Collection, Milwaukee County Historical Society (hereafter cited as Berger Col., MCHS); Ameringer, *If You Don't Weaken*, p. 283. Berger's awkwardness with his pen can be illustrated by his titling an editorial "1910 Was Born with Red Hair" in order to indicate the socialists' political prospects. *Social-Democratic Herald*, 12 February 1910.
21. Muzik, "Victor Berger's Early Career," 17-18. A Milwaukee legend suggests that from a successful debate with a socialist, he was led to a rigorous study of socialism and conversion.
22. Studies of the Socialist party tend to describe Berger casually as a Bernstein revisionist, but his career supports the argument of theoretical independence. Interestingly, his correspondence with European socialists, as disparate as Ramsay MacDonald and Karl Liebknecht, contains no letters exchanged with Edward Bernstein.
23. *Social-Democratic Herald*, 7 June 1913.
24. Ibid., 15 April 1905.
25. Ibid., 29 April 1905, September 1906, 5 February 1910, 26 February 1910.
26. Ibid., December 1907.
27. Socialist Party, *Proceedings of the 1908 National Convention*, pp. 38-39.
28. *Social-Democratic Herald*, 17 August 1912.
29. Socialist Party, *Proceedings of the 1910 National Congress*, pp. 119-120.
30. Berger to *Inquirer*, 22 May 1916, Berger Col., MCHS.
31. Berger to Morris Hillquit, 8 April 1905, Hillquit Collection, State Historical Society of Wisconsin (hereafter cited as Hillquit Col., SHSW).
32. Socialist Party, *Proceedings of the 1908 National Convention*, p. 15.

33. Herbert F. Margulies, *Decline of the Progressive Movement in Wisconsin, 1890-1920* (Madison: State Historical Society, 1968), p. 155; Robert S. Maxwell, *La Follette and the Rise of the Progressives in Wisconsin* (Madison: State Historical Society, 1956), pp. 200-201; Spargo, "Memoir," pp. 199-200.

34. Lincoln Steffens, "Eugene V. Debs on What the Matter Is in America and What to Do about It," *Everybody's Magazine* 19 (October 1908): 461-462.

35. Ibid., p. 468.

36. Wachman, *The History of the Social Democratic Party*, p. 10.

37. For a fuller treatment of Berger's early political activities, the best source is the one biography: Edward J. Muzik, "Victor L. Berger, a Biography" (Ph.D. diss., Northwestern University, 1960), pp. 32-112.

38. Socialist Party, Membership Reports, Socialist Party Collection, Duke University (hereafter cited as SP Col., Duke).

39. The Information Department of the Socialist party recorded that in 1912 there were party members in nine state legislatures and in many municipal offices, including several mayors. Ethelwyn Mills, ed., *Legislative Program of the Socialist Party: Record of the Work of the Socialist Representatives in State Legislatures, 1899-1913* (Chicago: Socialist Party, 1914), pp. 5-10. Debs received 901,062 votes for nearly 6 percent of the ballots cast for president.

40. Nathan Fine, *Labor and Farmer Parties, 1828-1928* (New York: Rand School of Social Science, 1928), pp. 236-243. This is one of the first histories of the Socialist party and was written by a colleague of those in the reformist faction. The study is valuable for its tracing of the party's effort to Americanize socialism, but it exaggerates the party's pre-World War I success in boring from within the trade union movement.

41. Ray Ginger, *Eugene V. Debs* (New York: Collier Books, 1962), pp. 313, 397. Whenever Debs battled Berger over an issue, he nevertheless recalled that it was Berger who introduced him to the works of Marx when he visited the imprisoned Debs in Woodstock jail after the Pullman strike of 1894. "I have loved him ever since. . . ." See Eugene V. Debs,

"How I Became a Socialist," *The Comrade* 1 (April 1902): 147-148.

42. Robert William Iverson, "Morris Hillquit: American Social Democrat" (Abstract of Ph.D. diss., State University of Iowa, 1951). This is the only biography of Hillquit. His autobiography, however, sheds some light on his early life.

43. The relationship between Hillquit and Berger grew from guarded hostility in 1901 to the polite cooperation of 1905 to full synchronization of forces by the end of the decade. Berger wrote to Hillquit on 9 March 1905: "Let me take the liberty of suggesting that the New York comrades. . . ." On 27 March 1905, he felt compelled to add: "Now I would not write this letter to you if I did not feel sure that we had made up our past differences and have both only one aim now, and that is to work for socialism, and the Socialist Party." Berger to Hillquit, Hillquit Col., SHSW. After Berger's death in 1929, Hillquit, while mentioning "the bond of friendship between us tightened with the advancing years. . . .", stressed Berger's role in Milwaukee and in Congress and minimized by omission Berger's significance in the national party. Hillquit, *Loose Leaves from a Busy Life*, p. 53.

44. Frederick I. Olson, "The Socialist Party and the Unions in Milwaukee, 1900-1912," *Wisconsin Magazine of History* 44 (Winter 1960-61): 110; Still, *Milwaukee*, p. 515.

45. Olson, "The Socialist Party and the Unions in Milwaukee," p. 112.

46. John Laslett, *Labor and the Left: a Study of Socialist and Radical Influences in the American Labor Movement, 1881-1924* (New York: Basic Books, 1970), pp. 44-46.

47. Wachman, *The History of the Social-Democratic Party*, p. 82. The total number of ballots cast grew in these years from 46,000 to 59,000.

48. Wachman gives the most comprehensive treatment of the early socialist electoral victories in Milwaukee. See Chapters 4-5. Among the elected aldermen were Frederic Heath, a member of the original executive of the Social Democratic party of America and the pride of the Milwaukee local because he was one of the few native-born among the leaders. Another successful candidate was Emil Seidel, who became the first socialist mayor of Milwaukee. Frederick Olson, after checking election returns by wards, found that the eight wards having the highest percentage of German-born voters gave the

Social Democrats twenty-six of their thirty aldermanic victories between 1904 and 1908. Olson, "The Milwaukee Socialists," p. 1.

49. Gilbert H. Poor, *Interesting Sketches: Blazing a Trail, the Story of a Pioneer Socialist Agitator* (1911), p. 85.

50. *Social-Democratic Herald*, 6 March 1906; Olson, "The Milwaukee Socialists," p. 261; Wachman, *The History of the Social-Democratic Party*, pp. 56-57.

51. Norman Thomas said in 1933: "America has produced three great socialists—Victor L. Berger was the great leader, Eugene V. Debs the great orator and Morris Hillquit the great philosopher of the American Socialist movement." See "Hillquit Memorial Issue," *New Leader*, 6 October 1934.

3

Reformist Domination and Defense

Participatory democracy was an ideal of the Socialist party. Stressing responsiveness to members, the party attempted to minimize bureaucracy. Like the radicals of the 1960s and 1970s in the United States and Europe, the leaders of the Socialist party objected in theory to the principle of representation. In addition, past experience in the monolithic SLP, subject to Daniel De Leon's absolute rule, inspired distrust of an entrenched executive. As the result of ideology and history, the party was resolved upon an open structure. Nevertheless, the Socialist party became enmeshed in formal parliamentary procedures.

A serious divergence of opinion existed between the party's factions, with leftists playing down the need of formalization and rightists maintaining that routine procedures were required for the party's effectiveness. The former drew back because of inherent suspicion of political processes, while the latter needed formalized channels for the implementation of its ideas. Personality was a factor, too; a spontaneous individual such as Debs was apt to find standard procedures stultifying and a calculating personality such as Berger thrived on them. Each faction's position was motivated by its basic approach and buttressed by mutual distrust.

The executive of the party consisted of a committee of varying numbers, usually about a half-dozen. These individuals were elected by the entire membership annually in order to prevent a particular clique from monopolizing the machinery of the party. The National Executive Committee was required to meet a dozen times during its year in office, and an Executive Secretary supervised the daily affairs of the party. The NEC was empowered to make routine policy decisions to be implemented by the Executive Secretary. Above the NEC in the hierarchy was the National Committee which met annually, but it was little more than a rubber stamp for the Executive.

Significant decisions were to be settled by a referendum of the membership. The reliance on direct legislation, including the recall, meant that the Socialist party was to be the embodiment of the principle of direct democracy. This commitment resulted in unwieldy machinery. Election to the various committees and posts often required more than a half-dozen ballots, and only a very small minority of the membership participated in the frequent referenda. Constant balloting and the necessity of conducting elections through the mails meant that only the most firmly committed remained active members. Moreover, the small staff under the Executive Secretary found itself continually bogged down. Due to the size of the country and the wide distribution of the locals, the party nearly strangled in paper.

Extraordinary policy decisions were to be determined in convention, involving great sacrifice of time. Normally, conventions were scheduled only for presidential election years, when elected delegates would meet to draw up the platform and select the candidate.

Therefore, the decision-making process of the party, while founded on the simple principle of majority direction, was nonetheless complex. The results were operational sluggishness and a power vacuum. The NEC stepped into that power vacuum and began to assume the essential policy-making role that had been intended to remain with the membership.

By the end of the party's first decade the reformist faction had come to monopolize the committee. The left's basic rejection of political action coupled with the right's attraction to it, the unwieldy party structure and the growing familiarity of the membership with leaders such as Berger and Hillquit who were elected again and again, invited easy domination of the party executive. The reformists occasionally faced a disagreeable issue in referendum initiated by a distraught local or individual. They reluctantly accepted Debs' recurrent candidacies and they met the revolutionists openly at each convention. But on a daily basis the reformists controlled the party through the NEC, routinely fending off revolutionists' attacks as an unwanted but tolerable burden. Not until spring of 1911 did the reformists find their rule challenged by a vociferous and articulate leftist on the NEC itself. But that proved to be only a temporary intrusion.

The reformists used their control of the executive in order to exploit party machinery and fashion policy in the image of their own conceptions. An example of reformists' molding and manipulating of the party is found in their retention and expansion of the principle of local autonomy. Berger was one of those most anxiously committed to this principle at the founding sessions of the party, and his wishes were implemented. The constitution of the party granted exclusive jurisdiction to the state organizations over the locals; only the states could expel an errant party member. In addition, the state organizations were dependent on the constitution, which insured that no executive committee cabal could ever intrude willfully. Even the vital power to discipline state branches for infraction of the constitution was granted to the NEC only grudgingly.

Berger, aided by other Milwaukee leaders and by members from other areas who were equally concerned over local autonomy, vigilantly guarded against any effort to weaken the principle once it became party doctrine. At conventions he led his forces against the inclusion of any local matters in the national program and platform. He pointed out: "You in Seattle do not know about the needs of Milwaukee. We in Milwaukee do not want to interfere in the affairs of New York." It was not uncommon for Berger to threaten to lead walk-outs from conventions if this principle were endangered, and the solid bloc voting behind him gave his word considerable weight.[1]

Not content merely to insure the sanctity of this principle, Berger effected various extensions of it. In 1913, for example, he prevailed upon the NEC to refuse in principle endorsement of any local initiative other than those which had worked their way through the party machinery. Thus, he deprived the executive of any inclination it might have to decide between two quarreling factions of a local, each of which claimed to be the legally recognized local branch of the party. Berger even persuaded the NEC to abandon its right to support local action.[2]

Berger's adamant stand, while initially strong, was intensified as the result of his recall from the NEC in 1905 because of his alleged support of a non-socialist candidate in local elections when no socialist was running. After that experience, he responded even to a suggestion of irregular policies in the Milwaukee local with charges that direct actionists were trying to smear him. Because of his counteroffensives, never after 1905 did the National Office investigate his organization, in spite of various controversies which surrounded him.[3]

In order to maintain reformist domination of the NEC, committee members often sought well-known and attractive figures, workers if at all possible, who might buttress the right's hold on the executive. For example, they persuaded a party member named Adolph Germer, an organizer of the United Mine Workers of Illinois, to seek election to the NEC. Thereafter Germer played an important role as a party functionary while simultaneously improving the reformist image through his own proletarian past.[4] In general the reformists tried to ram through tickets of their own choice, and as long as they controlled the committee and enjoyed not only the power but the inherent prestige, they were determined to maintain their hold on it.

Party machinery was exploited in order to shore up local popularity too. Berger was prone to manipulate the national party's assets to strengthen himself. While party custom frowned upon the release of lists of locals to outside organizations for any purpose, such as circularizing or fund raising, Berger nonetheless cajoled the National Office into granting him a list in order to solicit contributions to his newspaper. He also tried to win NEC approval of releasing the list to the Brewers' International Union in Milwaukee for their anti-prohibition campaign. Both times the accompanying publicity created party dissension and charges against Berger of using the party for his own interests.[5]

Originally the party had decided against publishing a newspaper, for although the power of the written word was respected, many in both factions feared any one person assuming the guise of party mouthpiece. Berger, no less than others, feared that eventuality. However, as time passed and party bulletins and newsletters were issued in lieu of a newspaper, many were persuaded of the need for a party-owned and -operated newspaper. Berger held back and used all the power at his disposal to prevent a reversal of the earlier decision. He himself as an editor appreciated the role of the press. In fact, he had encouraged the establishment of a national socialist press service for the privately operated socialist newspapers, and he was aware that the European socialists ran party newspapers and, in fact, prohibited privately owned socialist papers. Nevertheless, he did not waiver in his opposition to a party press, because he feared the possibility that an official voice of the party might one day be controlled by an opposing faction.

Neither Berger's arguments nor his threats worked, for other reformists felt secure in their increasing hold on the party. Berger, never acquiescing, sat on a committee of five which formulated detailed editorial policy, and he continued to grumble even though the member selected for the editorship was a newspaperman with whom he had worked easily. However, Berger's forebodings proved valid as, prior to the party schism in 1919, the NEC deemed it necessary to remove its left-leaning editor.[6]

But aside from a few instances where the reformists were not of one mind, they were accustomed to running the party to suit themselves. In 1912, for example, they appointed a reformist as campaign manager to Debs, and despite the candidate's own objections, the appointment held. While the reformists could not prevent the nomination of the popular Debs as their presidential candidate, they could through their choice of a manager attempt to mold his campaign.[7]

During the years before World War I, reformist control of the party solidified, while the left continually nipped at its heels. Only at the party conventions did the two factions confront each other publicly on relatively equal terms. At those times, the reformists lost their advantage and the revolutionists became serious challengers of party direction. When the party drew up its platforms, policy-making became more than the collaboration of a few comrades in entrenched positions. In the glare of the party eye, either faction might win the support of the delegates. The agricultural and immigration issues most clearly demonstrated their sparring back and forth in the conventions between 1908 and 1912.

There was so little agreement on the relevancy of the farmer to the class struggle that it was not until 1912 that the party could fashion an agricultural plank. The leftists maintained that until the farmer was divested of his property he was not a member of the working class, while the reformists insisted that he was an increasingly self-conscious and enlightened victim of economic forces. Both the conventions of 1908 and 1912 provided a framework for prolonged jousting over this issue, as did the party's only Congress, called in the 1910 non-presidential year to encourage wide exploration of issues.

Berger led the reformist faction's fight for an agricultural plank and received firm support from an erstwhile antagonist, A. M. Simons. Simons was a newspaper editor who moved from one socialist paper to another, as he made the ideological journey from revolutionist to reformist; in 1913 he joined the staff of Berger's Milwaukee *Leader*. Even in his leftist phase, however, he had urged the party to exploit what he saw as the farmer's predisposition toward socialism. As a reformist in 1908, Simons was that faction's expert on agriculture, and he strengthened Berger's arguments and broadened his understanding of the complexities of the farmer's life.

None of the major party leaders joined Berger in his effort to appoint a committee on agriculture. He persevered because of his commitment to deal with realities. He told the convention delegates that the conversion of American farmers was of vital concern to the party since their support would enhance the strength of the movement; after all, he pointed out, the United States was still in many ways an agricultural nation in which working farmers were locked in battle with economic forces. He believed that the party could only function with the backing of the majority of American workers, and it need not delude itself that antagonism existed between urban and agricultural producers. They had the same interests, he later wrote, and the Socialist party must be the political expression of the economic interests of the masses; socialists "must come as friends, not as 'class conscious' enemies." He denied vehemently the opposition's contention that support for the farmer meant an endorsement of individualism and private property.[8]

Although the delegates finally agreed to appoint a committee on agriculture, they rejected the program it produced. Berger agonized over this rejection, for it seemed to him both blind and distorted reading of the class struggle. He broadened his argument to the theoretical at the Congress in 1910. He pointed out that no socialist party had yet formulated an appropriate stand on agriculture because of the Marxist expectation of the disappearance of the small farmer. But the rate of agricultural concentration which Marx had sketched had not been approached; concentration in agriculture did not parallel that of industry. Agricultural methods and implements were not as fluid and open to combination; machinery had begun to eliminate hired labor but in outline little had altered. Berger's revisionist attack met with no more success, as a second time unconvinced leftists had enough delegate support to return the agricultural plank to committee.

When finally a plank was inserted into the party platform in 1912, it followed Berger's revisionist view of the farmer's role in the class struggle.[9] His triumph, he believed, had resulted from persuading revolutionists to the revisionist view that the party must preoccupy itself with the "everyday fight for the practical revolution of every day."[10] But, the fact that he did gain a victory in this matter despite vociferous opposition was due to the prestige he enjoyed in the party even more than to his arguments. The delegates who streamed into the conventions in Chicago and Indianapolis could not readily ignore a speech presented by Berger, whose name they had known since the founding of the party, and who invariably sat on the NEC. The representatives of the rank and file who came to the occasional conventions were far more receptive to the words of a famous reformist leader than they were to the arguments of revolutionists whom they did not know.

The cost to Berger of this type of triumph was the standard charge of opportunism. He was condemned by the revolutionists for his reformism and was told that his attitude was bourgeois. The left maintained that any step taken which might strengthen the principle of private property could not be endorsed by a Socialist party. Defeat on this issue was not accepted lightly and leftists spread the word that Berger and the reformists joining him were weakening the party and turning its orientation toward electioneering.[11]

Another consuming issue at the conventions, immigration policy, had a different outcome and saw Berger go down to defeat. The fact that his view did not prevail was indicative of reformist division rather than of revolutionist strength. Whenever a cleavage appeared among the reformists, their control of party machinery could seldom preclude the passage of distasteful policies.

Immigration policy was one of the most controversial issues at successive conventions of the pre-war years as it touched upon the party in a more intimate and emotional manner than did the agricultural plank. None of the leaders were connected closely with the agricultural issue, while on the other hand, many were immigrants themselves or supported by immigrant stock. Moreover, all were aware of the dynamite inherent in immigration policy because of the sensitivity of organized labor.

Delegates to the conventions tended to split three ways. Some, who clung to the pure Marxist principle of uniting the workers of the world, dismissed immigration as a transitory issue. Many reformists, including Berger, assumed the Anglo-Saxon (and Teutonic) chauvinism of the progressives and favored selective immigration quotas. This group found itself opposing a third group with whom it was normally allied, led by Meyer London, the representative of the Jewish section of the Socialist party, and more important, spokesman for the new immigrant. Those members recently arrived from Eastern Europe opposed limitations upon the open door policy. Thus, the lines were drawn at various party sessions for a complex struggle over immigration policy within the reformist faction, with the left able to stand aside and enjoy the bloodletting which would have to work to its advantage.

The fragmentation evident in this debate was indicative of a frequently manifested lack of cohesiveness. While the two factions generally held together within themselves, neither was monolithic. Members from each group might stray over particular issues, depending on temperament, timing, and topic. Moreover, there were many floaters in the middle of the party who favored now one faction and then the other, and who never formed their own firm bloc. Although the term "center" has been used, there was no center comparable to the left and right. Instead, there were numbers of people who might form a third or fourth segment in accord with the issue of the moment.[12]

An open door immigration policy was inimical to most reformist leaders, and a plank somewhere between principle and open expediency had to be hammered out. Berger's position, which was that of the majority of the Committee on Immigration, was rejected by the convention as untenable. Their report favored restricted immigration and full exclusion of Orientals on the grounds that imported labor was a weapon of the ruling classes in the class struggle.[13]

Berger was one of the most active defenders of the report. As was his habit, whatever he favored had his wholehearted support; he was virtually unable to commit himself on a partial basis. So despite the enmity he stirred in a party containing significant numbers of eastern Europeans, he insisted that much less time was required to educate a western or central European to class consciousness than the generation or more required to educate others. He made no attempt to minimize the importance of the issue. "This is a question of civilization mainly. I believe that our civilization, the European or Caucasian or whatever name you choose to call it, I believe that our civilization is in question."[14] His experience in Milwaukee where Germans were the nucleus of his movement, while Poles, Hungarians, and Italians remained hostile to it, served to reinforce his early sense of cultural chauvinism.

The minority report offered by reformist journalist John Spargo condemned restriction as irrelevant since Orientals were not inundating the country. Moreover, it emphasized the need to capture political power in order to prevent contract labor. Morris Hillquit criticized both reports as based on the same premise—the permissibility of exclusion. His substitute report condemned that principle but, in effect, endorsed the practice, not on racial grounds but in terms of deliberate importation of labor with resultant lower living standards. Hillquit's talents and position fit the occasion perfectly. He himself was a new immigrant, thoroughly schooled in Marxism but allied to the reformists. Thus in experience he cut across the three groups. His solution was the straddling of the issue and his compromise was accepted. Despite a subsequent battle, the resolution of veiled racial exclusion became permanent policy of the Socialist party of America.[15] The alienation of labor had been avoided.

The party's uneasiness in view of organized labor's hostility to an open immigration policy was understandable. Labor formed the essential arena of the class struggle. The relationship with organized labor was the main battlefield on which the two factions fought. While the Socialist party was committed through its original platform to support organized labor, socialists of both groups would have felt more comfortable with a labor movement which challenged American capitalism. The reformists, including Berger, believed that the Socialist party must work with the American Federation of Labor and coax it into a socialist orientation. The revolutionist wing, however, wished to avoid the conservative federation in favor of support for direct actionist labor organizations.

Berger attended conventions of the AFL for a twenty-year period as a representative from the Typographical Union. At the annual conventions he, along with Max Hayes of Cleveland and a few other socialist trade union leaders, led the opposition to President Samuel Gompers.

Berger was Gompers's bête noire because of his constant sniping, and the two of them agreed only on their mutual antipathy. Berger, while often disappointed, consistently tried to persuade the AFL to broaden its demands beyond Gompers's "pure-and-simple unionism." In 1902 he convinced the convention to seek disability insurance. The delegates accepted Berger's argument that the AFL favor disability insurance, but they opposed the idea of a pension plan, the second measure he proposed.[16]

At the 1904 convention he introduced a resolution which sounded suspiciously like industrial unionism. He suggested that a modern alignment of the entire working class replace trade union autonomy.

However, when the Wobblies appeared in 1905 he backtracked and dropped the subject.[17] In point of fact he never envisioned abandonment of the existing trade union movement either to industrialism or to De Leon's dual unionism. "Boring from within" the AFL remained his approach; such a posture emerged from his doctrine of party-union cooperation from relatively autonomous but related positions. But in time Berger became disheartened. Despite a few specific gains and a mildly encouraging trend, he came to view the AFL as hopeless and unworthy of expenditure of socialists' energy. In addition, Berger's interests and hopes in political action had broadened and he relinquished his role in the federation. He did not even attend the conventions of 1908 and 1909, and went to the St. Louis meeting in 1910 for a last appearance.

If Berger and other reformists began to turn away from the AFL and yet did not embrace the IWW, logically they might have sought some other means to reach the American working man. Most simply assigned the Socialist party more responsibility in the class struggle, but leftists began to suggest that the right was turning to another and unacceptable course. When the 1909-1910 term of the NEC was drawing to a close, a bitter controversy erupted between the reformist wing and a spokesman for the left, with the executive committee caught in the crossfire.

The NEC majority consisted of Berger, Hillquit, Simons, Spargo, and Robert Hunter, another writer and party propagandist. All five—four writers and one lawyer—were reformists.

The assault was led by William English Walling, an intellectual associated with the party and a founder of the National Association for the Advancement of Colored People. He frequently blasted Berger and other reformists as mere reformers who exploited socialist phraseology, and linked them to what he called progressive capitalists. Walling's allies included the influential *International Socialist Review* and Eugene Debs. While Debs never formally committed himself in this controversy, he cooperated with the critics of the NEC by attacking its members as "trimmers" in his articles in the *Review* and *The Appeal to Reason*.[18]

A. M. Simons attended the 1909 convention of the AFL and, while there, he became convinced that the American worker was sympathetic to socialist goals. In party circles, Simons argued that the party could easily capture the wage-earner if it abandoned its domination by intellectuals. He pointed out that the British Labour party had revitalized itself so that it more closely represented the worker than did the Socialist party of America. Simons suggested that the party redouble its efforts to recruit union men by engaging unionists as organizers able to appeal to workers from intimate knowledge of the class struggle. He maintained that he and the other members of the NEC would gladly relinquish their positions to real workingmen, but that they did not "propose to surrender to those who have never worked save with their jaws and who are tearing down every organization to which they belong."[19]

Walling and his associates considered Simons' remarks a threat. An accounting of his position before a New York local caused an uproar.[20] J. G. Phelps Stokes, who represented the left on the NEC, charged that the Berger-Hillquit faction sought to turn the Socialist party into a labor party which inevitably would be dominated by the AFL and, therefore, support the capitalist framework. Moreover, he claimed that the majority of the NEC intended to retain power by any means in order to effect the transformation. The evidence for this claim included a statement by Berger at an NEC meeting a month earlier in which he recommended that the Socialist party support an independent labor party if one arose.[21]

In this dispute, the left seized upon shadow rather than substance, for no conspiracy existed. Had there been a plan to maintain the NEC majority in power for any purpose, certainly Berger, who led most polls among the rank and file and therefore was indispensable to the other members of the right, would have been aware of it. Berger himself wrote of the "cabal" against the right which sought "to oust the Social Democrats from the NEC and to throw the Socialist Party into the hands of the impossibilists," and its existence convinced him to run again for the NEC specifically to prevent the party from falling to those who would destroy it as a constructive force. He urged that the reformists agree on a slate of candidates for the new committee and particularly on those who must be kept off it.[22]

A poll taken among the candidates for the executive committee revealed no support for a labor party. One of the most expansive statements from those polled came from Berger who reiterated a favorite axiom. The labor movement and the Socialist party must cooperate without abandoning their individual identities. "Both . . . must work in perfect harmony and help each other, but each . . . is to do its own work and shall not interfere with the other's business. . . . We want every trade unionist . . . to join the Socialist Party and every Socialist who is eligible to join his economic organization—thus we unite both activities in every worker.'' This view he proudly called the ''Wisconsin Idea.''[23]

The clamor ended rather abruptly. The elections in February resulted in the return to office of Berger, Hillquit, Spargo, and Hunter, with only Simons of the controversial five defeated. Not one leftist was elected to the committee.[24]

Walling believed the results to be a disaster for the Socialist party, and he woefully prophesized that the ''trimmers'' would be in a position to make policy at the National Congress in June. His evaluation of tightened rightist control of the party machinery was correct, but his prediction of the emergence of a capitalist-diluted labor party was not fulfilled.[25] Walling's effort to embarrass the right before its hold on the party permanently solidified had backfired. The left was without a voice in the highest echelons of policy-making and therefore was weakened not only for the party congress of 1910 which thrashed out policy but also during the more serious confrontation in 1911 and 1912 over direct action.

The debate in the party bore other significance as well. It was illustrative of the right's willingness to discuss and probe party problems as opposed to the left's lack of flexibility. The right's ability to analyze, to grapple with the meaningful though perhaps the unorthodox, in order to find a way to create a mass workers' party, sharply contrasted with the self-immobilized left which consistently opposed constructive probing to solve the party's dilemmas. That members of the NEC might examine other socialist parties and contrast other situations with their own should not have been notable; to ignore developments elsewhere would have been dereliction of duty. But the left wing saw their interest and discussion as rejection of socialist principles.

So while Simons sought to borrow from the British Labour party to strengthen the American Socialist party and to alter its middle-class composition into a proletarian base, and while Berger tried to weld together the union movement and the party, the left could not get beyond its own clichés. It continued to insist upon purity of doctrine, technique, and propaganda,[26] even though its orthodoxy was not reaching the worker. In its concentration upon absolutes, the left lost sight of the necessity to achieve progress along the way—which could give its struggle the chance for fruition.

It has been postulated that this party controversy marked the disintegration of the system of bargaining between the two antagonistic factions and that henceforth any method would be fair in the struggle.[27] But there is no evidence of a subsequent wider gap in the relations between the two groups. Nor can it be demonstrated that either side thereafter depended on illegal means to assert its will. Each side competed, exploited advantages, and campaigned as it had in the past. That both talked but neither listened is true, but this lack of communication was not a new development in the Socialist party. Since its formation it had been factionalized, and its lines were only hardened by this particular incident; the significance then was one of intensification rather than of alteration.

That the labor party issue subsided quickly indicated that in itself it was an artificial controversy. However, the dispute was revived later that year after a discussion within the confines of the right wing. In November 1910, Job Harriman, an attorney who had run as Debs' vice-presidential candidate in 1900, planned to capture California's labor leaders for socialism through the corrupt Union Labor party holding office in San Francisco. To achieve his goal, Harriman would have to travel the dangerous road of cooperation with a capitalist party. He sought Berger's opinion and was cautioned against such a move. Berger voiced his distrust of labor leaders heavily involved in politics and argued that any effort to reach labor ought to be directed toward the rank and file.

Berger insisted that Harriman was trying to unite labor on the wrong lines. He acknowledged that the Californian was not suggesting fusion with the Union Laborites, but he feared that cooperation might only serve to confuse political and economic spheres. Berger sought to convince Harriman to work with the trade union movement and to remain aloof from the so-called labor party. Harriman, unpersuaded, mentioned not running a socialist ticket in the next election, but when Berger warned that such a course could mean expulsion from the Socialist party, the discussion ended.[28]

A year and a half later when Harriman was assailed by a recall motion charging that he had contemplated selling out the party in San Francisco, Berger vehemently denied the accusations and maintained that Harriman only wanted to win labor support for the Socialist party. He admitted that Harriman's judgment may have been weak but nevertheless insisted that no actions detrimental to the movement had been taken.[29] Other reformists joined with Berger and, in spite of leftist support for recall, it did not pass.

Thus Berger, even with his own comrades, remained adamant in his labor party stand. Whereas he would support a genuine labor party, one had not emerged and he continued to recommend cooperation between the economic and political arms of the labor movement as the most fruitful avenue for advancement of his cause. Despite the charges of opportunism constantly leveled by his critics, he had counseled Harriman against joining with a bourgeois capitalist party in order to place socialists in office. While Berger, perhaps more than any other national leader, favored office-holding as a means toward the achievement of collectivist goals, he recognized that the cost of Harriman's plan was likely to be more than the opportunities were worth. He was not willing to pay the price of sacrificing the party.

The cleavage in the party did not entirely obviate cooperation between the factions on behalf of labor. In 1913 a joint effort to aid West Virginia coal miners occurred, but the association proved to be both temporary and superficial. For over a year the coal mines had been in turmoil as the United Mine Workers determined to unionize the area in the face of strong resistance by the companies. A strike began in April 1912 and a year later the men were still out. Violence by company guards had resulted in counterviolence, martial law, and the detention of the legendary organizer, seventy-eight-year-old Mother Jones, a local socialist editor and a UMW official. The atmosphere was wholly inimical to a settlement. In the spring of 1913 a new governor took office and, eager to end the strike, he released prisoners convicted by the military tribunal. To the mine owners he suggested submission to unionization and to the miners he threatened deportation from the strike area. The governor was so anxious to effect a settlement that he jailed editors of a socialist paper who rejected his conditions; the staff of another socialist paper saw its offices wrecked by National Guardsmen.[30]

At this point the Socialist party entered the struggle by sending a delegation into the strike zone to investigate conditions and to present their findings to President Wilson. Victor Berger, Adolph Germer, and Eugene Debs formed the committee. These three had been chosen through an appreciation of basic party divisions: the right, labor, and the left. The leftist press, however, was quick to point out that the result was a reformist-dominated committee. It not only demanded greater representation for the militants but also questioned the entire project, arguing that organizers and speakers were needed by the miners more than investigators. Further it was charged that if such a mission were advisable, the NEC had been negligent in its failure to send one earlier. It suggested that an apathetic NEC had been unable to act and only at a late date proposed an investigation because of increased pressure from West Virginia socialists.[31]

The failure of the NEC to take more than formal note of the West Virginia struggle earlier is difficult to understand. While Berger argued unconvincingly that inadequate finances prevented an on-the-spot investigation, Debs blasted the party leaders for the delay. In accepting his appointment to the committee, he noted that "the action is two months behind at best. Had the NEC acted on it . . . two months ago there would today be a different situation in West Virginia." Debs went on to personalize his attack with a venom he usually avoided. "Had it been Berger and Spargo in the bullpen instead of Mother Jones . . . the NEC would not have waited until the whole country was seething. . . ."[32]

Berger, Germer, and Debs visited the beleaguered coal fields and interviewed the governor, who promised that conditions would improve. At once the imprisoned socialists were released and the committee of three exonerated the governor of charges of arbitrary actions.

The strike was soon settled, with the role of the socialist delegation in that settlement negligible. The committee prepared a detailed report of its investigation for the NEC and the socialist press. Debs found himself in the unusual position of fighting off leftist charges pressed against the committee's conduct, which must have amused Berger and his comrades. Debs wrote in disgust that "the extremists wanted us to raise Hell with everybody. . . ." The three investigators denied that they had endorsed the governor's actions or that they had ignored the local socialists. They admitted that they had not condemned everything non-socialist, but argued that their mission was simply to ascertain the facts for the sake of the miners' cause.[33]

Along with these skirmishes in the field of labor, a similiar confrontation ensued in these years in one other area outside party circles. The party managed to display its internal dissension in its rivalries for the offices of International Secretary and delegates to the congresses of the Second International and to its Bureau, and indeed, during its participation in European meetings.

For most of its first decade, party delegations to the International consisted of members of the reformist wing, and they directed their animosity toward the Socialist Labor party in its claims to represent the American proletariat. But in 1910 the left achieved representation in the Socialist party delegation and thus made clear to overseas comrades the further division among American socialists.

Usually Victor Berger and Morris Hillquit served as the party's International Secretaries in recognition of their European backgrounds and connections with socialists abroad. Hillquit had represented the Socialist party at the 1907 International Congress at Stuttgart and Berger, making his first trip to Europe since his emigration, had attended the meeting of the International Socialist Bureau in Brussels in November 1909. At the Brussels meeting Berger tried to convince his European comrades that the Socialist party was entitled to both American seats on the Bureau. He insisted that the SLP had degenerated into a purely propagandistic organization with few followers, while in contrast the Socialist party had come to represent 97 percent of American socialists. His figures and analysis were disputed by a German representing the SLP, and the Bureau, unperturbed by the traditional American dissension, delayed the question until the Copenhagen meeting of the International the next year.[34]

Berger had enjoyed the role of visiting celebrity and was anxious for election to the party delegation to Copenhagen. He told Hillquit that he was one of the few in the party who could insure the capture of the second seat on the Bureau. Also, he argued, it was only logical that he be allowed to finish the work he had initiated at Brussels. He asked that Hillquit help him in the campaign for election to the delegation through various newspapers in which Hillquit had influence, such as the New York *Call* and the *Jewish Daily Forward*.

Both Berger and Hillquit were elected, along with their comrades John Spargo, Robert Hunter, and May Wood Simons, the wife of A. M. Simons. The right's desired homogeneity on the delegation was not achieved, however, because of the election of William D. Haywood, the leader of the Wobblies and the emerging hero of the Socialist party left. His election to the delegation marked a new tactic in the left's struggle to be heard, and it was a surprise to Haywood himself.[35]

As usual, much of the party's performance in the public debates centered upon its efforts to discredit the SLP. In the initial bargaining between the two American groups the Socialist party offered the SLP one vote of the fourteen to which the Americans were entitled, while De Leon insisted upon the three-and-a-half which he had held at the Stuttgart convention. The public jousting over the allotment of votes occurred between Hillquit and De Leon, with the Congress supporting Hillquit. While De Leon was reduced to one vote, he did retain his seat on the Bureau, and Berger could serve there only as Hillquit's nonvoting second.[36]

The sparring of the two American parties was supplemented by the struggle between the factions within the Socialist party. The left displayed such hostility to the right that occasionally it appeared to prefer actions against party interests rather than cooperation with the reformists. Both Berger and Haywood chose to serve on the labor commission at the Congress, and their mutual belligerence clearly demonstrated party division. Berger supported a clause in a resolution presented by the German delegation which vetoed the general strike in the event of war. Haywood opposed this successful measure and promptly excoriated Berger for his position.

Haywood's speech to the International stressed the reactionary composition of the AFL. The hope for American labor, he said, lay in the emergence and strength of industrial unionism in the United States. However, the report of the American delegation to the International, which was written and presented by Berger and Hillquit, emphasized the failure of that movement.[37] As usual, the reformists' hold on party machinery was of inestimable value to them.

The confrontation of the American socialists abroad had been bitter. But for once the Socialist party reformists and the SLP found something on which they agreed. De Leon's newspaper, *The Weekly People*, reported acidly that Haywood had distinguished himself to the European socialists as the savior of the American movement. The reformists told each other that it would be best for the party if Haywood and his followers were outside it.[38]

Two years later the left again successfully challenged the reformists over the party's international spokesmen. In 1912 Berger was disappointed when the post of International Secretary went to Mrs. Kate Richards O'Hare, a militant from Kansas City, while he secured only the position of second. It was permissible in Berger's eyes to wind up as second behind Hillquit, but he was extremely distraught over Mrs. O'Hare's election. Not only did he fear that the left's constant onslaught against the entrenched leadership might be gaining momentum, but he predicted that the new International Secretary would make the Socialist party look ridiculous to the European comrades; upon reflection, he added with disgust that "by doing so she will just represent the exact state of our American movement."[39] To Berger, the western radicals, with their unsophisticated approach to political and social questions, were unequal to party responsibilities.

In 1913 the left voted against sending a delegate to the International Socialist Bureau at Brussels, a move directed against Berger. Hillquit tried to persuade him that it was only a technicality and he could still go to Brussels, but Mrs. O'Hare as International Secretary went alone. The rivalry continued into 1914, with Berger and Hillquit finally elected to the party's major international positions in May. The left's strength in party elections had fizzled, probably because of the departure of the charismatic Haywood and the surrounding turmoil. But by that time the significance of the posts was lessened by external events.[40]

In these years before World War I, throughout party elections and arguments a recurrent pattern emerged. The reformist wing had to combine its plotting of the course of the party with self-defense against the left. While the NEC usually manipulated the party apparatus in accord with its own vision, much of its attention was fixed on the leftist challenge.

The expansion of the party in these pre-war years was remarkable in view of the party division. Membership, as reported by the locals, grew from 41,479 in 1909 to 84,716 in 1911, and to 95,957 in 1913. The list of newspapers related to the socialist movement numbered over two hundred in 1913. These newspapers were not clustered in any regional pattern but were spread across thirty-six states and Alaska. In the same period, up to two dozen different states across the nation saw socialists enter their legislatures and municipal governments.[41] There was clearly grassroots enthusiasm for the divided party.

The party successfully attracted support by offering channels of protest and promises of change. Its major policy-makers were critical of the status quo and promised long-range refashioning through a series of short steps. The socialist mayors and legislators on the local level utilized the same approach. They too won support through reformist arguments, and thus, throughout the party, it was those socialists who dealt with the existing American framework and the gradual curatives and modifications who were responsible for the expansion of the movement. The promise of abrupt revolution was neither made nor demanded.

What elected socialists offered to their constituents once in office was a combination of reform within the system and reformism to modify the system. Similar to the progressives, they endorsed direct legislation, public health measures, railroad regulation, and other ameliorative reforms. But unlike the progressives, they also offered the American public measures to transform the existing framework. In Wisconsin and other places, state legislators went beyond the regulation of public utilities to endorse state ownership of natural resources.[42] In this manner the Socialist party representatives across the country introduced new lines of thought and far-reaching ideas into the American forum.

By avoiding the impossibilism that they assigned to their party opponents, the reformists broadened the possibilities in American politics. Socialist views were becoming alternatives. Not only was it permissible for many to vote a third-party ticket, but it was becoming feasible to apply new perspectives to the problems besetting a recently industrialized society.

Within the Socialist party itself there remained basic differences of opinion on two pervasive issues. On matters as elementary as officeholding and direct action, furious struggles were waged which threatened to destroy the party. One swirled around Victor Berger and the other surrounded syndicalists in the party.

NOTES

1. Socialist Party, *Proceedings of the 1908 National Convention*, p. 13.
2. *The Party Builder*, 31 May 1913.
3. Berger to A. M. Simons, 14 November 1912, Berger Col., MCHS.
4. Robert Hunter to Adolph Germer, 17 December 1912; Germer to Hunter, 23 December 1912, Adolph Germer Col-

lection, State Historical Society of Wisconsin (hereafter cited as Germer Col., SHSW).

5. *American Socialist Official Business Supplement*, 7 November 1914, 20 February 1915, 27 February 1915; Berger to Walter Lanferseik, 3 June 1915, Berger Col., MCHS. The brewers obtained the list the next year, however.

6. *The Party Builder*, 16 May 1914.

7. H. D. Stettwagen to Berger, 12 July 1912; Debs to J. Mahlon Barnes, 2 July 1912; Barnes to Berger, 3 July 1912; Berger to Barnes, 8 July 1912, Berger Col., MCHS; Barnes to Hillquit, 27 June 1912, Hillquit Col., SHSW; *Social-Democratic Herald*, 10 August 1912; *International Socialist Review* 13 (September 1912): 276-277; Vol. 25. John M. Work, "Autobiography," II, chap. 5, pp. 14-15, typescript, John M. Work Collection, SHSW.

8. Socialist Party, *Proceedings of the 1908 National Convention*, p. 15; W. A. Glaser, "Algie Martin Simons and Marxism in America," *Mississippi Valley Historical Review* 41 (December 1954): 421-422; Victor L. Berger, "Socialism and the Farmers," Socialist Party, 1922 Convention Book, pp. 24-27. Norman Pollack in *The Populist Response to Industrial America* (Cambridge: Harvard University Press, 1962), has argued that a farmer-worker alliance in radicalism was a viable possibility in the 1890s.

9. Socialist Party, *Proceedings of the National Congress, 1910*, pp. 229, 239; Berger to Mrs. Kate Richards O'Hare, 12 April 1911, Berger Col., MCHS. By the time the plank was adopted, Simons had come around to the Marxist view. He believed that an agricultural revolution was occurring which the government should assist and channel toward greater concentration and, ultimately, collectivization. Kent and Gretchen Kreuter, *An American Dissenter: The Life of Algie Martin Simons* (Lexington: University of Kentucky Press, 1969), pp. 125-126. The report of the Farmers Committee which created the agricultural plank appears as Appendix D in Socialist Party, *Proceedings of the 1912 National Convention*.

10. Berger, Socialist Party, 1922 Convention Book, p. 27.

11. See a leftist analysis of the 1910 National Congress for an example of the charges of opportunism in the *International Socialist Review* 10 (June 1910): 1125.

12. For example, John Spargo, reformist and English

emigrant, offered a minority report which the new immigrants preferred.

13. The majority report cited the 1907 Stuttgart resolution of the Second International which actually condemned restrictions on open immigration despite the pleas of the Americans (led by Hillquit) who were affected by unrestricted immigration as were few other nations. To use Stuttgart for justification, the majority had been selective and distorted its intention. Socialist Party, *Proceedings of the National Congress, 1910*, pp. 75-77.

14. Ibid., pp. 119-120.

15. Ibid., p. 98. For an example of the left's delight in the temporary disruption of the right, see William English Walling, "Crisis in the Socialist Party," *The Independent* 72 (16 May 1912): 1048.

16. Philip Taft, *The American Federation of Labor in the Time of Gompers* (New York: Harper and Bros., 1957), p. 251.

17. Ibid., p. 199.

18. William English Walling to Eugene V. Debs, 14 December 1909, William English Walling Collection, SHSW; Walling, *Socialism as It Is: A Survey of the World-Wide Revolutionary Movement* (New York: Macmillan Co., 1912), pp. 179-180. Walling joined the party local in Stamford, Conn., only in February 1910.

19. Simons to Walling, 19 November 1909, Hillquit Col., SHSW, mimeographed copy. Simons later expanded his remarks in the New York *Call* of 6 December 1909. He explained that the NEC wished to make the Socialist party a true party of labor and he repeated that the party must attract men from the labor movement to leadership in the party.

20. John Spargo to Simons, 29 November 1909, SP Col., Duke.

21. J. G. Phelps Stokes to Hillquit, 2 December 1909, in *International Socialist Review* 10 (January 1910): 658. This issue of the *Review* was given over to the views of the prominent party members on a labor party.

22. Berger to Simons, 6 December 1909, SP Col., Duke.

23. Berger Statement, *International Socialist Review* 10 (January 1910): 598. The poll of candidates for the NEC appears on pp. 597-606. Debs wrote in a rather negative vein as he opposed both craft unionism and divisive dual unionism,

while acknowledging that both a political and an economic organization were needed. Ray Ginger, *Eugene V. Debs* (New York: Collier Books, 1962), p. 316. Historians have drawn distorted views of this controversy. Ira Kipnis maintains that Berger's labor party machinations were soundly defeated. Ira Kipnis, *The American Socialist Movement, 1897-1912* (New York: Columbia University Press, 1962), p. 15. Kipnis must be read in the light of his pronounced leftist bias. David Shannon, in his survey of the Socialist party, saw some truth in the charge of a right wing plot. David Shannon, *The Socialist Party of America* (New York: Macmillan Co., 1955), p. 68.

24. Berger to Hillquit, 13 February 1910, Hillquit Col., SHSW. Elected to the NEC, in order of votes received, were Hunter, Berger, Hillquit, Spargo, Lena Morrow Lewis, George H. Goebel and James F. Carey, all reformists. Stokes lost his seat and was unable to hand it over to a leftist.

25. Walling to Debs, 12 February 1910, Walling to H. M. Hyndman, 19 February 1910, Walling Col., SHSW.

26. See, for example, J. G. Phelps Stokes, "Campaign Methods," *International Socialist Review* 10 (March 1910): 837. Stokes' report on campaign methods had been rejected by the NEC at the January meeting.

27. Shannon, *The Socialist Party,* p. 68.

28. J. Mahlon Barnes to Berger, 22 June 1912, Berger Col., MCHS. Ira B. Cross, *A History of the Labor Movement in California* (Berkeley: University of California Press, 1935), pp. 245-247.

29. J. Mahlon Barnes to Job Harriman, 27 June 1912; Berger to Harriman, 22 August 1912; Berger to A. W. Harrack, 10 April 1912, Berger Col., MCHS.

30. John R. Commons, ed., *History of Labor in the United States*, Vol. 4, Selig Perlman and Philip Taft, *Labor Movements, 1896-1932* (New York: Macmillan Co., 1935), pp. 330-335.

31. *The Party Builder*, 7 June 1913, provides a view of the NEC side of the argument while the left spoke through the *International Socialist Review* 14 (July 1913): 895, 877.

32. *The Party Builder*, 31 May 1913; Debs to Germer, May 14, 1913, Eugene V. Debs Collection, Tamiment Institute (hereafter cited as Debs Col., Tamiment Institute).

33. Milwaukee *Leader*, 23 May 1913; Commons, *History*

of Labor, Vol.4, 335; Debs to Germer, 19 June 1913, Debs Col., Tamiment Institute; Debs to Germer, 14 June 1913; Germer to E. O. McPherron, 8 July 1913, Germer Col., SHSW; *Social-Democratic Herald*, 14 June 1913.

34. The Hillquit report on the Stuttgart convention appears in the 1908 Socialist Party National Convention *Proceedings*, pp. 64-66; Socialist Party, *Proceedings of the 1912 National Convention*, p. 174. Berger's visit in 1909 was eagerly awaited by some of the SPD. Karl Kautsky hoped that Berger's scheduled speech to Berlin workers might convince them that the American socialists were not opposed to the organized labor movement but to Gompers' reactionary trade unionism. Karl Kautsky to Algernon Lee, 11 October 1909, Algernon Lee Collection, Tamiment Institute.

35. Berger to Hillquit, 13 February 1910, Hillquit Col., SHSW; William D. Haywood, *Bill Haywood's Book* (New York: International Publishers, 1929), p. 232; *Socialist Party Official Bulletin*, June 1910. As an indication of Haywood's growing popularity, his vote for the delegation was the second highest. Only Berger's total exceeded his.

36. May to A. M. Simons, August 29, 1910, Algie M. and May Wood Simons Col., SHSW; Morris to Vera Hillquit, 30 August 1910, Hillquit Col., SHSW; *Social-Democratic Herald*, 24 September 1910. Berger spoke only once to the full convention and briefly outlined, in German and English, the history of American socialism. He stated that unity between the two parties was impossible because of De Leon's vilification of the Socialist party and his attacks on the trade unions.

37. Haywood, *Bill Haywood's Book*, p. 233; Socialist Party, *Report of the Socialist Party of the United States to the International Socialist Congress of Copenhagen, 1910*, p. 5.

38. Adolph Germer to Robert Hunter, 1 November 1910, Germer Col., SHSW.

39. Berger to Hillquit, 12 October 1913, Berger Col., MCHS.

40. Hillquit to Berger, 16 October 1913, Berger Col., MCHS; Berger to Hillquit, 13 February 1914, Hillquit Col., SHSW; *The Party Builder*, 30 May 1914.

41. The most elaborate figures collected on socialist newspapers and elected officials appear in James Weinstein, *The Decline of Socialism in America, 1912-1925* (New

York: Monthly Review Press, 1967). See Table 1 on socialist periodicals, pp. 94-102, and Table 2 on 1911-1913 elections, pp. 116-117.

42. The legislative program of socialists serving in state houses, with special focus on Wisconsin which elected 9 socialists in 1913, is given in Ethelwyn Mills, *Legislative Program of the Socialist Party* (Chicago: Socialist Party, 1914), p. 11.

4

Socialists in Public Office

In 1910 the Socialist party as a whole was measured against its platform commitment to political action. That commitment, in dispute ever since its fashioning in 1901, resulted in election victories for reformists across the country as the socialists approached the peak of their electoral strength in municipal, state, and congressional elections. The traditional left-right split over political action further solidified in the face of these victories. Leftists who had never accepted the revisionist principle of officeholding attacked the campaigning reformists with charges of opportunism. The strife reverberated before an American public beginning to listen.

Electoral triumphs in Milwaukee were the most significant in that they indicated persistent and durable socialist inroads into the community. Moreover, Milwaukee was the largest municipality to endorse the minor party. But the Milwaukee socialists and their leader Victor Berger found themselves placed in double jeopardy, facing both their legal constituents and the direct actionist left of the party.

Berger had sensed victory in Milwaukee ever since the municipal elections of April 1908, which had demonstrated that Milwaukee voters were no longer afraid of the label "socialist." In February 1910, the Social Democrats nominated the men who had proven to be their most successful candidates in the past. Emil Seidel, the party's first alderman-at-large, was the nominee for mayor, a uniquely appropriate candidate for the Milwaukee movement. Seidel was the son of German immigrants, able to campaign in both English and German, and a wood carver by trade with direct knowledge of the life of the workingman. Berger and six other apparently strong candidates ran for aldermen-at-large. The platform epitomized the concrete, reflecting the party's experience in municipal administration. The demand for home rule in Milwaukee, for example, was the number one plank in the platform.

Fierce denunciations of the Social Democrats appeared in the local press, and in response, the party was more systematic than ever in its publicity. It published papers and circulars in seven languages, and in the last weeks of the campaign, the bundle brigade, now expanded and using express wagons and even automobiles, distributed campaign materials throughout the city.[1]

Berger participated in all levels in the campaign. He gave several speeches, appealed for funds, and wrote editorials. He was most anxious to impress upon the national party the proximity of victory in Milwaukee and the necessity for contributions and well-known speakers. He arranged for John Spargo to convince the NEC to appeal to the locals for funds for the Milwaukee campaign. In his editorials Berger stressed the fact that while it was clear that socialism could not be attained through the capture of one city, it was nevertheless mandatory to begin within the municipal framework. He admitted that once in office, the Social Democrats would have to operate within existing laws; oppressive laws would be abolished as soon as feasible but while they remained in effect, implementation would be required. He insisted that there was a genuine difference between the socialist candidates and others: "the Social-Democrats aim at higher things than simply not to steal when they are in office. . . ." But he reminded his enthusiastic campaign workers that "we do not want any votes that are not at least in sympathy with both our aims and methods."[2]

In the midst of the campaign a scathing attack on Berger and the Wisconsin socialists appeared in the *International Socialist Review*, which then was enjoying the widest circulation of any socialist monthly. The *Review* denounced socialist participation in politics for any reason other than the encouragement of class consciousness. Berger had mesmerized the NEC and his local comrades into office-seeking, it charged, and his victories at the polls thus far had brought no enlightenment or benefits to the working class of Wisconsin.

The sniping from the left evidently did not lessen the Social Democrats' local impact, for on 6 April 1910, they were triumphant in one of the largest pluralities ever recorded in Milwaukee. They not only elected Seidel mayor with 27,608 votes out of 59,484, but the entire ticket, including seven aldermen-at-large and two civil judges, was victorious. Berger himself was elected to his first public office.[3]

Berger was jubilant over the fruits of seventeen years of uninterrupted labor, but he did not exult publicly on the night of 6 April. He asked his followers to take a solemn vow to help the elected socialist officials fulfill their promises, and reminded all of them that the country would be watching. Later he stressed the distribution of literature in accounting for the election victory, claiming that propaganda had made Milwaukee class conscious. He predicted that the philosophy of international socialism would now be applied to Milwaukee and would serve as an example for others. But, he cautioned, "we want to show our comrades all over the country that our principles will lose nothing of their revolutionary energy by being thus applied to a local situation."[4]

The assertion that Milwaukee was a class-conscious socialist municipality was debatable. The more probable reasons for the smashing victory were the support of the organized labor movement, the blatant corruption of the other parties, the enviable record established by Social Democrats in public office, the systematic propaganda spread throughout the city for over a decade, and the tactical skill, organization, and discipline with which Berger led the party.

The United States remained remarkably calm in the face of a socialist victory in its fourteenth largest city. The local press, licking its wounds after defeat, sought to sow dissension among the winners by depicting an authoritarian Berger as the puppeteer guiding the policies of Mayor Seidel; and such a picture was easily drawn due to the contrast between the bombastic, articulate Berger and the modest, earnest Seidel. The national magazines suddenly awoke to the socialist movement as a new phenomenon in American cities.

Up until then, coverage of socialist campaigns had been marginal, but in 1910 a flock of reporters converged upon the city and produced a multitude of articles on the election and its meaning. Their general tenor was that Milwaukee would receive clean government but that there would be no political upheaval. Berger was portrayed by all as the leader, organizer, and boss of the Milwaukee socialists.[5]

There was little unanimity in the socialist press. The New York *Call* sent congratulations to its comrades in the middle west. The *International Socialist Review*, while minimizing the importance of the election, was unusually generous in its comments. Although stressing the distinction between reformists and revolutionists, the *Review* argued that the left should not display exaggerated concern with the details of achieving worker emancipation. In this case, control of City Hall at least would enable the party to support the workers' economic organs and to exploit propaganda opportunities.[6]

Berger demonstrated increasing sensitivity to attacks now because he realized his own vulnerability. A month after the election he issued a clear warning to his comrades against the temptations of office:

> The Social-Democratic victory . . . might prove a serious misfortune and an obstacle to the growth of the socialist movement of America, if our comrades should for one moment forget that the administration and the management of the affairs of the city of Milwaukee are *not* the final aim of this great movement. We must not forget . . . that the government and administration of any city is only *a small incident* in our tremendous fight for the abolition of this system—only *a little stepping stone* in our line of progress. . . . I should be sorry for the party and wish the victory had never been won . . . if this victory should in the least interfere with the revolutionary spirit of the Milwaukee movement. . . .[7]

Berger settled into his role as chairman of the committee on legislation of the Milwaukee Common Council. There, he fought unsuccessfully for a minimum wage for municipal workers, public ownership of utilities, and home rule for the city. His one major accomplishment, and the aspect of his council service of which he was proudest, was his prevention of the sale of lakefront land to industry and its transformation into a public park.[8]

In the fall, Berger campaigned confidently for election to the United States Congress where he hoped to serve as a wedge for other socialists. As in his municipal campaign, Berger followed all possible avenues. To attract one group of voters, he condemned privately owned trusts and denounced high prices; to win over others, he stressed the revolutionary implications of his probable election. He invited Oscar Ameringer, an effective Oklahoma-based agitator, to use his fluent German in the agrarian areas of the Fifth Congressional District of Wisconsin. Karl Liebknecht, on a visit to the United States, spoke at a rally in behalf of Berger and Winfield R. Gaylord, a former minister and Christian Socialist and the party's candidate in the Fourth District.[9]

As in the spring, the subject of contributions to the Milwaukee campaign appeared on the NEC agenda. Robert Hunter proposed a large donation, arguing that the party's most important immediate task was to acquire a spokesman in Congress. Morris Hillquit suggested a lesser amount because of the financial problems of the party, while George H. Goebel, a New Jersey reformist organizer, demanded that the NEC first consider the other areas in which there were equally good chances for election. Berger, feigning embarrassment, argued that the financial hardship would be worth the election of two Wisconsin Congressmen who would give the party national representation at last. With only Goebel opposed, Berger's campaign chest was increased with party funds.

Berger received a 40 percent plurality in the 8 November election, while Gaylord went down to defeat. Fewer socialist votes were cast than in April, which Berger attributed to the sloughing off of reformer-progressive ballots, and he claimed that his victory was due to the hard core of the class-conscious. Congratulations rained down on him. Debs wrote, "Your election marks the beginning of the end of capitalism and the end of the beginning of Socialism in the United States." His reformist comrades Charles Edward Russell, who had been defeated in his gubernatorial campaign in New York State, and John Spargo telegraphed their good wishes, as did Ramsay MacDonald and Keir Hardie from the Labour Party and also Jean Longuet of the French socialist movement.[10]

Berger issued a victory statement in the *Herald* of 12 November that looked to the future. "While I am not a visionary and do not expect to revolutionize the congress of the United States singlehanded, I know that I have been elected to represent the views of the working class—to give voice to the hopes, fears and aims of that class—to shed a new light on every question before the House—to consider every question from a new point of view—whether it be beneficial or harmful to the proletariat."

John Spargo, whose telegram to Berger had compared his election in its significance with that of Lincoln's, predicted in a national magazine that although Berger would be a minority of one in Congress, he would not be unimportant. Spargo noted Berger's wide knowledge of socialist literature, while adding that "He cares for theories only in so

far as they relate to life and help in the solution of its problems."[11]
On the other hand, George D. Herron, a former Christian Socialist and
a founder of the Rand School, asked: "Does Victor Burger's [sic] socialism, which is the practical denial of everything I have understood
socialism to mean, and which is commended [by popular newspapers]
. . . as being sane and sound . . . does this represent the present and
future mind of the American socialist movement. . . ?"

At this time Debs, who evidently had decided to speak for the
revolutionist wing, cautioned the Socialist party against growth at the
expense of class consciousness. He regretted the fact that some party
members had become vote chasers and he denounced both the accumulation of bourgeois votes and cooperation with reactionary trade
unions. In order for political victory to be meaningful, the Socialist party would have to control economic power.[12]

It would be difficult to discover who Debs meant by "vote
chasers" if not Berger. The feeling between the two men was seldom
cordial and the antagonism stemmed perhaps as much from tem-
peramental differences as from policy disagreements. Berger was aware
of the danger that elective office could dazzle some socialists out of
their principles. A few weeks before Debs's criticism, a Berger editorial
in the *Herald* had reminded his Milwaukee comrades again that they
"must never forget that this party was not started and built up for the
purpose of getting political jobs. . . . This party was started for the
emancipation of the working class." But he thought that the need to
seek reforms dictated that risks be taken.[13]

The 1910 elections pleased Berger and other reformists, even
though they found themselves on the defensive. Berger and other socialists, such as Meyer London, who later succeeded him in Congress,
were attacked because of their election victories. That was to be the
standard pattern: assault in the face of political action on the one hand
and defense of any advances on the other.

When Berger went to Washington for the special session of the sixty-second Congress called by President Taft for 4 April 1911, he arrived there without a party directive on the role of a socialist congressman. He took with him to the capital only his own sense of optimism and his own conception of a Socialist congressional posture. As
he later wrote in a report to the party:

There were two ways before me. I could make a free-speech fight all alone, try to break down all precedent and all barriers, speak about the co-operative commonwealth, as long as my lung power would hold out and wind up my short parliamentary career by being suspended from the House, and thus also make an end to political action by this "direct action". . . . "Or I could pursue the other course, obey all rules and precedents of the House until they are changed—get the respect and attention of my fellow members, speak sparingly and only when measures directly concerning the working class are up for discussion, giving, however, close attention to all the business before the House of Representatives.[14]

In order to follow the latter path, Berger needed knowledgeable assistance from socialist sources, and he chose for his congressional secretary William James Ghent, a revisionist writer and the first director of the Rand School. Berger relied heavily on Ghent for the shaping of his bills in accord with his own sketchy directions. He borrowed ideas and suggestions from many sources and would leave Ghent to formulate the fragments into wholes. The two men worked harmoniously together at first, aided by their common ideological bond, but the strains of increasing pressure, combined with Berger's egotism, disrupted their relationship by the end of the term.[15]

Berger started his term without any other support, since the NEC had failed to present him with any guidelines. In his role as national spokesman for the party Berger was out on a limb; although the committee actually wished to support him, it was fearful of an exposed position and hesitated to make specific commitments. Had the committee shown more foresight at the start, it might have reduced its own, and Berger's, later embarrassments. As it was, not until Congress was in session and Berger had already initiated his course of action did the NEC finally discuss his position. At the April 1911, meeting in Boston Berger presented an outline of his congressional activities of the first few weeks and his future plans. He assured the committee that he considered the party platform his guide, and in return the NEC commended him for his efforts and resolved:

> That it is the sense of the national executive committee that,
> while representatives of the Socialist Party will at all times
> conform their conduct to the platform and principles of the
> party, they shall also confer with the national executive com-
> mittee on concrete measures introduced by them in Congress,
> and on the attitude to be taken by them on all pending
> measures of importance *wherever requested by the com-
> mittee*. [Italics added.]

But the lines of responsibility remained hazy and the committee did not
require consultation until the pressure of external criticisms was felt.
Berger resented the halfheartedness of a policy that was not a policy.
He would have preferred either independence or firm guidance; otherwise, he complained, the NEC was simply complicating his work.
Finally he himself suggested to the committee at its December 1911
meeting in Washington, D.C., that a subcommittee of three be elected
to whom drafts of all bills of socialist Congressmen could be
presented.[16]

The source of Berger's concern and the NEC's equivocation was
the harassment from the left. Throughout his term in Congress, he
found himself subject to greater criticism from socialist sources than
from those outside the party. From his first resolutions to his last bills
he was consistently badgered by a left wing unable to accept political
action.

Nonetheless Berger set sail on his course. He replied to messages
of good will with an ebullient statement in which he wrote: "A new
chapter in the history of American socialism has now begun. . . . The
United States . . . now takes its place with the other great and civilized
nations, since there will now be a representative of the working class in
the national legislature."[17]

He became a dynamic addition to the national political scene.
Berger was a vigilant freshman Congressman; he kept long hours, attended almost all House sessions, participated in many committee
hearings and introduced nearly two dozen bills and resolutions,
eight motions and minor resolutions, and many petitions from constituents. His bills were confined to two major areas—those which sought to
improve working conditions, such as a bill to regulate the labor of
women and children in the District of Columbia, and those which struck
directly at the capitalist system, such as one which provided for the

social ownership and operation of certain major industries. In addition, he had to serve his local constituents by the usual forwarding to the House of individual requests and petitions, by opposing prohibition in accord with Milwaukee interests, and by presenting to Congress resolutions from the Wisconsin legislature, which was then crowded with progressive Republicans and several socialists. Berger considered himself the spokesman of all socialist voters and sympathizers in the country and accordingly was preoccupied with social legislation and matters of national scope rather than measures specifically tied to his district. Nevertheless, he felt a particular responsibility to his local constituents. He was able to stimulate among his colleagues far more interest in a Milwaukee problem than could any other freshman Congressman. His notoriety more than compensated for his external concerns and lack of seniority, and in that way Milwaukee enjoyed an advantage.[18]

Some speculation was voiced that he might not be seated because of his frequent criticisms of the United States Constitution, but he took the oath of office with the other representatives. His first official act was to vote "present" rather than favor either of the candidates for Speaker of the House. That day, in order to counter the rumor that he would follow an obstructionist path, he issued a statement to curious reporters that he would "stand for every measure, no matter by whom introduced which gives greater political freedom or economic security to the working class."[19]

His first resolution was presented to Congress one month after the session began. He demanded the withdrawal of the American troops which had been posted at the Mexican border during that country's revolution. Although the resolution was incidental to his general efforts in Congress that term, it did represent the commitment to international solidarity of the socialist movement and served to distinguish Berger from his fellow Congressmen in the area of foreign affairs. It was also a portent of future events, the almost singlehanded attempt of the Socialist party to hold back the tide of war. The inception of the resolution and the manner in which it was implemented, involving socialist party machinery, is of interest. The pattern here was repeated in the presentation of other Berger resolutions and bills.

On 13 March, A. M. Simons, still a dependable collaborator, telegraphed Berger from Girard, Kansas, where Simons was editing the *Coming Nation*, and suggested that a petition be circulated among socialist locals demanding the recall of the border troops. Berger could present the petition to Congress. Berger agreed, and advised the National Executive Committee to forward petitions to secretaries of all locals. The NEC rubber-stamped the proposal and within a week locals throughout the country demonstrated against the presence of the troops, petitions were circulated, and the socialist press endorsed the demand "in the name of the workers of the United States. . . ." Less than a month after Simons's telegram, Berger was able to present his resolution to Congress, accompanied by a monster petition containing 90,000 signatures.[20]

After this official debut, Berger turned to matters of more concern to the party; he began to publicize the inadequacy of the existing political system. He denounced what he called antiquated government machinery and introduced a resolution to summon a constitutional convention. One generation should not legislate for another, he said, echoing Jefferson's teaching, or else the will of the people becomes stultified.

A second resolution provided for the abolition of the United States Senate and the veto powers of the President. His general aim was to make government more responsive to the will of the people, and therefore it seemed to him necessary to minimize the role of those officials who infrequently faced election. He was also particularly anxious to curb the power of the Supreme Court by invalidating its power of review. Although some in the Socialist party favored enhancing its powers at the expense of the more corruptible state courts, Berger believed the Supreme Court to be unresponsive to public opinion in general and hostile to labor in particular.[21]

During Berger's first year in Congress, American labor centered its attention on the McNamara case. Following a four-year struggle over the open shop between the organized structural workers and a manufacturers' association, the Los Angeles *Times*, owned by the association's director, Harrison Gray Otis, was dynamited on 1 October 1910, resulting in the loss of twenty-one lives. A nationwide manhunt for those responsible ensued. The following spring, J. J. McNamara, an officer of the International Association of Bridge and Structural Iron Workers, was arrested in Indianapolis and illegally extradited to California to stand trial with his brother, J. B. McNamara.[22] Labor saw in the treatment of J. J. McNamara a conspiracy to crush his union. The many ramifications of the case involved the entire American left, including the Socialist party, which threw its full support behind the defense of the McNamara brothers.

The National Executive Committee at its April meeting telegraphed its support to the accused men and their union and wired party locals to raise funds for the trial and for the election campaign of socialists in Los Angeles. Berger was the only member of the NEC to oppose these measures, arguing also against the motion that the National Committee investigate the case. He emphasized the opportunity to utilize government machinery. Party efforts would be superfluous, he believed; far more potent would be a resolution in the Congress demanding an investigation of the kidnaping of J. J. McNamara. The NEC and Berger proceeded with their respective plans and at the next meeting of the committee Berger claimed that his resolution had caused a stir; the innocuous measure merely demanded the protection of the constitution for the accused, but Berger insisted that the "interests" felt threatened.

Two hearings on his resolution convinced the House Rules Committee that the extradition of J. J. McNamara involved fraud and perjury, and led to consideration by the Judiciary Committee of the process of extradition.[23] Berger's efforts were approved by socialist and labor union locals, which endorsed his resolution and sent him congratulations. The majority of the Socialist party was behind him on this issue, beginning with the initial telegram from the *Chicago Daily Socialist* suggesting he offer a protest in Congress and concluding with the successful hearings. Following this, Berger was a star attraction at a Carnegie Hall rally for the McNamaras, where he exploited his opportunity to stress what socialists in Congress could accomplish.[24] But Berger's role in the McNamara case was not even mentioned in the leftist press.

After the May hearings on the McNamara extradition, Berger made his first formal speech to Congress. During the warm June days the House droned through its sessions on Canadian reciprocity, and Berger's appearance drew the largest audience of the debate. After he began to speak, word passed through the halls of the Capitol that the minority party of one had the floor, and curious members flocked into the chambers from the committee rooms, offices, and lounges. The aisles and even the area before the Speaker's dais were jammed.

Berger, after initially begging his audience to bear with his "Milwaukee accent," spoke for over an hour. He stressed the inefficacy of minor reforms within the system of capitalism and criticized above all the "fallacy" that the tariff protected the working man. The tariff, he explained, was intended simply to develop industry, and other rationalizations were only offered to secure the worker's vote. Labor needed, he argued, not the tariff but protection from sudden changes in the economy.

He did not wander far from the immediate issue and only included a few peripheral remarks on socialism. He concluded his speech by announcing that he would support the measure and explained that it was "of small immediate concern to the working class. In itself it means no material change in the conditions of the working man and the working woman. But because it is in line with social and political evolution, because it tends to destroy the old tariff superstition, because it tends to break down the barriers between nations, to bring into closer relations the various peoples of the world, I shall support the bill."

His audience followed his comments attentively, laughed at his humor, and asked questions respectfully. The reception strengthened his belief in using Congress as a forum for propaganda. As he told the NEC, he felt he was speaking beyond the Congressmen to the people.[25]

Berger's major success in Congress was a resolution to investigate the strike of the woolen mill workers in Lawrence, Massachusetts, and the hearings he sponsored on the strike. These hearings, which won national sympathy for the strikers, earned Berger the applause of all factions of the Socialist party. Even Big Bill Haywood had words of praise for the lone socialist congressman,[26] and the cooperation of the two men at Lawrence was unique in the history of the mutual animosity of the party and the IWW and of the two men as well. (See below, Chapter 5.)

His praise from the Wobblies could be contrasted with criticism from the AFL for his vote against the Dillingham Bill restricting immigration to the United States. Ghent had earlier feared that this issue, over which the party remained divided, could only hurt Berger as the one socialist who had to take a public stand.[27] However difficult the dilemma might have been, the Root Amendment excluding aliens who "conspire for the overthrow of a government recognized by the United States" insured the opposition of the Socialist party as a whole. Berger testified at the hearings on the bill and argued that the measure abolished the right of asylum. In addition, Berger opposed a clause, endorsed by the American Federation of Labor, which imposed a literacy test on prospective immigrants. He took this action confident that in this case all factions of the party would support him, but for several years thereafter he was forced to defend his vote against the bill before organized labor.[28]

In his various positions, Berger faced issues squarely simply because they existed, and he attempted to resolve them in a socialist direction. For example, when threatened with a railway strike that might endanger the national economy, Berger devised a resolution which provided for permanent nationalization of the lines and included a plan for financing a bond issue to cover the expenses of the operation. In his search for solutions to problems confronting the capitalist system, his answers invariably contained provisions for their execution. This practical approach may be seen in all his measures. Not content with arguing that unemployment would disappear with the arrival of socialism, Berger proposed that a federal loan fund be established to finance state-operated public works for the jobless. On the other hand, Berger was unafraid to condemn issues that he was certain were ephemeral, such as the level of the tariff.

Free of the dilemma which prevented some of his socialist comrades from acting in the political world, Berger made tactical use of immediate demands to reach long-range goals. He was able to initiate and support measures of direct legislation because of his firm commitment to democracy, and he embodied some of those resolutions in constitutional amendments as the most likely form to win acceptance from Congress. In addition, he explored his opportunities to bring every working-class issue before Congress; whether an issue involved conservative trade unions or the Wobblies, he believed he was justified in aiding by any means open to him criticism of the existing system.

However, an enormous blind spot obstructed his effort to represent American workers. Berger's committee assignment was that of the District of Columbia, thereby giving him the opportunity to represent that city's large and exploited black population. But his racist attitudes did not allow him to recognize that opportunity. He did introduce various measures for the benefit of District residents which, had they passed, would have aided blacks as well as whites: home rule, a cooperative store for the civil servants of the city, and limitations on working hours. In his speeches to his colleagues, he condemned what he called the starvation wages prevalent in the District. But to Berger, as to the party, the black was "the invisible man." While the party did not reject black membership, with the exception of a vocal minority it undertook no meaningful struggles against second-class citizenship, and the first socialist Congressman followed the same pattern: he supported black suffrage when the issue was before the House but he remained indifferent to the plight of the black population. Those most unrepresented and oppressed of Americans were invisible to the only congressional representative of the workers of the world.[29]

The major piece of legislation which Berger presented was an old-age pension. The bill provided four dollars per week for all impoverished workers who were over the age of sixty, were citizens of the United States for at least sixteen years, and were not convicted felons. In his presentation of the bill, Berger told the House of Representatives that his object was to provide a pension for veterans of the industrial wars who, unlike Civil War veterans, had been forgotten. "Any toiler who has faithfully labored for a meager wage for twenty years or more has created more wealth than a pension in old age can repay. Every toiler produces more than he is paid. . . . The word 'pension' is a misnomer. The payment ought to be called 'Partial restitution.' . . ."

An unusual clause in the bill forbade the courts to rule on its constitutionality. Motivated by the socialists' contempt for the American judiciary, Berger had carefully researched this point and, with the aid of Simons, found that the Reconstruction Congress had deprived the Supreme Court of the power to review a piece of legislation.

Berger hoped that the bill might initiate national agitation for an old-age pension, but instead it stirred up wholesale controversy in the Socialist party. While Berger had been wary of leftist criticisms of the pension, he never anticipated the severity of the storm that broke throughout the party. On all sides he was assailed. The NEC, to which he had shown the bill before its introduction to Congress, had insisted the age limit be reduced from sixty-five to sixty, and then endorsed the bill. But beyond the committee, Local New York, among others, was so incensed over the meagerness of the pension and the exclusion of aliens that it demanded that socialist congressmen be required to submit bills and resolutions to the NEC before their introduction to Congress.[30] It was this pressure that forced the NEC to assume its full responsibility. The reformist leaders as a whole had had to be prodded into a realization that electing public officials involved commitments.

Berger's staff insisted that the schedule of payments was in align-

ment with the existing conditions of capitalist society. The iniquity of
the alien clause was acknowledged but termed unavoidable until re-
ciprocal arrangements existed between nations for the pensioning of
one another's nationals. The bill's critics were called "ultradoc-
trinaires," but many reformists joined the leftist condemnation of the
exclusion of felons, who were described as products of the capitalist
system. Some leftists announced that even a good pension bill would be
misguided, and Daniel De Leon added to the chorus by lambasting the
entire bill, clause by clause. He said that such a measure from a
bourgeois source was understandable but "Coming in the name of Socialism, the bill is an insult to Socialism and to the working class
alike."[31]

Within the party, Walling attacked Berger's measure for nation-
alizing railways and telephones, arguing that ownership by a capitalist government would not be "even a partial installment of Socialism. . . ." The result would be state capitalism rather than socialism.
Another leftist complained that Berger's measure to abridge the Supreme Court's jurisdiction implicitly admitted to the Court powers
which in fact it had seized.[32] Berger was condemned for his
"constructive" delusions. While he might have whittled away some prej-
udices against socialism, he nevertheless had not demonstrated through
his bills what socialists would do once in power, an impossibility within
the capitalist framework. Berger was criticized for introducing far too
many measures. Had he concentrated on analyzing bills from the working-class perspective, he at least would have followed the sensible example of European socialists. The next American socialist elected to Congress must realize his proper role. The left, dissatisfied with Berger's
congressional performance, insisted that in the future the party tightly
guide the policy of its representatives.

Gene Debs, however, was generous in his remarks and commented
that Berger had demonstrated effectively the value of even a single socialist in Congress. He voiced the hope that several socialists would
soon be elected.[33]

But apart from a smattering of commendation, the leftists remained either opposed to a socialist in Congress or ambivalent. To
some, the very fact of Berger's election was sufficient to prove his lack
of principle; others denounced him for participating in parliamentary
processes once he took his seat in the House. Every bill he introduced
met condemnation for its violation of the essence of socialism. The

most common denominator of the criticism leveled at Berger by members of the left was opposition to his presence in the Congress.

The right-wing socialists praised his work for breaking down hostility against the party and for widely publicizing the cause. His ability to impart his knowledge of economic conditions to the public in terms a laborer could understand was applauded.[34] But because of Berger's willingness to face all issues, he was often deep in controversy even with the non-revolutionists. Labor's support for him as a trade unionist was dependable only until he opposed a measure calculated to decrease immigration to the United States. That vote also alienated those socialists who were tied very closely to organized labor. The NEC, from which he might have expected solid support, proved negligent initially and then, although generally endorsing his work, tried to straddle responsibilities until it could no longer dodge party pressure.

When Congress adjourned in August 1912, Berger returned to Milwaukee to campaign for re-election on the basis of his record. He boasted at rallies of his various accomplishments, saying "They told you that you would never hear from me in Washington but you did. . . . I was the representative of not only the Fifth district but of the working class of the United States as well. You people in Milwaukee elected the first congressman-at-large."

Running against a fusion ticket, he bragged of forcing the two opposition parties to combine, proving the lack of principles and differences between them. The major issue, he said, was not the tariff discussed by his opponents but the fact that the workingman received so little of the amount he produced.[35]

It was unfortunate for Berger's re-election prospects that he had not spent more time in Milwaukee during the congressional sessions or contributed editorials regularly to his newspapers. One of his closest colleagues had warned him that the influential Milwaukee *Journal* had initiated a campaign to win the organized workers away from the socialist ticket. She begged him to counterattack through frequent articles, but despite Berger's conviction that the consolidation of local control was of major importance for a party with national aspirations, he had never found the time to submit more than a few items. The pressures from his national involvement were simply too heavy. Thus, his absence from home forced him to campaign from a weaker position than that of two years earlier, and he was overwhelmed by the fusion ticket.

Defeat found Berger philosophical. He accounted for it in terms of fusion and the organization of the Catholic vote against socialism. But he believed that he had only lost a skirmish in a long war for the emancipation of the working class. He regretted that socialist voters would not be represented in the sixty-third Congress, but felt he had at least demonstrated to the country that socialists were capable of constructive action.[36]

The question of the efficacy of Victor L. Berger as a public spokesman of the Socialist party may be analyzed on a variety of levels. While the contemporary socialists argued about his success in building a positive image of socialism, the type of symbol which Berger became to the American public was in fact of importance.

The first socialist in Congress was the antithesis of the late nineteenth-century view of the radical as bombthrower. Berger was impeccable in dress, polite to his colleagues, learned in his arguments. Indeed he was a model of respectability who spoke a language not incomprehensible to indigenous radicalism and therefore seemed entitled to a hearing. He made Marx appear less unacceptable. Congress, the press, and the public in general found him unique only in his role as representative of a minor party.

In the House of Representatives Berger was cordially received by his colleagues. He was given opportunities to speak and a committee assignment, and he never had to complain about his treatment. The national press showed genuine curiosity about him and gave him far more coverage than any other freshman Congressman.

His franking privileges enabled him to mail thousands of copies of his speeches throughout the country; the National Office of the Socialist party distributed more copies to the locals. The public seemed to respond and joined the party faithful in showering Berger with so much mail that his clerical staff required continual expansion. As evidence of public interest, Berger received an ever increasing number of speaking requests. Through a lyceum bureau hired to handle booking arrangements, he spoke in and around Washington, and, between sessions, he traveled as far west as North Dakota to fulfill engagements.[37] The attention he received validated his original belief in the educational value of elective office. The logical schoolhouse for mass enlightenment was the public forum, Berger was convinced.

But the effect of Berger's term on the Socialist party was far from positive. In fact his congressional term, and the elections of the Milwaukee socialists and others to local offices, resulted in the hardening of opposing beliefs, and thus exacerbated the party division. To the left the office-holders clearly could not advance the cause, while to the right they merited support. Neither was ready to alter its stand. Perhaps a few socialists here and there became persuaded by the performance of reformists in office that active participation in American politics effectively promoted socialist goals, but the number of such conversions appears to be insignificant. A few reformists in office for a term or two were inadequate to accomplish the wholesale transformation of the party's outlook which Berger hoped to effect. Moreover, the fact of disunity was a harsh liability to the elected socialists. Had the party been united in its support of political activists, their performance in office might have nourished the party. Because of the factionalization, the achievement of representation meant little.

Berger and the other office-holders effectively forced the party to take positions on current issues, causing the public to awake to the Socialist party as an increasingly realistic, viable choice in the political arena. But the party's internal weakness prevented its full assumption of a responsible role in the nation's political dialogue.

NOTES

1. Carl D. Thompson, "How the Milwaukee Socialists Distribute Literature," p. 1, mimeographed paper, SP Col., State and Local Files, Wisconsin, 1898-1920, Duke; Frederick I. Olson, "The Milwaukee Socialists, 1899-1941," pp. 176-177; Marvin Wachman, *The History of the Social-Democratic Party of Milwaukee, 1897-1910*, pp. 68-69. From 1910 through the entire decade a newspaper entitled the *Voice of the People* appeared before every Milwaukee primary and election and during major strikes and other crises and was distributed to each household.
2. *S.P. Official Bulletin*, February 1910; *Social-Democratic Herald*, 12 February 1910, 19 March 1910.
3. Henry L. Slobodin, "What's the Matter with Wisconsin?" *International Socialist Review* 10 (February 1910): 686-688; mimeographed statement issued by the Milwaukee

Social Democratic Central Committee and found in the SP
Col. State and Local Files, Wisconsin, 1898-1920, Duke. This
total represented 46.4 percent of the votes cast.

4. Milwaukee *Free Press*, 6 April 1910; Victor L. Berger,
"What Is the Matter with Milwaukee?" *The Independent* 68
(21 April 1910): 841; *Social-Democratic Herald*, 9 April 1910,
3 September 1910. Years later Mrs. Berger recalled that on
the night of the victory, Seidel would not respond to the
cheering crowd until Berger made his appearance. Milwaukee
Journal clipping of 14 December 1939, in the Emil Seidel
Collection, MCHS.

5. Abraham Cahan, "Milwaukee Socialists Attacked,"
New York *Call*, 19 April 1910; Milwaukee *Journal*, 27 July
1910; Frederic C. Howe, "Milwaukee: A Socialist City," *The
Outlook* 95 (25 June 1910): 411-421; "Victor L. Berger,"
American Magazine 70 (May 1910): 41-43; "Victor Berger,
the Organizer of the Socialist Victory in Milwaukee,"
Current Literature 49 (September 1910): 265-269.

6. Cahan, "Milwaukee Socialists Attacked"; Mary E. Marcy,
"The Milwaukee Victory," *International Socialist Review* 10
(May 1910): 991.

7. *Social-Democratic Herald*, 28 May 1910. Berger entitled this editorial, "What's Best for the Movement the Only
Question."

8. *Political Action*, 29 October 1910, 11 February 1911,
28 February 1911.

9. *Social-Democratic Herald*, 3 September 1910; Edward
J. Muzik, "Victor L. Berger, a Biography" (Ph.D. diss., North-
western University, 1960), pp. 205-207; *Voice of the
People*, 5 November 1910; Oscar Ameringer, *If You Don't
Weaken* (New York: Henry Holt and Co., 1940), p. 284;
Political Action, 29 October 1910. The rally where
Liebknecht spoke included all the elements of a typical Mil-
waukee socialist program—speeches in English and German
and musical entertainment from the local socialist singing
societies. *S.P. Official Bulletin*, October 1910.

10. Mimeographed statement issued by the Milwaukee Social Democratic Central Committee, SP Col., State and Local
File, Wisconsin, 1898-1920, Duke; *Social-Democratic
Herald*, 12 November 1910; *Political Action*, 19 November
1910, 3 December 1910; *S.P. Official Bulletin*, December
1910.

11. John Spargo, "Victor Berger, First Socialist Congressman," *Survey* 25 (3 December 1910): 337-339.

12. George D. Herron to Hillquit, 10 January 1911, Hillquit Col., SHSW; Eugene V. Debs, "Danger Ahead," *International Socialist Review* 11 (Janurary 1911): 413-414.

13. *Social-Democratic Herald*, 3 December 1910.

14. Socialist Party, *Proceedings of the 1912 National Convention*, p. 234.

15. Berger to William James Ghent, 28 March 1911, 13 March 1911, Berger Col., MCHS; Ghent to Morris Hillquit, 27 June 1912, Hillquit Col., WSHS. Ghent had to abandon work in the spring of 1913 when he contracted tuberculosis. Harold Sherburn Smith, "William James Ghent, Reformer and Historian" (Ph.D. diss., University of Wisconsin, 1957), p. 36.

16. *S.P. Official Bulletin*, May 1911, August 1911, November 1911, January 1912; Ghent to Ernest Untermann, 17 October 1911, Berger to Ghent, 16 November 1911, Berger Col., MCHS; *Social-Democratic Herald*, 30 December 1911.

17. Berger Statement, 14 November 1910, Berger Col., MCHS.

18. See *The American Labor Year Book* (New York: Rand School of Social Science, 1916), p. 101. This contains a review of Berger's record in Congress, including all his measures. His record is also reviewed in the Social Democratic Party, Milwaukee County, *Campaign Manual*, 1912, pp. 20-26, and in Socialist Party, *Socialism in the United States Congress: The Work of Victor L. Berger* (Chicago: Socialist Party, 1912).

19. *Social-Democratic Herald*, 19 November 1910; U.S., *Congressional Record*, 62d Cong., 1st sess., 1911, 47, Part 1, 6; *Social-Democratic Herald*, 8 April 1911. Berger's newspapers served to forecast his actions, report them, and parry thrusts of his critics.

20. A. M. Simons to Berger, 13 March 1911, Berger to Simons, 21 March 1911, Berger Col., MCHS; J. Mahlon Barnes to Hillquit, 23 March 1911, Hillquit Col., SHSW; *Social-Democratic Herald*, 25 March 1911. Hillquit drew up the petition.

21. U.S., *Congressional Record*, 62d Cong., 1st sess., 1911, 47, Part 1, 430, 707; Ghent to Louis B. Boudin, 17 April 1911, Berger Col., MCHS.

22. John R. Commons, *History of Labor in the United States*, Vol. 4, Selig Perlman and Philip Taft, *Labor Movements, 1896-1932* (New York: Macmillan Co., 1935), pp. 319-322.

23. *S.P. Official Bulletin*, April 1911, May 1911; Socialist Party, *Minutes* of the National Executive Committee, 29 April-1 May 1911; Berger Statement, 31 May 1911, Berger Col., MCHS. At the hearings Berger said that he assumed neither the guilt nor the innocence of the accused but was concerned with breaches of their civil rights by public officials. He called only two witnesses—the president of their International and the brothers' attorney—in order to demonstrate that a full congressional investigation must be held. U.S., Congress, House, Committee on Rules, *Hearings On House Concurrent Resolution 6 for the Appointment of a Committee of Investigation*, 62d Cong., 1st sess., 1911, pp. 3, 7.

24. J. Louis Engdahl to Berger, 24 April 1911; various resolutions in commendation sent to Berger, May 1911; Simons to Berger, 3 June 1911, Berger Col., MCHS. Ultimately, on the advice of Clarence Darrow, their attorney, the brothers pleaded guilty in order to save their lives. The outcome of the case hurt labor before public opinion, and the Socialist party failed to elect Job Harriman as mayor of Los Angeles, although pre-trial chances had been good.

25. *Political Action*, 1 July 1911; U.S., *Congressional Record*, 62d Cong., 1st sess., 1911, 47, Part 1, pp. 2026-2030. At the 1912 party convention, Berger tried unsuccessfully to get the party to take a stand on the tariff. Though admitting that it was an unreal issue, he argued that it assumed importance from its role in the national dialogue. S.P. *Proceedings* of the 1912 National Convention, p. 107. *S.P. Official Bulletin*, May 1911.

26. William D. Haywood, *Bill Haywood's Book* (New York: International Publishers, 1929), pp. 49-50.

27. Ghent to Ernest Untermann, 17 October 1911, Berger Col., MCHS.

28. U.S., Congress, House, Committee on Immigration, *Hearings on Dillingham Bill, S. 3175, to Regulate the Immigration of Aliens to and the Residence of Aliens in the United States*, 62d Cong., 2d sess., 1912, pp. 9, 14; mimeographed statement on Berger's vote on the Immigration Bill, 11 January 1915, SP Col., State and Local, Wisconsin 1898-1920, Duke; Milwaukee *Leader*, 14 February 1913.

Samuel Gompers had only contempt for Berger as a representative of organized labor. He wrote that Berger did not support any legislation favored by the American Federation of Labor and particularly excoriated his vote to support Taft's veto of the Sundry Civil Service Bill, which organized labor believed prevented appropriations for criminal prosecution of labor under the Sherman Anti-Trust Act. Berger opposed that measure as a "swindle of the workers" and said that the Sherman Act had never been applied to labor but funds would always be found for labor prosecutions when desired. Samuel Gompers, *Seventy Years of Life and Labour* (London: Hurst and Blackett, Ltd., 1925), Vol. 2, p. 293. Berger to *Inquirer*, 4 March 1914, Berger Col., MCHS.

29. See Berger note of 17 April 1911, Berger Col., MCHS.

30. U.S., *Congressional Record*, 62d Cong., 1st sess., 1911, 47, Part 4, p. 3699; Simons to Berger, 8 April 1911, Berger to Simons, 1 May 1911, Berger to Inquirer, 31 May 1911, Berger Col., MCHS; *S.P. Official Bulletin*, May 1911, August 1911.

31. *Social-Democratic Herald*, 23 September 1911, contains an article by Ghent entitled "The Old Age Pension Bill." *The New Review* 1 (1 March 1913): 293; Daniel De Leon, *Berger's Hits and Misses* (New York: New York Labor News Co., 1917), p. 64. These columns from *The Daily People* were published again in 1931 in a book entitled *Revolutionary Socialism in the United States Congress*.

32. William English Walling, "Government Ownership," *International Socialist Review* 12 (April 1912): 652; Louis B. Boudin to Ghent, 15 April 1911, Ghent to Boudin, 17 April 1911, Berger Col., MCHS; Louis B. Boudin, "A Serious Blunder," *International Socialist Review* 11 (June 1911): 758-759. Many times Berger had explained the differences between the systems of state capitalism and socialism but in his zeal to move toward a socialist system of government ownership, he saw this as a necessary first step.

33. *New Review* 3 (15 January 1916): 291-294; Eugene V. Debs, "Meyer London in Congress," *American Socialist*, 4 December 1915.

34. Milwaukee *Leader*, 27 February 1913, 4 April 1913. The latter issue reprinted an article from the *Western Comrade* by Carl Sandburg in praise of Berger. Sandburg later worked for the *Leader* during World War I.

35. Milwaukee *Leader*, 4 November 1912, 13 October

1912. His campaign featured a collection entitled "Some Anti-Socialist Voices of the Press on Victor L. Berger and his Work in Congress," typescript, Berger Col., Tamiment.

36. Elizabeth H. Thomas to Berger, 14 July 1911, Berger to Clifford Pinchot, 13 November 1912, Berger to Simons, 16 November 1912, Berger Col., MCHS. Berger won over five hundred votes more than he had in 1910, but they were only 14,025 of 38,615 ballots cast. Wisconsin, *Blue Book*, 1913, 37: 267.

37. *S.P. Official Bulletin*, May 1911; Julius Gerber to Elizabeth H. Thomas, 13 June 1911, Thomas to Gerber, 15 June 1911, Germer to Emil Seidel, 15 June 1911, Gerber to Berger, 28 October 1911, Berger Col., Tamiment; Ghent to Coit Lyceum Bureau, 31 May 1911, Berger to Coit Lyceum Bureau, 5 May 1911, 25 June 1911, Berger Col., MCHS. For an article on Berger's role in Americanizing Marx, see Roderick Nash, "Victor L. Berger: Making Marx Respectable," *Wisconsin Magazine of History* 47 (Summer 1964): 301-308.

5

Syndicalism Resolved

The issue of direct action finally erupted simultaneously with the struggle over office-holding. The appearance of the Industrial Workers of the World pitted the Socialist party against a labor organization seeking economic collectivism through a policy of confrontation.

The Wobblies were organized in 1905 in Chicago following years of frustration experienced by radicals unable to ameliorate working conditions through existing labor unions. The new organization was a product of native conditions which combined both French-style syndicalist ideas and American socialist and radical impulses.[1] Much of its early history was related to the Socialist party as a result of overlapping ideas and personnel, and even when the two groups went their separate ways in 1913, they were still associated together in the public mind.

The moving organization behind the new group was the Western Federation of Miners, a union which had been shaped by its history of industrial conflict into an indigenous class-conscious radical force,[2] and consequently divorced from the American Federation of Labor. Aware of its physical and geographic isolation, the WFM was determined to broaden its base, and called an organizational meeting of radical labor leaders and socialists. Of the thirty-six who were invited, only Victor Berger and Max Hayes declined to attend.

The meeting in January 1905 produced a manifesto for the organization of workers along class lines, a decision against affiliation with any political party, and a summons to a founding convention to be

93

held in June. The projected union would be composed of workers from various crafts and industries who would strive to achieve the immediate aims of the proletariat while simultaneously pushing for the ultimate goal, an industrial cooperative commonwealth.

From the first the IWW suffered from internal friction between syndicalist and socialist ideals. As personnel changed, the originally somewhat political, socialist perspective was transformed into a non-political, direct actionist outlook. Due to its acceptance of the idea of the class struggle and of the theory of labor value, the IWW favored the control of the means of production and distribution by industrialized unions, the minimal use of political action required for worker conquest of the state, and the state's immediate abolition once in power. The fear of the state, based on its coercive character, and the concurrent desire to exploit its power during the transition to the new society, lent the IWW its French syndicalist coloration.[3]

At its birth, and for some years afterward, the IWW flirted with the concept of political action. Its original preamble endorsed both political and industrial means. But with the trend toward economic action alone, conflict flared and the parent WFM departed, and Daniel De Leon, one of the founders, was ousted.

Other socialist founders, such as Debs, Simons, and the first and only president of the IWW, Charles O. Sherman of the United Metal Workers, also departed. With the barely legal unseating of Sherman, the abolition of his office in 1906, and the generally changing tenor of the organization from socialist industrial unionism to anarcho-syndicalism, the political orientation disappeared. In 1908 the political clause was dropped,[4] and thereafter the membership was dominated by militant unionists who disparaged political organization. Ironically, the IWW turned against political action just at the time when the Socialist party, and Berger in particular, offered support via political methods. Despite the change in orientation, many Wobblies retained their membership in the Socialist party and sought its assistance for four more years.

The direct actionist tactics to which the IWW was committed included economic pressure, free speech agitation, boycotts, strikes, and sabotage. The organization did not advocate the use of violence except in self-defense, despite its portrayal in contemporary sources.[5]

An examination of the IWW, especially its publications, reveals that to the organization the word "sabotage" was not synonymous with violence; the meaning was distorted by capitalist and socialist enemies of the IWW. Sabotage included passive resistance, such as loafing on the job, or the disabling of machinery to reduce profits and production. Elizabeth Gurley Flynn, in an IWW publication, defined sabotage as "either to slacken up and interfere with the quantity, or to botch in your skill and interfere with the quality of capitalist production so as to give poor service. It is something that is fought out within the walls of the shop. Sabotage is not physical violence, sabotage is an internal industrial process."[6] The definition of sabotage was to be an integral part of the later struggle between the IWW and the Socialist party; indeed it was the very point upon which the connection was ruptured.

The man who symbolized the IWW in its first fifteen years was William D. Haywood, who came out of the west to stand on the national stage as one of the most zealous and dedicated of native American radicals.[7] His youthful years were spent in the Western Federation of Miners and the Western Labor Union, where he served his agitational apprenticeship and became a socialist. It was Haywood who chaired the first convention of the IWW and it was his influence that made the Wobblies the one national labor organization to concern itself with the black, the migrant, and the immigrant.

Haywood was involved personally in every significant event in the history of the IWW. The 1906 illegal extradition of Haywood, Charles H. Moyer, president of the WFM, and former IWW member George A. Pettibone, from Colorado to Idaho, and their subsequent trial for the murder of former Governor Frank Steunenberg of Idaho, led to the IWW's suspension of its organizational work and the defection of the WFM; and the 1913 recall of Haywood from the Socialist party hierarchy triggered the IWW exodus from the party.

Gene Debs welcomed the IWW, for he thought that industrial unionism and a socialist party were fundamental to progress. He was optimistic that the new organization would be more responsive to the needs of the workers than was the stodgy AFL.[8] But Victor Berger, whose position on the relationship of economic and political action was more rigidly defined than was Debs's, and who had a vested interest in the AFL-connected Federated Trades Council in Milwaukee, shunned the new organization; he maintained that while he actually favored industrial unionism, he opposed the IWW on the basis of an overemphasis of the economic phase of the class struggle.

Berger saw the history of the labor movement in the United States as a constant struggle between political and economic partisans. At first, he noted, the socialists attempted to treat the unions as a mere appendage to the party and denounced their insubordination. As a result, angry labor leaders convinced their membership of socialist hostility.

> And while they [who opposed a two-armed movement] formerly tried to inject socialist politics into the trade unions . . . they now try to inject trade unionism into socialist politics and to solve political questions by the trade union. The trade union is now the fetish before which we must bow down. And "industrialism" . . . is in future to be considered by socialists as the magic key which will open the gate of freedom to the American proletariat. The result of this . . . extreme [sic] was the foundation last June of the IWW in Chicago, which in its platform demands that the trade union should also do the work of a political party. That is its sense if any sense can be made out of its contradictions.

Berger hated what he labeled a new version of nineteenth-century anarchism and flung out the condemnation that "a syndicalist is simply an anarchist too cowardly to admit it." He belittled and ridiculed the IWW as offering only the chaos of individual competition in every aspect of life, and he tried to discredit the Wobblies by falsely maligning their industrial conflicts as the substitution of "savage and barbaric warfare for the civilized warfare of the twentieth century." He considered the Wobblies essentially anti-social, and while he genuinely feared that they would damage the left's image before public opinion, he was most concerned over their threat to his party and his own position. Such self-interest was sufficient in itself to dictate vociferous opposition to the Wobblies.

But Berger was not unable to recognize and applaud some of their strengths. He lauded their ability to frighten exploitative employers and he appreciated their energy. "This must be said for the IWW. . . . even though its methods are poor, [it] has the spirit of rebellion, the heat of fanaticism, and the heroism of the poor who have nothing to lose, all of which are great elements of strength. . . ."[9] But the Wobblies did underestimate the need for organization, which he considered a serious tactical error.

Berger's relations with the IWW were seldom cordial and often hostile, and to the federal government he boasted that the Wobblies probably hated him more than any other man in America.[10] But despite ideological differences and even personality clashes, he usually aided the IWW when he was in a position to do so. Since both opposed the existing order their occasional cooperation was logical.

Berger as Congressman twice came to the rescue of his antagonists. Ironically, those two incidents he later considered the outstanding accomplishment of his term. In the Lawrence strike, his assistance was responsible for the Wobblies' major triumph; in the second incident, he was credited with forcing the retirement of a federal judge who had harassed an IWW member.

In January 1912, a strike involving 25,000 immigrant workers erupted in Lawrence, Massachusetts, in protest against a reduction of wages. The employer was the powerful American Woolen Company and the strikers were mainly unskilled recent immigrants of various nationalities, few of whom were organized. The handful of skilled workers belonged to the United Textile Workers, which was affiliated with the AFL, while a fraction of the unskilled belonged to the IWW.

The strike leaders telegraphed the Wobblies for assistance, and Joseph Ettor, a member of the executive, went at once to Lawrence. His participation brought the strike to the attention of John Golden of the United Textile Workers, whose anxiety to prevent the strengthening of the IWW served only to antagonize both the strikers and his own conservative organization.

A clash between strikers and the activated militia led to the death of a woman striker and the subsequent arrest of Ettor and Arturo Giovanitti, also of the Wobblies, as accessories to the murder. The loss of Ettor resulted in the substitution of Haywood as the leader of the strikers.[11]

At this time, Berger, in response to Haywood's appeal, introduced a resolution in Congress for an investigation of conditions at Lawrence. In his remarks Berger called attention to the violation of the constitutional rights of the workers and the forcible detention by the police of the strikers' children within the city. He described the low wages and inhuman conditions at the mills, and he inserted a dramatic United Press report into the record. He even managed to see President Taft, of whom he demanded a Department of Justice investigation of the case.

Taft appeared visibly aghast at the picture of Lawrence which Berger sketched, and it was his interest which led to immediate hearings by the Rules Committee of the House.[12]

In the meantime Haywood and Berger quarreled during a meeting of the NEC over the most effective manner in which the Socialist party might assist the strikers. Berger, pointing out that congressional hearings were already scheduled for the next week, unsuccessfully opposed Haywood's suggestion of party protests to Taft and Governor Foss of Massachusetts.

At the hearings, Berger enjoyed his prominence thoroughly. He stressed the routine brutality of the company which held a near monopoly in its field, benefited from the tariff, and yet paid lower wages than other trusts. He called the strike a rebellion of the working class against unbearable conditions. Berger's effectiveness, however, was weakened by his posturing, and the irritated Rules Committee decided that only committee members could question witnesses. When Berger protested that he alone of the Congressmen was familiar with conditions at Lawrence, he was finally allowed to feed questions to committee members.[13]

The testimony of working children impressed the committee and the public as well, as the strike leaders had hoped. The strike was settled the week following the hearings, resulting in wage boosts for the workers and short-term membership gains for the IWW.

The city of Lawrence proceeded with its murder trial of Ettor and Giovanitti. The Socialist party raised funds for the defense and, after the acquittal, Lawrence came to symbolize cooperation between the Wobblies and the party.[14] For focusing national attention on the strike, Berger won praise from reformist socialists and even, years later, from Big Bill Haywood in his memoirs. A few months after the events, however, Haywood had entirely ignored Berger's role during an address to the Socialist party convention on the significance of Lawrence. But the *International Socialist Review* cited Berger's "invaluable assistance" to Haywood and the IWW. The *Review* celebrated the cooperation of the two organizations and announced the discovery of successful tactics by the Socialist party: industrial unionist direct action in combination with political action.[15]

In that same session of Congress, Berger again stepped forward to aid the IWW. On 13 May 1912, the Milwaukee *Leader* reported that Judge Cornelius U. Hanford, Federal Judge of the western district of the state of Washington, had cancelled the citizenship papers, granted in 1910, of a Wobbly named Oleson solely because of his alleged membership in the union.

Within the month, Berger moved to impeach Judge Hanford for his violation of the constitution by "frivolously" annulling the naturalization of an individual. He charged the judge with a series of illegal decisions as well as with drunkenness and other personal conduct inappropriate to his position. Berger submitted a resolution instructing the Committee on the Judiciary to investigate and also filed a stack of affidavits with the Department of Justice testifying to the personal and judicial unfitness of Judge Hanford. He even met with the Attorney General to inquire whether the Justice Department had approved the Oleson ruling.[16]

Oleson's membership in the Socialist Labor party was no deterrent to Berger's interest in the case. He was anxious to determine if government policy now sanctioned nullification of citizenship for political reasons. If so, such action could be applied to members of the Socialist party, including Berger himself. But while his interest in the case was not entirely academic, he insisted: "We must resist any encroachments of the judiciary . . . no matter whether the victim is a member of our party or not; no matter whether he be a Socialist, a Bull Moose, or a Knight of Columbus."[17]

Berger succeeded in his efforts to unseat Judge Hanford; in the midst of the investigation of the impeachment charges by the House Subcommittee on the Judiciary, Hanford suddenly resigned. Later Berger successfully moved that the Socialist party contribute funds to Oleson to allow him to appeal the loss of his citizenship.[18]

There were a few occasions, however, when Berger not only refused aid to the IWW but actively opposed it. He and Bill Haywood confronted each other during NEC meetings over the issue of Socialist party support for the Wobblies' free speech struggle on the west coast. The right of free speech meant, to the IWW, the use of street corners for agitational purposes. It was a practical rather than a constitutional or ideological issue to the Wobblies, because without that right the IWW would be unable to recruit members. When the agitators were prohibited from holding street meetings, they would fill the local jails and endure tactical hunger strikes, until the local authorities were forced to surrender. The peak of the free speech struggle occurred in 1912 in San Diego, where it assumed "the character of open class war, in which conservative unions . . . aligned with socialists and the IWW in a common defense against a united employer attack.'' The tension was exacerbated by the rise of extra-legal vigilante groups who tried to push aside legal authorities in their zeal to persecute the agitators.[19]

In April, Haywood moved before the NEC that the Socialist party give moral and financial aid to the free speech movement in San Diego and that it take steps to bring about a congressional investigation of conditions there. Berger, to whom the latter part of Haywood's motion was directed, had no intention of helping direct actionism. He would assist the Wobblies in a strike, but he would not associate with what he called a brawl. He amended the motion so that action was delayed until the California State Committee of the Socialist party investigated and reported to the NEC. The report arrived the next month and the NEC responded with a donation to help only its own local in the fight. At the party convention which immediately followed, Berger argued that the NEC had already taken action and, therefore, no further party response was needed. But the delegates voted to send telegrams of support to all free speech groups.[20]

Berger's reformist comrades shared his fear of the twofold Wobbly threat to attract potential socialists and to frighten the American public into reaction. Adolph Germer and Robert Hunter, for example, discussed the possibility of a national conference to debate political action. They recoiled, however, from the possibility of inviting progressive trade unionists on the one hand, and from programming the general strike for debate on the other. They felt too threatened to move in either direction.[21]

Hunter was particularly agitated about the aggressive image that Haywood might be foistering on the Socialist party. He proposed that the party issue a statement to the press reiterating support for its trade union resolutions of the past and differentiating its attitudes from those of the Wobblies. He mourned the increasing activity of revolutionists of all types, whom he described as controlling "every paper in the movement," and feared that soon constructive socialists would lose control of most locals. Hunter finally became so despondent that he decided not to stand for re-election to the NEC and he abandoned his activism. His tone in letters to Hillquit vividly portrayed the demoralization of a few of the reformists.

I can not stand the bitter attacks and villanous [*sic*] statements that some comrades seem to consider their most useful
work in the Party, and I am becoming more and more ir-
ritable. I fear that my usefulness as an official is over. How
you, Berger, . . . and Spargo can stand these poisoned arrows
and remain so fair to those who never cease to pepper you, I
do not see. I suppose it is only because you have been in the
fight all your lives and can not give it up. I have been simply
thunderstruck to see how every act of ours has been misrep-
resented, to see ourselves accused of every crime, to have
words put in our mouths that we never uttered and to see us
condemned for policies that we never dreamed of adopt-
ing.[22]

Reformist Carl D. Thompson, director of the party's Information
Department, prepared a file on syndicalism and sabotage, and issued
party pamphlets condemning economic action exclusive of political action. He wrote to Helen Keller, a perplexed supporter whose loyalty he
was particularly anxious to insure, that it was most important that the
long continuing struggle over political action be settled in the Socialist
party as it had been in most European Socialist parties. He argued that
"here more than in all the earth the political method has the greatest
possibilities and other methods the least." He vowed that the party
would settle the issue in favor of political action.[23]

Thompson's pamphlets demonstrate typical reformist manipulation of party machinery, but public discussion always saw party factions
compete on equal terms. Such a confrontation between the two points
of view occurred at Cooper Union in New York City on 11 January
1912, when Morris Hillquit and Bill Haywood debated "What shall the
attitude of the Socialist party be toward the economic organization of
the workers?" The reformists were anxious to deflate Haywood, and
they sent encouragement and suggestions to Hillquit. Socialist Mayor
George R. Lunn of Schenectady reminded him that the party depended
on Hillquit's at least holding his own, and Ghent wrote that he was coming from Washington to witness the debate.[24]

Haywood argued that the socialists must encourage industrial
unionism and the eventual control and ownership of industry by those
unions, or preferably, by one big union. He accused Hillquit of com-
promising with the labor establishment and admonished him for his

concern with "safe" union tactics. Haywood emphasized militant party support of all strikers and a commitment to the general strike.

Hillquit asserted that Marx never supported a general strike. He explained patronizingly that the Socialist party aimed at the emancipation of labor by the workers themselves through both economic and political activity. The political movement must dominate, however, because the "ultimate goal of the entire labor movement is political in nature, and the accomplishment of that aim, no matter how brought about, will be a political act." He argued that while some socialists exaggerated the importance of the form of economic organizations, it was not the task of the Socialist party to support any particular type of structure. He pointed to what he called the growing strength of the socialist movement in the country, and he finished with a challenge, "Shall we now . . . charge front and revert to the tactics which have ruined the Socialist Labor party and retarded the socialist movement every time they have been resorted to? . . . that is the only issue between us."[25]

The debate served neither to settle the issue nor to clear the air between the two factions. It was merely a skirmish en route to a major confrontation that could not be avoided.

Direct action was debated in 1908 at the first Socialist party convention following the formation of the IWW, and a constitutional amendment was adopted which provided for the expulsion of members who opposed political action. Berger, as the spokesman for those backing this alteration of Article II, Section 6 of the constitution, discussed the growing tendency to depreciate political action and the ballot. He spoke of the need for a political party and the importance of excluding those out of harmony with that policy: "We must have the powers of the political government in our hands, at least to a great extent. . . . So everybody who is talking to you about direct action and so on, and about political action being a humbug, is your enemy today because he keeps you from getting the power of political government."

Two years later, the McNamara case and its culmination forced the Socialist party to focus its attention on violence and sabotage. Berger said that the tactics of the old line labor leaders inevitably led to frustration and the subsequent use of dynamite: "a 'pure and simple' trade union leader is often only a step removed from syndicalism, sabotage, slugging and violence." His only weapon is the strike, Berger continued, and faced with its loss he may become desperate and go to any extreme to win that strike. He hoped that the McNamara tragedy might awaken labor to the knowledge that the field of its struggle had shifted largely to the political and that the workers must turn to the ballot and the Socialist party.[26]

The revolutionists agreed that the McNamara case pointed up the inadequacy of the traditional unions to lead the workers' struggle against capital. The decay of craft union organizations necessitated the adoption of the new weapon of industrial unionism, to be utilized in coordination with a courageous and aggressive political party. However, the revolutionists continued, the party's emphasis on the ballot demonstrated its inability to teach class warfare on the industrial front, causing the worker, disappointed in his union and his party, to turn toward the use of dynamite.[27]

The debate between the right and the left, with the revolutionists supporting the syndicalists, would not be stilled. It continued in the various socialist press organs and was echoed in debates between the factions. The issue was resolved formally at a tumultuous party convention in May 1912.

The Socialist party met in Indianapolis for the first time since its initial convention eleven years earlier. The delegates came to the convention as a confident group of native American [28] professional men and women accompanied by a few of the foreign-born and a smattering of workers. Enthusiasm, even exuberance, prevailed. The party's prospects appeared bright as membership and votes climbed ever higher. The future was obviously theirs. It was necessary only to smooth over a few ruts in the path.

Indicative of the probability that a pre-convention reformist strategy existed was Berger's prediction that the Socialist party would rid itself of those who were attempting to destroy its effectiveness and reputation. The presence of Karl Legien of the right wing of the German Social Democratic party and an officer of the German General Federation of Labor Unions supports that conjecture. Legien, on a lecture tour of the United States paid for jointly by Gompers and the Socialist party, addressed the delegates on the dangers of sabotage and syndicalism and of the necessity of supporting existing trade unions.[29]

For the first few days the Socialists' convention proceeded without major incident. Advances on one side were offset by gains on the other. The resolution dealing with the party's relationship to the labor movement did not explicitly endorse industrial unionism, but the implicit acknowledgment of its existence was satisfactory to Haywood and his

group. Similarly a compromise was reached by the Committee on Platform, which stressed the importance of the class struggle and its ultimate goal but also endorsed immediate demands.

The presentation of the report of the Committee on Constitution
forced a showdown. Hillquit, as spokesman, recommended the
modification of Article II, Section 6 to provide expulsion not only for
opposition to political action but also for endorsement of crime against
persons or other methods of violence. Winfield R. Gaylord of Berger's
delegation offered an amendment from the floor that would prevent a
party member from advocating "crime, sabotage, or other methods of
violence."[30] Debate was lengthy and bitter. Berger, who had not been
a member of the Committee on Constitution, led its defensive team.

He used his ammunition against anarchism, dismissing any differences between that and syndicalism, as was his custom in debate.
"Those of you who stand for political action and for an effective and
sane economic movement—who stand against the bomb, the dagger
and every other form of violence will know how to vote on this amendment. . . . I for one do not believe in murder as a means of propaganda,
I do not believe in theft as a means of expropriation, nor in a continuous riot as a free speech agitation." In perhaps his most emotional
speech before a party convention, his voice rang on:

> Every true socialist will agree with me when I say that those
> who believe that we should substitute "Hallelujah, I'm a
> bum," for "The Marseillaise," and for the "International,"
> should start a bum organization of their own. . . . I am ready
> to split right here. . . . You know where anarchism leads to.
> . . . It made individual brigandage possible under the cloak of an
> idea. I am not willing that our party should stand godfather
> for any business of that kind.[31]

The left argued that sabotage was not violence and that the issue
was raised to obscure the question of industrial socialism. One delegate
confronted Berger with an editorial Berger himself had written some
years earlier inciting the workers to violence and sabotage. Berger, who
was subsequently embarrassed in every Milwaukee election by that in-
criminating editorial, published in 1909,[32] replied that the advice
must be read in context. He insisted that he had never advised that the
ballot be backed by bullets, but in fact had argued that a line must be

drawn between "a real social revolution on the one side and anarchy, murder and sabotage on the other. . . . The socialist movement is undoubtedly revolutionary. . . . But we do not mistake a riot for a revolution. . . . We do not preach the revolution in that way."[33]

The convention voted to include the anti-sabotage clause by a vote of 191 to 90. The character of the opposition to the clause was analyzed afterward by Ghent, who determined that forty-six of the eighty-four delegates whom he checked had middle-class occupations, while only twenty-eight were industrial workers. That middle-class delegates were on both sides in the voting seems to refute Haywood's charge of a non-proletarian coalition. But the vote should not be seen as an accurate indication of sentiment on syndicalism. Undoubtedly, had the clause not been phrased so that a favorable vote appeared to be an endorsement of bloodshed, more non-reformists would have supported the left. The right had boxed its antagonists into a corner and cleverly divided their forces, thereby destroying their effectiveness.[34]

The United Press reported that much hostility to Berger existed. Gossip at the convention held that he wanted the clause in order to curry favor with the anti-socialist press. Berger himself was very well pleased with the convention. "The sabotage clause. . . is a necessary declaration which puts us in thorough accord with the historic position of the party everywhere." He was not beyond bragging to a congressional hearing at which he testified that it was he who had written that anti-sabotage clause. This created resentment among the others who had worked for the clause at Indianapolis, but it was neither the first nor the last time that Berger irritated or angered his comrades.[35]

The syndicalists never forgave Berger for his role at the convention. During a lecture tour on the West Coast two years later, syndicalists in the audience hooted him off a platform.

The *International Socialist Review* claimed victory for the left at the convention. It reported that the old line reformists had won only one of the points at issue, the insertion of the anti-sabotage clause, and that it was the strength of the left wing that had forced the reformists to unite in that fight. Finally, it exulted, the working class was beginning to control the party, and mistakenly predicted that the referendum on the clause would be defeated because the word "sabotage" was undefinable.

But those of the left who recognized their defeat did not accept it passively. At the annual meeting of the National Committee in May

1913, an unsuccessful motion was presented to strike Article II, Section 6 from the constitution, and months later a leftist spokesman addressed a local of the Hungarian Federation of the Socialist party and recommended that the members join the Wobblies.[36]

The right was as zealous in its execution of the new policy as was the left in its efforts to amend it. As soon as the presidential campaign ended, the reformists set out to remove Haywood from the NEC. Ever since Haywood had become a popular and powerful figure in the Socialist party, the right had tried to diminish his role in party politics. The romantic and rebellious idealist, the one-eyed giant, could not be hidden by the journalists and lawyers who had been accustomed to dividing the party stage among themselves. With Haywood's election to the NEC in December 1911, Berger and his friends, still in control of a majority of the committee and of the socialist press, felt their entrenched power threatened. They had begun to be lulled into assuming the permanence of their control of the party and lacked perspective as to the extent of the sudden threat. In no other way can their irrational fear of Haywood and exaggerated conception of his power base, which was of course outside the Socialist party, be understood.

The reformists marshaled their strength in the press and the party and even strained at legal limitations in an effort to get rid of Haywood. A close watch was kept on everything the Wobbly leader wrote and said. In December 1912, the New York State Committee, supported by the New Jersey State Committee and local Washington, D.C., initiated a recall of Haywood from the NEC. The party did not normally include evidence or charges in its referenda but the hierarchy preceded the recall question with a resolution.

> Whereas W. D. Haywood, a member of the National Executive Committee, has stated in public meetings in New York City that he never advocated the use of the ballot by the workers, but indeed advised them to use direct action and sabotage, a violation of Article 2, Section 6, of the National Constitution: therefore, be it
>
> Resolved, By the state committee representing the Socialist party of the State of New York, that W. D. Haywood is unworthy to remain any longer a member of the National Ex-

ecutive Committee, and the committee therefore initiates a motion for his recall . . . as provided by the National Constitution.[37]

John M. Work, then the executive secretary of the party, insisted (in his unpublished memoirs) that he conducted the recall vote strictly in accord with all party rules despite his own predilection for the removal of Haywood.[38] There is no evidence to cast doubt upon Work's statement, but it obscures other matters. First, the inclusion of the resolution instead of merely the question "Shall W. D. Haywood be recalled from the National Executive Committee?" (a violation of traditional party practices), clearly involved excessive manipulation of the party machinery by the National Office. Secondly, the recall of a member of the NEC for violation of the anti-sabotage clause was not in accordance with the constitution, which provided for the expulsion of such an offending member from the party. It may have been that the right feared to expel Haywood and thereby provoke a mass exodus from the party, but its use of the recall had no legal basis. And finally, the confusion which surrounded the recall lay in the indefinability of the word "sabotage." Haywood was charged with recommending direct action and sabotage, but whether he urged violence, which in essence was what the party condemned, was debatable.

The *Review* sprang to his defense with published excerpts from Haywood's writings and speeches to convince its thousands of readers to vote against the resolution and to assure them that behind the recall was the intention to drive industrial unionists out of the party.

Both sides agitated throughout the balloting. Algernon Lee, director of the Rand School, assured Hillquit, whom the *Review* had attacked along with Berger for using arbitrary methods, that "From all I hear, the vote . . . is going very well in this city [New York]; and if one may judge by the tone of the State Committee, it will be the same all over the state." Adolph Germer, who regularly opposed Haywood within both the labor and the socialist movements, attacked him in the February issue of the *Miners' Magazine* and afterward described Haywood's defense in *The Industrial Worker* as indefinite and evasive. Germer confidently wrote that "The party is being cleansed of that turbulent element that has marred its growth in the past. It might result in a split and if so . . . the constitutional wing of our movement will build up an organization that will challenge the admiration of the world.''[39]

Although a few socialist locals, such as Butte, Montana, and the Minnesota State Committee protested against the form of the recall, the resolution passed by more than a two-to-one margin, 22,495 to 10,944.[40] The majority of the NEC had successfully ousted Haywood within nine months of its initial maneuver against him.

That it was necessary to use extraordinary methods did not trouble the reformists, for a superficial view did not reveal that fact to the rank and file. The intensity of the rightists' fears of Haywood and the IWW momentarily overwhelmed their basic commitment to democracy.

But Berger and his comrades saw no reason to dwell on this dark aspect of their triumph. At any rate, Berger could claim consistency in his opposition to non-political methods. He had fought direct actionist tendencies among the Milwaukee socialists, in the Socialist Labor party, in the predecessors to the national Socialist party, and in the party ever since its formation. He made a standing threat at conventions to withdraw the Milwaukee organization if the party rescinded its cooperation with the established trade union movement in favor of the industrial union. In accordance with his views, Berger refused to attend the organizational meeting of the IWW, he ridiculed it and distorted its policies in countless speeches, and, when it appeared to threaten the nature of the Socialist party, he did not scruple as to the methods necessary to eradicate its presence.

The reformists' determination in the Haywood affair stemmed not only from the threat they saw in him but also from their belief that the new force of industrial unionism, while possibly a progressive catalyst in the labor movement, could only discredit the Socialist party before American public opinion. Since they chose to achieve socialism through political methods requiring the capture of votes and offices, the reformists could not tolerate the outright alienation of the voting public by any segment of the party, or indeed, by any outside force with some connection to the party. This reason alone was sufficient to lead Berger to fight aggressively against industrial unionism. But in addition, he saw industrial unionism as a potential threat which might discredit the leadership of the Socialist party before its own membership.

The party leaders, old and familiar, were incapable of stirring the rank and file as was the fresh and dynamic Haywood. His vigorous presence, linked to a forceful organization, challenging routine and tired methods in the labor and socialist movements, offering criticism from an anti-capitalist perspective which appealed to the party membership, could not easily be dismissed. That they exaggerated the possibility of their defeat at Haywood's hands seems evident, but their response is understandable.

The party leaders set out to prove that the IWW represented violence through its endorsement of sabotage. Thus, they smeared the young organization, as did the national press and the federal and state governments. Berger never attempted to define sabotage to the members but said that its endorsement, which the constitutional clause linked with crime and "other methods of violence," would lead to expulsion. The IWW never denied that sabotage was one of its methods. It only denied that sabotage necessarily meant violence, but to that no one listened.

It is ironic that Berger had the same aggressive aura about him as did the Wobblies. Just as he was able to manipulate the image of the industrial unionists because of their careless talk, so Berger's enemies took advantage of his sometimes reckless phraseology to link him with anarchism. Throughout his career he heard the taunt "bullets and ballots" from old party politicians, labor union foes, and antagonists in the party. Even within his own faction his popularity was limited because of his assaults with pen and voice. It was his closest party associate, Morris Hillquit, who freely admitted that Berger's tone often smacked of anarchism.[41]

The undaunted party leaders in 1913 found themselves with fewer followers than in 1912. Yet while it is true that Haywood's departure from the Socialist party after his recall stimulated some of his followers to quit in sympathy, it cannot be demonstrated that a serious membership decrease resulted from the resolution of the syndicalist issue.

The fact that the membership shrank from 118,000 in 1912 to 95,957 the next year was explained by a left wing journal, exaggerating the loss, in terms of the anti-sabotage clause. Leftists argued that the clause, passed in order to impress capitalists, had become a basis for inquisitional procedures against whomever the party leaders selected, with Haywood the first victim. Hatred of boss rule, the journal claimed, was forcing out members.

In an effort to discourage such analyses, Carl D. Thompson issued a report to demonstrate that the only meaningful method through which to evaluate membership figures was the comparison of statistics over a number of years. He compared the 1909-1913 membership to the

1905-1909 period to illustrate, through the most favorable manipulation of figures, the vitality and growth of the party.[42]

That the membership decreased in 1913 cannot be debated, but this is partially attributable to the fact that, as in most political parties, membership declined following the enthusiasms of an election year. This natural phenomenon was undoubtedly intensified at this time by the withdrawal of an indeterminate number of IWW sympathizers, or at least Haywoodites. A third factor not to be overlooked was the attraction of the new President, Woodrow Wilson, for some of the less committed socialist supporters. To interpret the membership losses only in terms of the syndicalist struggle is to oversimplify.

Historians of the Socialist party long interpreted the events of 1912-1913 as marking the end of party growth and radicalism. While they discuss internal shrinkage and political eclipse, they clearly misread figures and their significance. David A. Shannon cites the year 1912 as the start of the party's gradual but steady drift toward conservatism under the leadership of the reformist faction. The reformists' clever separation of the revolutionists into divergent syndicalist and non-syndicalist camps insured their own grip on the party which they led further away from radicalism.[43] However, this explanation is not sufficiently penetrating.

Other historians have read even greater significance into the power struggle. Ira Kipnis argues in sweeping generalizations that the loss of the syndicalists led to an immediate and sharp decrease in membership and a modification of socialist militancy so that the party became no more than the left wing of the progressive movement. His conclusion, however, is not validated by events. Daniel Bell also sees 1912 as the turning point in the history of the party. His analysis on several different levels concludes that the party peaked in influence then and began a retreat into isolation from the realities of American politics. Isolation led to a loss of faith in the inevitable triumph of the cause.[44] But there is no evidence that the Socialist party leaders felt increasingly isolated and powerless. On the contrary, they were optimistic that future elections would open more doors to socialist reforms.

A recent study has begun to impose perspective on this period. James Weinstein accurately demonstrates that no sharp decline occurred in party membership. Compiling the most comprehensive figures extant, he proves that a "patchwork pattern" of growth and leveling off characterized the pre-war years.[45] With shrinkage thus discredited, a more pertinent assessment of the party turmoil is required. If no decline occurred, there had certainly been a bloodletting, the effect of which could not be negligible.

The party had been moving away from a revolutionary spirit ever since its formation, and the withdrawal of the syndicalists represented only another step in the same direction. Certainly Berger's faction was left more confident and secure, but party policy did not change markedly. The same long-range socialistic goals were sought through the tactic of immediate demands, with the goals distinguishing the party as Marxists rather than as progressive reformers. Only personnel shifts had occurred and the right had maneuvered into the more comfortable position of having to fend off only one group on the left, a faction that grudgingly lived with the concept of political action. A party dialogue appeared to be somewhat easier to maintain with organizational socialists than with confrontationist socialists. A greater sense of agreement existed than in the previous nine years, and policy-making was expected to be a less torturous procedure.

Thus the party entered the cataclysmic year of 1914 with one less division, and the reformist leaders had no knowledge that their opportunity to conduct policy relatively unhindered would be fleeting.

NOTES

1. Because the IWW was the only syndicalist organization to appear in the United States, it is generally termed an unqualified example of syndicalism, but Haywood said that the Wobblies sought to organize along lines existing in industry while syndicalism attempted to coordinate different trades. William D. Haywood, *Bill Haywood's Book* (New York: International Publishers, 1929), p. 231. The massive new history, *We Shall Be All: A History of the IWW* by Melvyn Dubofsky (Chicago: Quadrangle Books, 1969), holds that the IWW moved toward acceptance of a belief in the syndicalist organization of the new society. See pp. 73-74, 147.

2. For the western background of the IWW, see Dubofsky's early chapters in *We Shall Be All*, and especially pp. 36, 55-56.

3. Vincent St. John, *The IWW: Its History, Structure and Methods*, rev. ed. (Chicago: The Industrial Workers of the World, 1919), pp. 3-4; Paul F. Brissenden, *The Industrial Workers of the World: A Study in American Syndicalism* (New York: Columbia University Press, 1919), pp. 62-63; Eldridge Foster Dowell, *A History of Criminal Syndicalist Legislation in the United States* (Baltimore: Johns Hopkins University Press, 1939), p. 27; James Oneal and G. A. Werner, *American Communism: A Critical Analysis of Its Origins, Development and Progress* (New York: E. P. Dutton and Co., Inc., 1947), pp. 24-25.

4. Brissenden, *The Industrial Workers of the World*, pp. 177, 222.

5. Dowell, *A History of Criminal Syndicalist Legislation*, p. 30; Oneal and Werner, *American Communism*, pp. 24-25, 30. James Oneal, a top ranking reformist Socialist party leader and a labor historian, cites the IWW as a major example of what he calls the "force tendency" in the American labor movement. He sees the IWW in the tradition of nineteenth-century radical groups whose impatience with and lack of confidence in the efficacy of political means led them to favor the qualified use of force. He argues that the force tendency in the Socialist party disappeared with the departure of the Wobblies. On the other hand, Dubofsky and Conlin both argue that the IWW opposed the use of violence. The Wobblies' volatile rhetoric and their enemies' distortions painted them with a violent brush, but they actually believed violence to be both unnecessary and fruitless. Dubofsky, *We Shall Be All*, pp. 146, 153-170; Joseph R. Conlin, *Bread and Roses Too: Studies of the Wobblies* (Westport, Conn.: Greenwood Publishing Corp., 1969), pp. 69-70.

6. Dowell, *A History of Criminal Syndicalist Legislation*, pp. 32-36.

7. Haywood, *Bill Haywood's Book*, p. 31.

8. Ray Ginger, *Eugene V. Debs: A Biography* (New York: Collier Books, 1962), pp. 255, 273.

9. Milwaukee *Leader*, 6 May 1913, 15 August 1913; *Social-Democratic Herald*, 2 December 1905, 10 August 1912, 17 August 1912. He sometimes played loosely with the terms "trade" and "industrial" unionism.

10. Berger in interview with the *Seattle Daily Times*, 4 August 1913.

11. Brissenden, *The Industrial Workers of the World*, p.

282. John R. Commons, *History of Labor in the United States*, Vol. 4, Selig Perlman and Philip Taft, *Labor Movements, 1896-1932* (New York: Macmillan Co., 1935), pp. 266-270.

12. Haywood, *Bill Haywood's Book*, p. 249; U.S., *Congressional Record*, 62d Cong., 2d sess., 1912, 48, Part 3, 2485-2486; Social Democratic Party, Milwaukee County, *Campaign Manual*, 1912, p. 26; Milwaukee *Leader*, 27 February 1912. A number of strikers vainly attempted to send their children to friends outside Lawrence both for their safety and for publicity.

13. *S.P. Official Bulletin*, March 1912; U.S., Congress, House, Committee on Rules, *Hearings on House Resolutions 409 and 433: The Strike at Lawrence, Massachusetts*, 62d Cong., 2d sess., 1912, pp. 8-10, 124.

14. *S.P. Official Bulletin*, June 1912; Milwaukee *Leader*, 7 June 1912; Commons, *History of Labor in the United States*, Vol. 4, pp. 271-273.

15. New York *Call*, 3 May 1913: Haywood, *Bill Haywood's Book*, p. 257; *International Socialist Review* 12 (April 1912): 627, 629.

16. U.S., *Congressional Record*, 62d Cong., 2d sess., 1912, 48, Part 8, 7799.

17. *S.P. Official Bulletin*, September 1912.

18. Ibid.

19. Commons, *History of Labor in the United States*, Vol. 4, pp. 236-238, 240; Dubofsky, *We Shall Be All*, pp. 189-193.

20. *S.P. Official Bulletin*, May 1912, June 1912; Socialist Party, *Proceedings of the 1912 National Convention*, pp. 60-63.

21. Robert Hunter to Adolph Germer, 18 March 1910, Germer to Hunter, 28 March 1910, Germer Col., SHSW.

22. Hunter to Hillquit, 21 December 1910, 27 December 1910, 10 December 1911, Hillquit Col., SHSW. Hunter attacked anarcho-syndicalism in his book *Violence and the Labor Movement*, published in 1914.

23. Carl D. Thompson, "Political Action vs. Direct Action," n.d., SP Col., National Office File, 1896-1922, Duke. The Information Department was required to abstain from controversial matters. These pamphlets were issued after the party went on record against direct action, but during the period when the membership was still torn by the issue.

Thompson to Helen Keller, 22 December 1913, SP Col., Duke.

24. George R. Lunn to Hillquit, 5 January 1912, Ghent to Hillquit, 9 January 1912, Hillquit Col., SHSW.

25. "Report of Discussion Meeting under the Auspices of Local New York," 11 January 1912, typescript, Hillquit Col., Tamiment Institute.

26. Socialist Party, *Proceedings of the 1908 National Convention*, pp. 241-242; Victor L. Berger, "Socialism vs. Sabotage," in "Larger Bearings of the McNamara Case, A Symposium," *Survey* 27 (29 December 1911): 1422; Milwaukee *Leader*, 6 May 1913.

27. Frank Bohn, "The Passing of the McNamaras," *International Socialist Review* 12 (November 1911): 403-404.

28. The 1912 Socialist Party *Campaign Book* reports that 71 percent of the membership was native-born.

29. New York *Call*, 9 May 1912; Samuel Gompers, *Seventy Years of Life and Labour*, II (London: Hurst and Blackett, Ltd., 1925), 35. Legien addressed the U.S. Congress and afterward, in Berger's office, witnessed a violent argument as Gompers charged Berger with discrediting the American labor movement to European workers during his visits abroad in 1909 and 1910. Thereafter Gompers and Berger avoided all contact. Gompers's account would indicate that Legien was far to the right of the American reformist socialists. Socialist Party, *Proceedings of the 1912 National Convention*, p. 60; the *International Socialist Review* of June 1912 (p. 815) declared that Legien's comments had been inspired by prominent German-speaking party members.

30. Socialist Party, *Proceedings of the 1912 National Convention*, pp. 122, 195-198, 366.

31. Ibid., p. 130. Berger cited this speech at the congressional hearings to unseat him as evidence of his opposition to the IWW. U.S., Congress, House, Special Committee, *Hearings before the Special Committee Appointed under the Authority of House Resolution No. 6 Concerning the Right of Victor L. Berger to be Sworn in as a Member of the 66th Congress*, 1919, 1, 356-357 (hereafter cited as *Berger Hearings*).

32. See *Social-Democratic Herald*, 31 July 1909. "In view of the plutocratic law-making of the present day, it is easy to predict that the . . . hope of this country will finally be in one direction only—that of a violent and bloody revolution.

Therefore, I say, each of the 500,000 Socialist voters . . .
should besides doing much reading and still more thinking, also have a good rifle and the necessary rounds of ammunition
in his house and be prepared to back up his ballot with his
bullets, if necessary. This may look like a startling statement.
Yet I can see nothing else for the American masses today."
Berger must have written this in despair, although generally
he felt confident of electoral success. After the election
triumphs of 1910 he never again wrote in this vein.

33. Socialist Party, *Proceedings of the 1912 National Convention*, p. 133.

34. Ghent's analysis appears in David Shannon, *The Socialist Party of America: A History* (New York: Macmillan
Co., 1955), p. 73; Haywood, *Bill Haywood's Book*, p. 257;
Ohio was the only state delegation to vote against the insertion of the clause, thus foreshadowing its later left wing commitment. For a full treatment of the convention, see Ira Kipnis, *The American Socialist Movement, 1897-1912* (New
York: Columbia University Press, 1952), pp. 391-408,
balanced by the shorter work by David Shannon, *The Socialist Party of America*, pp. 71-74.

35. United Press dispatch, 18 May 1912; clipping in
Debs's Scrapbook, IX, 1910-1915, Debs Col., Tamiment
Institute; Berger Statement, 22 May 1912, Berger Col.,
MCHS; *The Party Builder*, 28 February 1914; Ghent to Hill-
quit, 14 April 1914, Hillquit Col., SHSW.

36. Nettie May Rankin to Thompson, 2 April 1914, SP
Col., Duke; *International Socialist Review* 12 (June 1912):
824, 873-874, and 13 (June 1913): 878; Hungarian
Translator-Secretary to the NEC, 24 December 1913, SP
Col., Duke.

37. *S.P. Official Bulletin*, January 1913.

38. John M. Work, "Autobiography," II, Chap. 5, 16,
typescript, John M. Work Collection, SHSW.

39. *International Socialist Review* 13 (February 1913):
625; Algernon Lee to Hillquit, 22 January 1913, Hillquit
Col., SHSW; Germer to John H. Walker, 7 February 1913, to
J. Keir Hardie, 18 February 1913, to Thomas Kennedy, 9
March 1913, Germer Col., SHSW.

40. *International Socialist Review* 13 (February 1913):
625; *S.P. Official Bulletin*, 1 March 1913.

41. Morris Hillquit, *Loose Leaves from a Busy Life* (New
York: Macmillan Co., 1934), p. 59.

42. Haywood, *Bill Haywood's Book*, pp. 230, 260; *The New Review* 1 (August 1913): 673, 677-678; Carl D. Thompson, "Bigger, Better and Stronger Than Ever," typescript, SP Col., National Office File, 1896-1922, Duke.
43. Shannon, *The Socialist Party of America*, p. 79.
44. Kipnis, *The American Socialist Movement*, pp. 418-419, 427; Daniel Bell, *Marxian Socialism in the United States* (Princeton: Princeton University Press, 1967), pp. 79-80.
45. James Weinstein, *The Decline of Socialism in America: 1912-1925* (New York: Monthly Review Press, 1967), pp. x, 114-115.

6

Fissures on the Right

The outbreak of the war found Berger and the other American delegates to the International Socialist Congress at sea, both literally and figuratively. As Europe marshaled her armies and governments maneuvered to force each other into declarations of war, the scheduled opening of the full Congress of the International in Vienna was thrust forward from the end of August to the first week of that month and moved to Paris. On 30 July Berger and Oscar Ameringer left Milwaukee for New York where they met the other delegates—Morris Hillquit, Emil Seidel, George R. Lunn, and Meyer London, an unofficial member of the delegation. Only Charles Edward Russell had left earlier. The delegation gathered in Hillquit's home to debate whether or not to proceed to a congress that might never open. The majority argued that duty required that they try to get to Europe. They boarded the *Vaterland* but switched to the English *Oceanic* after the German ship was detained. The *Oceanic* had sailed only ninety miles out of the harbor when the delegates received a cable from the National Office informing them that the congress had been cancelled. All except London, who decided to proceed, returned to the New York harbor by tug, and Berger, Ameringer, and Seidel left at once for Milwaukee.[1]

Berger's initial comment on the war to the press was a prediction of a struggle between Russian autocracy and western democracy. German participation in the "historical struggle" would be determined by the five million German Social Democrats, he said, rather than by the Kaiser. However, he hoped that the war somehow could be localized.[2]

117

Once back in Milwaukee, Berger had time to reflect on the momentous reality of European war. Conflicting emotions resulted from his three distinct allegiances: to Germany, to world peace, and to the United States, and he remained faithful to his various loyalties throughout the ordeal of the war.

Berger's racist world-view, shaped through a prism of belief in German superiority, led to an instinctive reaction to the war. Ever since his immigration to the United States, Berger had been a participant in and supporter of German cultural activities. He and his family patronized the German theater in Milwaukee, and German was always used freely at home. During the war the Berger family reverted more and more to the use of their native tongue and participated in bazaars and other events to raise funds for German victims of the war. Berger publicly admitted two months after the war began, albeit with qualifications, that his sympathies were with Germany.[3]

Despite all his bombast and excitability, Berger always advocated peace, and his deep commitment led him to participate in non-socialist peace groups which aroused party hostility toward him. But on the other hand, Berger never considered himself a pacifist and, indeed, ridiculed pacifism as cowardly. He felt contemptuous of anyone who would refuse to defend family, home, and country, and this, too, brought him into conflict with members of the party who maintained that the worker was without a country to defend.

Berger's belief that the worker did have a country involved an admission of American nationalism. He said that by virtue of his vote the worker enjoyed citizenship in the United States and its concomitant responsibilities. In an interview in Seattle in 1913, Berger had explained that socialism was identical with patriotism because it strove for the greatest good for the mass of the people. "I want it understood that the Socialist movement is not anti-national. The Socialist movement is international. I'll even say that the Socialism is intensely national. If this country should ever be attacked by a foreign enemy the Socialists would be found in the very front ranks, defending their homes and their families."[4]

The composition of the Milwaukee community placed Berger and his newspaper in an anomalous position. The *Leader* could not follow a course that would satisfy socialist readers, who interpreted the war in economic terms, and at the same time please nationalistic German leaders, who thought that any position less than endorsement of the

Central Powers was pro-British. Some of the other dailies in Milwaukee exploited the *Leader*'s dilemma; when Berger wrote that he would not fight for the Kaiser, the Milwaukee *Free Press* headlined that his sympathies were with the British, and the *Leader*'s circulation ultimately suffered.[5]

The *Leader*'s initial comment on the war was confined to a general statement that there was no choice in the clash between German kaiserism and Russian czarism. Mankind's only hope lay with the United States and with the rising tide of democratic socialism. "Here in America we must make the fight for industrial democracy—for the rule of the people—lest civilization itself may perish." In this editorial Berger did not even discuss the causes of the war but limited himself to an automatic plug for socialism. At the time he did not know that most European socialists voted to support their own governments in the war.

Not until another month passed did Berger offer an analysis of the causes of the war. He emphasized that fear of social democracy and its growing strength had caused the Kaiser and the Czar to seek a diversion from the "inner enemy." Berger also cited militarism and the desire of the ruling class to try out its fighting machines. He touched upon nationalism and the traditional rivalry between Teuton and Slav as one important factor, and added an indictment of England: English jealousy of growing German trade was responsible for transforming an economic rivalry into a military rivalry. He concluded: "This war is the disgrace of the twentieth century. And it is a misfortune that international Socialism has proved itself too weak to prevent it."

Berger was keenly disappointed by the German Social Democrats, the majority of whom supported the German government and voted for the war credits. The SPD had long been Berger's inspiration as the finest and most successful socialist organization in the world, and as an apologist he now stressed that the international socialist movement was only fifty years old and therefore its component parts could not yet overwhelm the power of nationalism. The socialists needed more time to transform primitive nationalism into international solidarity. Berger's own German racism and his personal reconciliation of nationalism with internationalism should have tempered any criticism he may have had of the SPD. In fact, it is difficult to imagine Berger as a member of the Reichstag opposing the party decision that summer of 1914.

In August the *Leader* published an editorial entitled "Let the Nation Feed the Nation," which predicted that the American export trade would soon become a veritable flood resulting in the spiraling of domestic prices beyond the reach of the worker and his family. The *Leader* demanded that doors be closed upon war exports and that the control of food distribution be placed in the hands of the government. The government "should run the warehouses and distributing agencies through which the people's food must flow." And it concluded: "Starve the war and feed America!"[6] The Socialist party soon adopted this expression as its slogan.

As Berger's initial reaction to the war was a personal, instinctive response rather than a theoretical one, his comrades also reacted as individuals. Morris Hillquit, who was born in Riga in the Russian Empire, had no such loyalty for the land of his birth. Reared as a Jew without the right to Russian citizenship, Hillquit lacked even a sense of national identity such as Berger experienced as a Jew in the Austro-Hungarian Empire. His disappointment expressed itself in concern for the fate of socialism in general without regard to a particular country. "I was dismayed," he later wrote, "by the sudden collapse of human reason, . . . the realization of the failure of the Socialist International in the supreme hour of the crisis, the shattering of cherished illusions about the temper and power of the Socialist movement, and the desertion of so many of its trusted leaders."[7]

Algie M. Simons and his wife, May, who until 1914 had been a leader of the Women's Committee of the Socialist party and an effective socialist agitator, experienced the same type of intense emotional reaction to the war as did Berger. Although both were born in the United States, they shared a love for England developed through several visits there and nourished by warm relationships with English friends. The outbreak of the war was excruciating for them, and they early decided that the hope of socialism and internationalism lay with the English cause. Their involvement became very real through their uncomfortable residence in German Milwaukee, and by the second year of the war the Simonses began to withdraw from the social life of the city. Algie Simons even found his editorial position on the Milwaukee *Leader* somewhat circumscribed when Berger brought to the staff the German-born Ernest Untermann for the sole purpose of neutralizing Simons's obvious predilections.[8]

The reformist leaders of the Socialist party must have faced the war and the responses of their European comrades with the hollow feeling of defeat. They now commanded their own party almost unchallenged, but to what end? To explain a war across the sea? To rationalize the behavior of socialists to whom they were tied through long tradition? They desired only to be left alone with the problems of American society and their solutions, but the inexorable movement of world politics engulfed them.

The first party pronouncement on the war was issued on 14 August 1914, before policy could be formulated. The statement was little more than routine, a reiteration of opposition to all wars and condemnation of the ruling classes of Europe for the current one. "By their action in this crisis" it read, "they have conclusively proven that they are unfit to administer the affairs of nations in such a manner that the lives and happiness of the people may be safeguarded." The Wilson administration was called upon to prove its peaceful intentions by opening negotiations for mediation at once and "extending every effort to bring about the speedy termination of this disastrous conflict." No mention was made of the causes of the war, but the party demanded that the United States government insure the domestic food supply by nationalization and called for resolutions and demonstrations to prevent American exporters from aiding the war effort.[9]

At once, the party's campaign committee ordered one million anti-war leaflets and ten thousand anti-war posters. The Executive Secretary, Walter Lanferseik, cabled ten socialist parties in neutral countries suggesting a conference to lay the groundwork for immediate mediation of the war.[10]

Although party leaders were without a policy, the NEC unwisely vetoed Berger's proposal that it meet at the end of August to formulate a constructive position. It also ignored the suggestion of the editor of the party organ that a specific group be organized to handle the party's peace campaign.[11] Finally, that winter, the leaders realized that discussion was needed in order to formulate a substantive war policy and a subcommittee drew up a peace program.

Declaring that there were no conflicts between workers of the various countries, the subcommittee presented peace proposals, most of which later would be acceptable to non-socialist peace circles. The subcommittee favored a peace without indemnities or forced territorial transfers, an international court to settle disputes and an international league to keep the peace, national disarmament, internationalization of strategic waters, neutralization of the seas, and the extension of political and industrial democracy. The National Executive Committee approved the proposals in January 1915.[12]

Thus five months after the war began, the Socialist party was finally able to offer a peace program, but one which sorely divided its members. A. M. Simons first flung down the gauntlet with the charge that the program, lacking a straightforward denunciation of militarism, was undistinguishable from a bourgeois proposal. To Simons, the explicit opposition to offensive wars involved an implicit acceptance of defensive wars. If the party wanted to compromise its principles, Simons wrote, it ought to announce that a socialist in Congress may vote for a defensive war. He charged that the NEC position allowed the socialists to assume the posture of opposition to war while depending on the bourgeois politicians to vote the arms which the socialists secretly favored. Simons proposed a statement of opposition to capitalist war, support for universal disarmament without "any piffle about a 'citizen army' " and consistent opposition to military appropriations, the very problem over which the European socialists stumbled. Simons's demand for an absolute commitment against war is of special interest because of his later loyalist activities. Indeed, he was already labeled a jingo by some socialists.[13]

Charles Edward Russell was critical of the endorsement of national disarmament, arguing that it was impossible even to discuss disarmament until all countries were prepared to discard their weapons. Otherwise the gesture was futile at best, and at worst suicidal. Russell stressed the importance of focusing upon the fundamental fact that the war was the result of competitive systems and consequently even more severe wars might occur.

Morris Hillquit urged the widest possible discussion of the program before a vote by the National Committee on its formal adoption. If any anti-war program were passed by the party without sufficient discussion, Hillquit warned, there was a great danger of extreme dissatisfaction among the membership. He cited a referendum then circulating which demanded a national vote on a war declaration and which included a clause specifying that those who favored war be the first to enter the armed forces; the impracticality of that radical-sounding clause would only serve to embarrass the party. Full and open party discussion could insure the necessary healthy and vital give and take.

On the other hand, John Spargo immediately accepted the peace proposals and proceeded to the next point: that the major task of the American socialists was to curb a demand for military preparations in the United States.[14]

The mail pouring into the National Office revealed that great confusion existed in the party over the peace proposals and that clarification of the issues remained the most urgent need. The left wing journals were actively pushing their views, and this led reformists once more to wring their hands over "impossibilism" and to bombard their various newspapers with "reasonable" proposals.

Hillquit was more occupied with the war than perhaps any of the other leaders of the party. He wrote a series of articles for *Metropolitan*, gave several lectures on the war before chapters of the Intercollegiate Socialist Society, and debated preparedness advocates before huge New York crowds. When dealing with the general public, Hillquit listed as the causes of the war artificial political boundaries, historical grievances, commercial rivalries, imperialism, and militarism. He opposed American defensive measures by dismissing the danger of attack and picturing the evils involvement would bring—the brutalization of the nation and the end of social progress. Before socialist audiences, Hillquit dwelt on colonialism and commercial rivalries and on the problems of the socialists. He sympathetically portrayed the dilemma of the European socialists in August 1914 against the background of various resolutions of the Second International, and discussed the socialists' role in the eventual settlement and the way in which the war might affect the international socialist movement.[15] Morris Hillquit, at home both as a lecturer and as a writer, reached the epitome of his fame during the war as a major spokesman for the party and author of its war statements.

The vocal left expounded its own policies. Leftists condemned the reformist NEC peace proposals for an inadequate economic analysis of the origins of the war. One editorialist endorsed the general strike as the most likely measure to prevent American participation in the war. Another critic denounced the reformists for weighing party tactics and strategies when they ought to be injecting the masses with idealism in preparation for the impending struggle against American militarism.

This critic, now beginning his career as Louis C. Fraina and later to be better known as Lewis Corey, singled out Berger particularly for his attacks on pacifism. If the Socialist party thought it was feasible to oppose the existing capitalist system, then it could also oppose nationalism and militarism, Fraina argued, and there was no need to compromise with those forces. He identified Berger, and Hillquit too, with "the reactionary elements of bourgeois progressivism." He condemned the proposal for an international peace force which, he said, could be used against proletariat uprisings or so-called backward races. Fraina ruled out Berger's old concept of a "citizen army" as tainted with militarism, and added that it was not necessarily democratic. He denounced defensive wars, insisting that socialists must be against war without exception and that those who opposed disarmament were nationalists subordinating the class struggle to national struggles. "The economic nationalism of the Socialist conservative is more reactionary than that of the Capitalist because Capitalist nationalism by the very law of motion of its development tends to economic internationalism." Thus, Fraina denounced the leadership of the party in ringing tones that summoned the left to a new confrontation with a dividing right.

An old nemesis of the right then joined the fray. William English Walling, who had led a previous attack on the right wing, criticized its peace proposals and omissions to prove that the leadership of the party had lined up with the Central Powers. The demand for an immediate peace and the prohibition of indemnities were favorable to the German Empire, he declared, and the refusal to call a general strike had the same effect. For a second time, Walling stood apart from policy-making and contented himself with the promulgation of serious charges against the party's leadership.[16]

As the National Committee gathered in Chicago in mid-May to formulate a peace program following eight months of harrowing debate, the committee members were aware of the need to develop a constructive program that would be acceptable to the membership and not especially vulnerable to the poised left wing.

Victor Berger had not been inactive during this period of policy discussions. He had approved in December 1914 preliminary peace proposals and in March 1915 he contributed a lengthy article to the party organ in which he optimistically predicted that the war would strengthen the socialists in Europe and result in democratization and the emergence of the socialists as the most significant political factor. But Berger's optimism was only for public display. Inwardly he was agitated over the resurgence of the left. In April he wrote several letters to the Open Forum of the *American Socialist* dismissing disarmament as a viable policy. Disarmament meant suicide, he argued, and in personal correspondence he denounced those who proposed such a policy as phrasemongers.[17]

Amid much discussion and dissension the National Committee managed to pass both an Anti-War Manifesto and a Peace Program. The manifesto, issued to the American public, warned against allowing "interests" to stampede the United States into the war. "The Socialist Party of the United States raises its voice in solemn and emphathatic protests against this dangerous and criminal agitation, and proclaims its opposition to militarism and war. No disaster, however appalling . . . justifies the slaughter of nations and the devastation of countries. . . . We call upon the people of the United States . . . to throttle all efforts to draw this country into the dangerous paths of international quarrels, imperialism, militarism and war."[18] The "disaster, however appalling" to which the manifesto referred was the sinking of the *Lusitania* by the German navy on 7 May. The Socialist party was most circumspect in its response. It had become obvious that the chief task of the party was not to attempt to end the war in Europe, which was clearly beyond its reach, but to concentrate on stemming the tide of militarism which had begun to rise in the United States. The *Lusitania* sinking stimulated that spirit and the party was uncertain how best to meet its challenge. Indeed, Berger's *Leader* kept an editorial silence on the matter for ten days and finally struck out at England for creating the naval war zone and warned Americans against acting as shields for the Union Jack.[19] The party did not go so far and felt it easier to dismiss the sinking as tragic but insignificant as measured against war as a whole.

The comprehensive peace program followed the lines set by the subcommittee's proposals in December. The Socialist party recommended peace terms without indemnities or forced annexations, an international federation whose decisions would be effected without recourse to arms, universal disarmament "as speedily as possible," and the prohibition of private profit from the manufacture of arms. Both political democracy, including extension of suffrage and popular control of diplomacy, and industrial democracy, which would work toward the removal of economic causes of war, were specified as major goals.

The National Committee had tried to avoid arousing the left by insertion of the vague phrase "as speedily as possible." But the reformists realized criticism from the left was inevitable. Within the committee the few representatives of the left wing vigilantly peppered the opposition with objections and criticisms. Kate Sadler, National Committeewoman from the state of Washington, added an amendment limiting the use of arms to wars of self-defense. Berger very heatedly condemned this amendment; he opposed any measure which would limit action in case of extenuating circumstances.

To the Milwaukee socialist, motions of this nature struck at the essential right to fight for national existence. Berger delivered an impassioned speech which was not totally relevant to the specific issue under consideration but was indicative of his mood during that trying session. "There are things worse than war. Slavery is one of them. I would take up a gun and fight against slavery and I would fight against the invasion of my home. You can't resist an invasion with resolutions, any more than you can destroy capitalism by resolutions." With the support of his comrades, his motion to table Mrs. Sadler's amendment passed, but Berger was not satisfied. He would have preferred an overt commitment to the right of self-defense.

The party approved the peace program in referendum and also amended the constitution to provide for the expulsion of any socialist elected to public office who voted for war or war appropriations. The amendment, Article II, Section 7, passed by an overwhelming majority of 11,141 to 782.[20]

On the left, Walling analyzed the peace program and found it to be as favorable to the German war position as earlier proposals. He charged the party with a lack of neutrality, noting that its positions seemed to agree consistently with those of Edward Bernstein and Karl Kautsky but never with the English socialists. He approved the new clause for the expulsion of those voting for war appropriations and noted that it repudiated the 1913 position taken by the German Social Democrats. But the tone of Walling's criticisms indicated the initial acceptance of the reality of the war by an erstwhile spokesman for the left.

It was also charged by the left that the approach the right wingers took to the war involved the acceptance of that war. Such resignation led to the premise that the United States was likely to become engulfed in the war and the next logical move, the left taunted, was to prepare for involvement.[21] Fundamentally, these attacks struck at the leadership for staking out a war stand that attempted to solve the socialist dilemma of participation in the world. Through this approach, the left was reviving after a few years of depression and discouragement . But the effort to come to terms with the war situation *in order to avoid* American participation was in accord with the consistent position of Berger and his comrades, and was necessary if the Socialist party were to play an effective role in the struggle against preparedness waged by other peace groups.

Walling's specific charges were presented by others prominent in the party as well. George D. Herron, writing from abroad in the midst of the war, complained to Hillquit that the American party and all its auxiliary institutions, including the Rand School of which he was a founder, were blatantly pro-German. "Though you conceal it from yourselves [*sic*], you certainly do not conceal it in your writing."[22] Those who felt deep distress for the disasters experienced by England and France and a concomitant hatred for Germany were unable to accept the claim that the Socialist party leaders had mapped out a just peace which was realistic and which would leave the fewest scars. The party's insistence on its own neutrality seemed hollow to some.[23]

Meyer London, who had become the second socialist Congressman in November 1914, introduced a resolution asking that the President convene a congress of neutral nations to offer mediation to the warring powers. The Socialist party supported London with demonstrations and petitions and sent a delegation, including Hillquit and London, to see President Wilson, who told them that he was not certain that the so-called neutrals were entirely impartial.[24] But the party knew that its real challenge lay in the United States.

Berger's own activities during the war differed from those of the other leaders of the party. Like them, he learned to live with the defection of the German Social Democrats from the principles of the International, but his analysis of that defection differed from most. He praised their support for their country based on their belief that Germany acted in self-defense. "We cannot very well blame the Socialist parties of the various European nations for standing with the rest of their people in this world crisis. And least of all can we blame any Socialists for defending their homes . . . wherever they were face to face with invasion." Berger went on to justify socialist nationalism by the declaration that socialism could never be anti-national if it were to fulfill its mission. He predicted that a new and stronger International would be organized, an International "with less illusions—that will realize that nations are here and that their existence must be recognized. . . . In short, we will build a new International Socialist movement with the knowledge and upon the basis that Socialism is not anti-national, but that it is international.''

Berger expected to see a postwar realignment of forces, both between nations and within nations, with socialism achieving greater strength than ever before. In private correspondence he wrote that Marxism *per se* and its prophets might be weakened by the war, but eclectic socialism would attain greater strength than Marxism ever could.[25]

In Berger's initial peace efforts he tried to utilize his Washington, D.C., connections. He asked Congressman William Kent of California, a progressive Republican with whom he had served in the sixty-second Congress and developed a warm friendship, if he thought President Wilson would communicate a peace plan to the German Social Democratic party. But Kent replied that it would be useless to petition Wilson, since such a move would be seen as meddling in the internal affairs of another country. In November 1914, during a visit to Washington, Berger tried to obtain an appointment with the President in order to urge him to assume a more active peacemaking role. Despite Congressman Kent's assistance, Berger was told that the President's calendar was full and he was not granted an interview. While in the Capital, Berger also attempted to acquire letters of introduction for Hillquit for his contemplated visit to the European conference of neutral socialists, but again he met with frustration. He was told by both the British and German Ambassadors that they needed their governments' approval first. This fiasco was of no consequence, however, when Hillquit, despite his instructions to represent the Socialist party, decided not to attend the conference, since only Scandinavian socialists would be attending.[26]

Berger's quest for peace was not merely a war-induced reaction. In June 1914, he attended a conference held in Philadelphia by non-socialist peace enthusiasts to consider the formation of a peace league. His attachments to such groups were always cautious; he endorsed ''plain and simple'' peace agitation guardedly, warning that there would be no avoidance of the threat of war until international socialism triumphed.

In July 1915, Berger accepted the vice presidency of the League to Enforce Peace, an outgrowth of the Philadelphia conference. He told the League's officers that while he opposed some of their tendencies, a world war was no time to stress differences among peace advocates. At once, the Information Department of the party sought confirmation from Berger of charges that he was an active member of a bourgeois peace organization whose honorary president was William Howard Taft. But Berger, as usual, did not let criticism sway him. He maintained his membership and a year later willingly provided former President Taft with names of those in the Milwaukee area who might be interested in the League.[27]

Berger was not the only member of the party hierarchy to cooperate with non-socialist peace organizations. Carl D. Thompson, who later was ousted from the party for his participation in the Public Ownership League, became active in the Emergency Federation of Peace Forces during the first year of the war. His enthusiasm for the Emergency Federation brought a word of caution from Morris Hillquit, who advised Thompson to bear in mind the substantial differences between the bourgeois approach to peace and that of the Socialist party. However, Hillquit himself addressed a conference of the Emergency Federation on 18 February 1915.[28]

The reformists' interest in peace led them to consider aligning the party formally with the National Peace Conference. Though Berger was willing to invite criticism for the sake of his personal beliefs, his concern for party integrity caused him to oppose official association with the non-socialist peace group. He was the only member of the National Executive Committee to vote against permanent representation for the party at the conference in the spring of 1915.[29] His stand here was not consistent with his traditional effort to encourage the party to cooperate with other progressive forces. It may be that he preferred such cooperation in a purely political vein, where results might be quickly forthcoming.

After the war began, Berger experienced the loss of some prestige in the city of Milwaukee. The German population there was divided in its loyalty: some were vociferous German patriots, such as those belonging to the Milwaukee branch of the National German-American Alliance; others were sympathetic to the German cause; and a third group remained entirely aloof.[30]

Berger's predilections lay with the second group. He was sympathetic both because of his cultural ties and because of his belief that the socialists in Germany were gaining strength as they were in no other nation. However, he did not favor an overwhelming victory because the crushing of one nation by another invariably led to resentment and hostility in the next generation. Berger hoped for a draw, but one in which Germany was somewhat ahead. These ideas drew him into conflict with the majority of the German community of Milwaukee.

The *Leader* followed a policy which Berger described as "pro-English, pro-German, pro-French, pro-American, pro-Russian, pro-humanity." He freely admitted that he instructed his staff to stress items from the German news service, reasoning that they would be closer to the truth than Allied reports, since the British controlled all cables.

Berger's very efforts to present a reasonable and quietly German newspaper cost him circulation and advertising revenue. The other Milwaukee newspapers, unhindered by socialist restraint, pandered to the emotions of German Milwaukee and struck out at the *Leader* as an English sheet. Berger remarked, not without wit, in the bitter congressional election campaign of 1914, that he was charged with being an Englishman who immigrated in the days of William the Conqueror.[31]

The Milwaukee socialists were caught in the war-induced nationalist dilemma. Men like the American-born Seidel felt pained at the need to proclaim their loyalty. They did not want to see Germany crushed, but more than that they could not, in good conscience, claim.[32] Berger lost the race to regain his seat in Congress. His opponent, William H. Stafford, the fusionist incumbent, catered to German nationalism. Stafford was a conservative Republican with whom Berger seemed to alternate as congressman, and in this race he was aided by German resentment of Berger's unaggressive stance.[33]

The effectiveness of the national party was also decreased at this time but for different reasons. The party's ability to publicize its peace program was hampered by inefficiency and dissension in the National Office in Chicago. Walter Lanferseik, the Kentucky businessman who became Executive Secretary late in 1912, angered the party's leaders by his handling of the war crisis. No quarrel over Lanferseik's politics was involved, for he was as far from the taint of impossibilism as were the other leaders. However, the Secretary's concern for party finances had led him to delay and prevent meetings of the National Executive Committee throughout the first year of the war when, in reality, party activities would have expanded its coffers. In September 1914, Berger fumed that Lanferseik's approach made the NEC seem superfluous. In the face of a European war and the coming congressional elections, the NEC had not met since May, and policy had been in the hands of the Secretary. Berger maintained that it was the duty of the NEC to convene rather than to rubber-stamp Lanferseik's moves.[34]

In addition to Lanferseik's shortsighted use of party machinery, he clashed with Carl Thompson, whose Information Department operated out of the National Office. The lack of harmony decreased the staff's effectiveness and led to the suggestion that the Information Department be abolished. Those who, before the war, had successfully won dissolution of the Lyceum Department as an expensive extravagance, attacked the Information Department on the same grounds. Berger, who believed that the department served as a necessary clearinghouse for information and as a means of propaganda, and who had faith in the abilities of fellow Milwaukeean Thompson, fought for its retention. At the NEC meeting in September 1915 he voted against merging its functions into those of the Secretary's, but he and the Information Department went down to defeat.

At the same meeting, the National Executive Committee asked for the resignation of both Thompson and Lanferseik in an effort to clear the National Office and start the 1916 campaign with fresh personalities. Thompson submitted his resignation but the Secretary refused. Berger, who had been willing to go along with the Secretary, was now convinced that Lanferseik lacked too many of the qualities necessary for such a party post and therefore must be replaced.[35]

A consensus existed among the right wing leaders that the National Office was in chaos and a new reformist-oriented Secretary was needed to reorganize headquarters, but they disagreed as to whom they would support in the election. The two men most frequently mentioned were Carl Thompson and Adolph Germer. Berger preferred Thompson, one of his political proteges. Both men, he said, were radical in the basic Greek definition of the term, "rooted in the ground." Neither was tainted with extreme revisionism, he wrote to a Finnish Federation member who suggested that perhaps Germer, whose candidacy was less divisive, would be a better choice. The Milwaukee socialist stormed against the artificial lines set up in the party between radicals and reformists, "reds and yellows," and wrote that most of the English-speaking radicals were no more than former Populists under a thin veneer of socialism. Their ability to pepper their conversation with revolutionary phrases served only to lead others to call them radical. Thus Berger, in encouraging a particular candidacy, went to great lengths to obliterate real party differences. But in practical terms, he added that Thompson had more initiative and a greater familiarity with the socialist movement and was therefore more qualified than was Germer.[36]

Carl Thompson, however, was vulnerable because of his having antagonized some of the leaders years before. Despite Berger, the right threw its support to Adolph Germer, who defeated Thompson and the scuttled Lanferseik who tried for re-election. Berger's major regret was the failure of the retiring Executive Secretary and the NEC to prepare for the 1916 campaign. They had even neglected to authorize the traditional campaign manual. Omissions such as this, as well as the wounds caused by the election of the Secretary, left the party in poor shape to conduct a presidential campaign.[37]

Moreover, serious policy divisions over the war were widening. Berger himself added fuel to the incendiary atmosphere through his views on preparedness. As the issue of American participation in the war became a national one, the Socialist party could not avoid a firm stand. Since the autumn of 1914, the party had had skirmishes over disarmament, which the National Committee tried to resolve by compromise in its peace program. But the issue had been neither shelved nor solved, and in 1916 it became a major, divisive controversy.

In January, Berger published his views on preparedness in the *Leader* and issued a similar statement to the *American Socialist* in its poll of candidates for party offices. Berger's remarks led to a motion to recall him from the NEC and to additional factionalization within the party. At a time when all its strength would have been expended on the presidential campaign, the party was reduced to helplessness.

Berger titled the *Leader* editorial "National Service."

A standing army is always the tool of the ruling class . . . a menace to our democracy. Any nation, class or individual that is defenceless, however, will soon be enslaved or cease to exist. . . . The *Leader*, therefore, is in favor of a "preparedness" that shall protect and unite the bulk of our nation, that is, the working class. For that purpose we must train the bodies and minds of all our young folks. . . . We want all of our people to be able to defend themselves and the common weal.

The preparedness that Berger proposed involved academic education as well as calisthenics. He forecast that the public school would become the center for the country's defense. At age nineteen the youngster would give one year to public service, in which he would learn basic industrial and agricultural skills, essentials of first aid, and the use of weapons.

> This preparedness will absolutely guard the national independence until such time as we shall have complete disarmament and world's peace [sic] by international agreement. . . . It will protect the working class against further subjugation and enslavement at home until all class distinctions are abolished. . . . In short, we refuse to be carried away by any hysteria caused by this world war. We socialists are as much opposed to militarism now than [sic] we ever were. But the Socialist party is not for peace at any price. War may be hell, but there are some things in this world worse than "hell." Real socialists are willing to fight these things.[38]

Berger's views echoed those of William James in his "The Moral Equivalent of War." Whether or not Berger was familiar with James's work is not known, but whatever the connection, there was no way to stave off Socialist wrath from descending on the audacious Berger. After his election to the NEC in March, the storm broke. Local Marion, Indiana, whose most famous member happened to be Debs, moved for Berger's recall from his position on the basis of his advocacy of preparedness, contrary to the principles of the Socialist party. The recall demand was accompanied by a charge that the *Leader* was as inflammatory a sheet as any Hearst-owned newspaper, and it recommended that Berger be succeeded on the NEC by the candidate with the next highest number of votes in the recent election.

Berger was furious over the recall motion and the unorthodox presentation permitted by the outgoing Lanferseik. This time it was not a revolutionist like Haywood being victimized. To defend himself, he solicited and published supporting letters from his influential friends, meanwhile becoming more and more agitated. He wrote to Hillquit demanding to know if the New York Central Committee had endorsed his recall as rumor held. He was so upset by critical letters in the *American Socialist* suggesting the scuttling of the *Leader,* that he considered proposing the abolition of the party newspaper. His initial hunch that an official organ could develop into a vicious instrument seemed to him now vindicated.[39]

In self-defense, Berger pointed out the difference between militarism and his conception of preparedness and stressed the importance of a constructive program. He said that a socialist party could never be pacifist, because to one degree or another the capture of the capitalist system would involve the use of force. He also struck out at improprieties in the form of the recall and then demanded that the essential freedom to differ within socialist principles be retained. Finally he attacked the resurgent left, claiming that "a group that is opposed to all political action is now using the 'peace-at-any price' hysteria as a means of punishing me for my well-known constructive views. It is the same group that scoffs at preparedness but applauds the throwing of bombs. It is the same group that every little while starts some 'freedom of speech' fight in some town. In our own party, however, they want to forbid all discussion that is not to the taste of the group."[40]

Berger won support from some radicals on the basis of his plea for freedom of speech, but his imaginative charges of bomb-throwing served only to stir up further animosity against him as the spokesman of the right. He was accurate in his delineation of the left's exploitation of the war hysteria in the party and its antecedents in the party struggle of the previous few years, but he certainly realized that some of the personnel had changed and that the tactics had become more subtle.

Berger more openly declared his hostility to the principle of nonresistance and proceeded to articulate his own definition of patriotism. He wrote that patriotism could only be based on the possession of a share of the *patria,* and the workingman's inadequate share was not likely to encourage him to patriotism. The socialists, who tried to bring all men into the national and the international communities, would, by changing the system, involve the workers in the wealth and the welfare of the country, thereby giving them a reason to fight in its behalf.

In mid-September, Berger was vindicated by the defeat of the recall motion, 11,212 to 8,014.[41] His pleasure was tempered by his increasing bitterness toward the party for failing to appreciate his contributions.

In the face of the strife within the party, in the National Office itself, about the shoulders of a major leader, and over the proper stance on preparedness, it was inevitable that the Socialist party would run sluggishly in the presidential election of 1916. In addition to the above handicaps, the party had chosen a candidate who was incapable of attracting much support outside the membership.

In 1913 the western radicals had pushed through a proposal to name the party's candidates by referendum, a move reflective of faith in direct democracy and distrust of the eastern-dominated conventions. Debs refused to run, to the relief of some of the party leaders, including Berger, who had remarked earlier that it would be disastrous to name Debs again. In addition to their mutual animosity, Berger believed the nomination of the same candidate for a fifth time would be a confession of bankruptcy. Berger well knew, though, that the Socialist party was poor in presidential candidates, for those with national reputations were invariably of foreign birth. There is no evidence that he pushed any particular nomination, but of those in the running, he probably preferred reformist James H. Maurer of Pennsylvania, who shared with Berger a background in the labor movement and in local politics.

Allan L. Benson, a journalist and propagandist whom Berger readily called a crank, won the referendum. Benson was known in the party through his books and his articles which had appeared in *The Appeal to Reason* and in other magazines, and he was popular with western members especially for his prolific writing against preparedness. His unsuccessful referendum calling for a national vote on war brought him particular attention among the rank and file. In his campaign, Benson stressed only the preparedness issue, to the distress of those who thought the campaign ought to concern socialism, and he gave few public speeches. His chances for a successful race were further handicapped by the divisive presence of Carl Thompson as his campaign manager. Benson himself disliked Thompson, and Thompson was so unpopular with some segments of the party because of his ministerial background, his firm commitment to political action, and his connections with non-socialist progressive organizations, that a New York local tried to recall him from his position.[42]

Another harmful factor in the socialists' campaign was the defection of some socialist voters to Wilson's camp. Defectors included not only those dazzled by the Wilsonian reforming veneer, but also a few of the party's intellectual prizes who were swept in by Wilson's promise to keep the country out of war. Upton Sinclair, a founder of the Intercollegiate Socialist Society a dozen years earlier, dropped out of the

Socialist party in order to support the Democratic candidate. John Reed, who had been discouraged by the surrender of the European socialists to nationalism, devoted all his writings in *The Masses* to preventing the United States from joining the slaughter abroad. He and *The Masses* supported Wilson on the basis of the President's efforts to eliminate war-enthusiasm. Reed, with others, published an appeal to party members. "Every protest vote is a luxury dearly bought. Its price is the risk of losing much social justice already gained and blocking much immediate progress." He lashed out savagely at the party in a letter to the National Office in which he proclaimed his own socialist commitment but harangued Hillquit, Berger, Spargo, and others as "unbelievable smug fakirs. . . . As for Benson, I think he is too small to be spoken about with much seriousness. I have yet to feel any real soul or vision in the American Socialist Party, with its lies, and its petty politics, its Milwaukee, Schenectady, etc."[43]

The socialist vote totalled a paltry 585,113, a shocking decline from Debs' tally of over 900,000 in 1912. In Milwaukee, Berger again failed to win a seat in Congress. Although his vote climbed from 11,674 in 1914 to 15,936, apparently aided by the socialist victory in the mayoralty election that spring, the exigencies of the German-American mood again defeated him. The election of Mayor Dan Hoan, formerly the city attorney, had been achieved on a platform of municipal reform, as in the case of Emil Seidel's election in 1910, but Berger's campaign had revolved around international events.[44]

The years of the European war had not been bright ones for the American socialists. Not directly involved, they nevertheless had bent all their efforts at the start toward curtailing the war and then toward limiting it to its current overwhelming scale. Though three thousand miles away, the war had caused defections on the right of the party and a resurgence of the ambitions of the left.

The party seriously stumbled in its policy-making. Its moves were ridiculed and condemned as treason and its inactions were attacked as weakness. Unity was absolutely necessary to preserve the party for the major test of its career, the prevention of American involvement in the European war. But whether that necessary unity could be achieved was debatable in those dark days following the 7 November election. The decrease of protest votes and the growing and alarming loss of members who had brought the party renown served to cripple the organization severely. Racial politics and alien issues blocked the path to electoral success that hitherto had appeared open to the Socialist party, and divided members who shared faith in political action.

It was questionable whether or not any one leader could reverse the party fortunes. Benson could only be ignored by the hierarchy after his ineffective campaign, while Debs, who had lost a race for Congress about which there had been considerable confidence, was not capable of pulling the organization together; nor were the reformist leaders willing to have him try. Berger, too, had lost an election and also suffered seriously from the effects of the recall motion which had impaired his prestige. As 1916 ended, there was little reason for optimism.

NOTES

1. Oscar Ameringer, *If You Don't Weaken* (New York: Henry Holt and Co., 1940), pp. 300-301; Victor Berger telegram to Morris Hillquit, 30 July 1914, Berger telegram to Emil Seidel, 30 July 1914, Berger Col., MCHS; *New York Sun,* 1 August 1914, *New York Tribune,* 2 August 1914 (clippings in Hillquit Scrapbook), Hillquit Col., SHSW; Milwaukee *Leader,* 30 July 1914, 3 August 1914; *United States of America v. Victor L. Berger, Adolph Germer, J. Louis Engdahl, William P. Kruse and Irwin St. John Tucker,* District Court of the United States, Northern District of Illinois, Eastern Division (1918-1919), IV, 3101. This is a five-volume stenographic typescript (hereafter cited as *Berger Trial*).

2. Milwaukee *Leader,* 30 July 1914.

3. John M. Work, "Autobiography," II, chap. 4, 1; typescript, John M. Work Collection, SHSW; related by Heinrich Bartel of Berger's editorial staff to Frederick I. Olson, reported in Olson's "The Milwaukee Socialists, 1897-1941," Ph.D. dissertation, Harvard University, 1952, p. 337; Milwaukee *Leader,* 17 October 1914; Baryd Still, *Milwaukee: The History of a City* (Madison: State Historical Society, 1948), p. 456.

4. Berger to Ernest Untermann, 15 May 1915, Berger Col., MCHS; Milwaukee *Leader,* 6 August 1913.

5. Ameringer, *If You Don't Weaken,* pp. 305-306; *Berger Trial,* IV, 3233.

6. Milwaukee *Leader,* 5 August 1914, 5 September 1914; Berger quote on the age of the socialist movement in Cincinnati newspaper, clipping in Berger Col., MCHS, n.d.

but internal evidence suggests January 1915; *Milwaukee Leader,* 21 August 1914.

7. Morris Hillquit, *Loose Leaves from a Busy Life* (New York: Macmillan Co., 1934), p. 145.

8. Diary of May Wood Simons, 12 August 1914, 18 September 1914, Simons Col., SHSW; Kent Kreuter and Gretchen Kreuter, *An American Dissenter: The Life of Algie Martin Simons* (Lexington: University of Kentucky Press, 1969), pp. 155-158; Berger to Untermann, 4 September 1915, Berger Col., MCHS; Untermann to Paul Gauer, 22 January 1954, Untermann Collection, MCHS. Untermann resigned less than a year later, charging that Berger complained that his writings were too favorable toward the Germans. Untermann to Berger, 26 April 1916, Berger Col., MCHS. Untermann asked Berger at the time he was hired (1915) what Berger would do if the United States was eventually drawn into the war against Germany. Berger was stumped and all he could say was that the socialists would go down with colors flying. Untermann to Gauer, 22 January 1954, Untermann Col., MCHS.

9. William English Walling, ed., *The Socialists and the War: A Documentary Statement of the position of the Socialists of all Countries: With Special Reference to their Peace Policy* (New York: Henry Holt and Co., 1915), pp. 212-213; Alexander Trachtenberg, ed., *The American Socialists and the War* (New York: Rand School of Social Science, 1917), p. 10; Walter Lanferseik telegram to Berger, 9 August 1914, Berger Col., MCHS.

10. Telegram of 14 September 1914, Berger Col.

11. *American Socialist Official Business Supplement,* 29 August 1914; J. Louis Engdahl to Berger, 19 September 1914, Berger Col., MCHS.

12. Carl D. Thompson to Debs, 23 December 1914, SP Col., Duke; *American Socialist,* 26 December 1914; Walling, *The Socialists and the War,* pp. 468-470; *American Socialist,* 16 January 1915. Berger voted for the peace proposals: Berger telegram to Lanferseik, 28 December 1914, Berger Col., MCHS. The NEC was then composed of Berger; Adolph Germer; James H. Maurer, the Pennsylvania trade union leader and currently a representative in the State General Assembly; J. Stitt Wilson, socialist mayor of Berkeley, California, in 1911; and Lewis Duncan, mayor of

Butte, Montana, in 1911. There was never at any other time such a homogeneous NEC wholly committed to step-at-a-time socialism, political action, and cooperation with the conservative trade unions.

13. A. M. Simons to Thompson, 20 January 1915, Simons Statement, 20 January 1915, SP Col., National Office File, 1896-1922, Duke. The proposals which Simons opposed included an endorsement of declarations of offensive wars only through referendum. For rumors of Simons's jingoism, see Julius Gerber to Hillquit, 9 December 1914, Socialist Party Col., Tamiment Institute.

14. Charles Edward Russell to Thompson, 18 January 1915; Hillquit to Thompson, 30 January 1915; Spargo Statement, 25 December 1915, SP Col., Duke.

15. Thompson to Hillquit, 2 February 1915; Thompson to Hillquit, 11 February 1915, SP Col., Duke. Morris Hillquit and Augustus P. Gardner, *Must We Arm?* (New York: Rand School of Social Science, 1915), pp. 36-38; Hillquit, "The American Socialists and the War," pp. 18-23, typescript of three lectures, SP Col., Tamiment Institute.

16. Henry L. Slobodin, "Our Robertarian NEC," *International Socialist Review* 15 (March 1915): 544-545, 561; *The New Review* 2 (December 1914): 619; Louis G. Fraina, "The Menace of American Militarism," *The New Review* 3 (February 1915): 133-142; Walling, *The Socialists and the War*, pp. 470-472.

17. Berger, "War Strengthens Socialism," *American Socialist*, 6 March 1915; see various issues of *American Socialist* for April 1915: Berger to Untermann, 15 May 1915, Berger Col., MCHS.

18. Trachtenberg, *The American Socialists and the War*, pp. 14-15.

19. Milwaukee *Leader*, 18 May 1915.

20. *American Labor Year Book* (1916), pp. 125-126; for Berger's statement, see *New York Times*, 14 May 1915 (clipping in Hillquit Scrapbook), Hillquit Col., SHSW; *American Socialist Official Business Supplement*, 22 May 1915.

21. William Walling, "The Peace Programme of the American Socialist Party," *The New Review* 3 (15 June 1915): 90; Louis B. Boudin, "The Socialist Party and Preparedness," ibid., 3 (1 December 1915): 339.

22. George D. Herron to Hillquit, 5 April 1915, Hillquit Col., SHSW.

23. *American Socialist,* 1 September 1915.

24. Meyer London Resolution of 6 December 1915, Meyer London Collection, Tamiment Institute. London stood alone on several preparedness issues in the House but his performance failed to satisfy many in the Socialist party. Lanferseik to Hillquit, 23 December 1915, Hillquit Col., SHSW; Hillquit, *Loose Leaves from a Busy Life,* p. 16.

25. Berger, "Greetings of the First Socialist Congressman to His Successor," *American Socialist,* 4 December 1915, 10 July 1915; Berger to Hillquit, 3 June 1916, Hillquit Col., SHSW.

26. Congressman William Kent to Berger, 6 August 1914, Berger Col., MCHS. Ibid., 30 November 1914, Hillquit to Berger, 17 December 1914, Berger telegram to Hillquit, 28 December 1914, Berger Col., MCHS. Ibid., Hillquit to Lanferseik, 21 November 1914, Hillquit to NEC, 28 December 1914, Hillquit Col., SHSW. A full account of European socialists' efforts to fashion a satisfactory war program is found in Merle Fainsod, *International Socialism and the World War* (Cambridge: Harvard University Press, 1935).

27. Berger to Secretary of Peace Organization, 4 June 1914; Berger to Secretary of League to Enforce Peace, 8 July 1915, SP Information Department to Berger, 18 August 1915, Berger to Taft, 22 May 1916, Berger Col., MCHS. Berger's membership in the league was not an inactive one. At its June 1915 conference, he unsuccessfully proposed a resolution against the munitions export trade and argued for the prohibition of a member state of the anticipated peace association from sending arms to another nation in order to prevent opposing militarism with militarism. Frederick L. Paxson, *American Democracy and the World War* (Boston: Houghton Mifflin Co., 1936), I, 279; "International League of Peace," *Survey* 34 (8 August 1915): 293.

28. Hillquit to Thompson, 6 January 1915, Thompson to Hillquit, 13 January 1915, Hillquit to Thompson, 9 February 1915, SP Col., Duke.

29. Lanferseik to Berger, 2 March 1915, Berger Col., MCHS.

30. Clifton James Child, *The German-Americans in Politics, 1914-1917* (Madison: University of Wisconsin Press, 1939), p. 117; Karen Falk, "Public Opinion in Wisconsin

during World War I," *Wisconsin Magazine of History* 25 (June 1942): 393.

31. As early as 29 August 1914, Berger was criticized by a Milwaukee Social Democratic local for being anti-German and, it was inferred, therefore unsocialistic. Milwaukee *Leader*, 30 August 1914; *Berger Trial*, IV, 3094; Milwaukee *Leader*, 30 October 1914. Berger won 11,674 votes of 33,481 cast. Wisconsin, *Blue Book*, 1915, 38, 230.

32. Francis Hackett, "How Milwaukee Takes the War," *New Republic* 6 (17 July 1915): 272-273; Milwaukee *Leader*, 17 October 1914. A national magazine reported that Berger and his socialist organization were condemned as traitors to Germany by the *German Herald* and the Milwaukee *Free Press* in August 1914, for demanding the prohibition of trade in arms, a demand picked up by the German-American Alliance in 1915 when that prohibition would have harmed the English war effort and provided Germany with an advantage. "Victor Berger Reproaches His German Friends for Inconsistency," *Current Opinion* 59 (August 1915): 80.

33. Milwaukee *Leader*, 30 October 1914; Berger to Charles W. Thompson of the *New York Times*, 13 November 1914, Berger Col., MCHS. Oscar Ameringer wrote to the National Committee endorsing Berger for the NEC after the latter's one-year absence from it, and said that despite Berger's internationalism, he lost in Milwaukee for being pro-British. Ameringer was trying to counter party gossip of Berger's Germanism. Ameringer to National Committee, January 1916, ibid. Frederick Olson, "Victor Berger: Socialist Congressman," *Wisconsin Academy of Sciences, Arts and Letters* 58: 34-35.

34. Berger to James H. Maurer, 4 September 1914, Maurer to Berger, 19 September 1914, Berger Col., MCHS.

35. Berger to Thompson, 4 September 1915, 19 October 1915, Berger to National Office, 20 August 1915, Berger Col., MCHS.

36. Hillquit to Berger, 25 September 1915, Berger to T. Hiltunen, 30 January 1916, Berger Col., MCHS.

37. J. Mahlon Barnes to Hillquit, 14 December 1915, Hillquit Col., SHSW; Milwaukee *Leader*, 22 April 1916; Berger to Inquirer, 24 May 1916, Berger Col., MCHS. Germer criticized the *Leader* for excessive electioneering.

38. Milwaukee *Leader*, 11 January 1916; *American Socialist*, 15 January 1916. Simons had once suggested that the

solution of the problem of military preparedness lay in the government supplying each man with a rifle. This would obviate the need for a standing army and lead toward the transition to disarmament. Simons to Berger, 14 January 1911, Berger Col., MCHS.

39. *American Socialist,* 20 May 1916; Berger to Germer, 5 July 1916, Hillquit to Berger, 30 June 1916, Berger Col., MCHS. Hillquit dismissed the rumor. Berger to Hillquit, 3 June 1916, Hillquit Col., SHSW. The *Leader* published letters in defense of Berger by Ghent (5 February), Untermann (17 June), and Hillquit (19 August 1916). Reformist James Oneal, however, supported the propriety of the charges, *American Socialist,* 15 July 1916. At the time his name was linked with the left. See George H. Goebel to Berger, 20 July 1916, Berger Col., MCHS.

40. Milwaukee *Leader,* 9 August 1916.

41. Frank P. O'Hare to Berger, 17 August 1916, Berger to Inquirer, 22 May 1916, Germer telegram to Berger, 15 September 1916, Berger Col., MCHS. *The American Socialist Official Business Supplement* of 30 September 1916 gives the figures as 12,349 to 8,362. The issue did not die. In March 1917, Charles E. Ruthenberg of Ohio insisted that Berger's leaflet on military training, authorized by the NEC, be reviewed by the National Committee before publication "because Berger's views on this subject were so bitterly resented by part of the party membership. . . ." National Office to Berger, 22 March 1917, Berger Col., MCHS. The NEC's selection of Berger to write that particular leaflet was incredibly naive.

42. Berger to Inquirer, 19 July 1915, Berger Col., MCHS; Harold W. Currie, "Allan L. Benson, Salesman of Socialism, 1902-1916," *Labor History* 11 (Summer 1970): 300-301; *The Masses* 8 (June 1916): 26. Walling called Benson a pacifist who was not representative of the party, arguing that socialists were opposed to peace at any price. The Thompson recall motion appears in *American Socialist Official Business Supplement,* 14 October 1916.

43. Upton Sinclair to President Woodrow Wilson, 22 December 1917, SP Col., Duke; *The Masses* 8 (August 1916): 10; Granville Hicks, *John Reed: The Making of a Revolutionary* (New York: Macmillan Co., 1936), p. 223;

John Reed to National Office, 13 October 1916, SP Col., Duke.

44. *American Socialist,* 18 November 1916. The winner, Republican Stafford, received 18,585 of the 43,153 votes cast in the three-man race. See Wisconsin, *Blue Book,* 1917, 39, 289. Also see ibid., 1915, 38, 230, and Baryd Still, *Milwaukee,* p. 522.

7

Assessment on the Brink

The force of American public opinion has been cited as moving the United States inexorably toward intervention in World War I, stimulated by the warmongering of influential figures such as Theodore Roosevelt and his National Security League. But such an interpretation demonstrates undiscerning hindsight. Noninterventionism was the pervasive note sounded throughout the din of conflicting voices between August 1914 and April 1917.

At the start of the European war, American public opinion was a mass of contradictions. Natural antipathy to war mixed with the traditional sympathies and hostilities felt by those of German, Irish, English, and Slavic heritage was further complicated by economic commitments. These various factors were molded by the daily incidents of the war and finally cemented into a resolution to join the allies in their fight against the Central Powers. But in no sense was there an early and persistent hysterical insistence upon war.

If the pattern of events forced public opinion, it was that pattern which placed pro-German sentiment in the United States on the defensive as early as the invasion of Belgium, and the defensive posture persisted. Allied propaganda skillfully exploited events, and was aided by allied control over communications and also by inept German espionage and sabotage efforts in the United States. Ultimately war prosperity, which was linked to the well-being of the allies, pushed the American public toward a commitment to intervention.

Strong disagreement, focusing on the preparedness controversy, persisted for long months before the decision was made. Those who opposed American intervention—pacifists, pro-Germans, anti-English, or those whose decision was non-ideological—argued for the reduction of arms in order to preclude the possibility of intervention. The proponents of preparedness encouraged an active association with the allies and were joined by a segment of the public which, while not interventionist, feared the belligerent international atmosphere and hence supported preparedness.[1] By the end of 1916, public opinion had seemed to crystallize into a firm allegiance to the allies. With the resumption of submarine warfare by the German navy on 1 February 1917, a kind of hysteria finally overwhelmed the American public which then demanded war against the aggressor who threatened the nation.

The Socialist party was not blind to the trend of American opinion, and after the pathetic election campaign of 1916, attention was focused with renewed vigor on efforts to stop the war before the United States was pushed into it. Victor Berger, whose war stance was derived perhaps out of greater agony than that known by any other American socialist, was forced by his private torment to take some kind of action that might terminate the slaughter. He proposed to the National Executive Committee that it contact the socialist parties of the other neutral nations, and of the warring nations, to arrange for an international conference on means of bringing the war to a conclusion. Berger recommended that the meeting be held during the second week of April 1917, or any early date that was more convenient, and that the basis of representation be that of the cancelled Vienna Congress.[2]

Because of the significance of the proposal and the impossibility of a full discussion by mail, consideration was delayed until the NEC meeting a few weeks later. The meeting revealed that a deep rift had appeared within the committee. The members were Berger, Hillquit, John M. Work, John Spargo, and Anna A. Maley, a Minnesota organizer and lecturer. All five were staunch and long-standing members of the right wing, committed to political action at home and peace abroad. But the war views of Spargo had evolved differently from the others.

Spargo opposed any attempt to achieve an armistice which might result in a peace based on the status quo. The English-born socialist indicated that such a peace would be favorable to Germany and that any German victory would mean the end of international social democracy for a generation. Spargo noted that no committee members were partisans of either side, but unfortunately, he said, actions of the party leadership had appeared to be sympathetic to the German cause. Spargo failed to dilute Berger's motion significantly, but the NEC agreed to send the International Socialist Bureau a telegram, as Spargo had suggested, requesting that the Bureau call an international congress. If the Bureau took no action within a few weeks, the Socialist party would assume the initiative in accord with Berger's proposal.

The NEC appointed Berger and Spargo, the two primary antagonists, to a subcommittee to compose a party declaration in clarification of the proposed conference. The two men sparred quietly and then agreed on a statement. They resolved that the future peace must achieve a wider measure of democracy than existed before the war, must be sufficient to rally the workers to prevent other wars, and must retain wartime collectivism. Spargo prevailed in his insistence on a speedy rather than an immediate peace, and Berger's sentiments were expressed in a clause stressing lasting peace as of more significance than incidentals such as indemnities. The NEC unanimously approved the statement, although Hillquit, ever sensitive to potential vulnerability, informally objected to the quasi-endorsement of the wartime collectivism which so many socialists scorned as inadequate. This important meeting concluded with the appointment of Berger and Work to an emergency committee with which Secretary Germer could consult between sessions of the NEC.[3]

The next months witnessed a series of frenzied actions by the Emergency Committee and the NEC in a futile effort to stem the tide of war. In order to meet the emotional response of the American public, including some party members, to the renewal of German submarine warfare, state secretaries were notified to organize mass meetings against a declaration of war, to cooperate with all anti-war groups, and to flood Congress with anti-war messages. Berger utilized his unique background to offer moral support to those congressional progressives who offered last-minute opposition to American intervention. He telegraphed both Congressman Claude Kitchin and Senator Robert M. La Follette to encourage their "heroic struggle" which, he said, would earn the vindication and applause of history.[4]

The Emergency Committee met on 2 February and sent Wilson a telegram demanding a full embargo. Spargo, alone on the NEC, protested that such a demand placed the Socialist party in support of the most militarist nations against those less prepared. Critics outside the committee denounced the reformist wing of the party as pro-German, while simultaneously attacking the composition of the Emergency Committee. The right defended itself and replied that quick action was necessary before Washington severed diplomatic relations with Berlin. John Work especially stressed his personal neutrality and pointed out that his own ancestry was English.[5]

On 6 February the NEC issued an anti-interventionist statement maintaining that neither side deserved the support of the United States and calling for greater public demonstrations. Again Spargo found himself a minority of one against the Hillquit-drafted and Berger-edited proclamation.[6]

Peace groups across the country agitated feverishly to counter the mounting war pressure. On 27 February Berger presided over a demonstration of 4,000 socialists and non-socialists in Milwaukee; he asked the crowd:

> Where does America come in? America does not come in at all unless it breaks in. . . . The submarine warfare, while vicious, is not waged primarily against the United States, but against the allies . . . an answer to the British war zone of the sea. If America wanted to go to war about it we might have gone to war two years ago when it was first originated by England. . . . There are many Americans who will protest against the war because America has nothing to gain and a great deal to lose. We are bound to lose lives, civil liberties and money. . . .

The audience adopted Emil Seidel's series of resolutions denouncing war for the protection of commerce, recommending prohibition of travel on belligerent ships, and demanding a complete embargo; and Berger sent the resolutions to President Wilson. That same day he telegraphed the House Committee on Expenditures in the name of the Socialist party, protesting that the proposed ''spy'' bill ''abolish[ed] freedom of speech and freedom of press. It is an unwarranted and insane attack caused by the prevailing war madness upon the liberties which have been achieved through long years of struggle.''[7]

In Milwaukee, an unofficial referendum on intervention held by the German-American Alliance was reported to run three hundred to one against war. The only official referendum on the war in the United States was held in nearby Monroe, Wisconsin, a community of Swiss extraction. The referendum, under the auspices of the city council, overwhelmingly rejected intervention, 954 to 95.[8] All such evidence of public opposition to intervention the socialists publicized.

The NEC was weary from its exhaustive efforts, and the majority favored calling an emergency convention to allow a greater portion of the membership to formulate a war policy which no doubt would soon be necessary. Hillquit, Secretary Germer, and Anna Maley wanted a convention, even though the NEC lacked the constitutional authority to summon one. However, Berger was not certain that a convention was necessary, while John Work was adamantly opposed. Work insisted that the committee could write a better anti-war manifesto "than could be written in [*sic*] hurly-burly of a convention in which there would be scheming impossibilist delegates." Nevertheless, for the sake of unity, Work agreed after Berger was persuaded by the other three, and the NEC wired members of the National Committee suggesting an emergency convention. The proposal was approved and the convention was scheduled to convene on 7 April wherever adequate facilities could be found.[9]

In the few weeks before the convention, the Emergency Committee continued its harried and futile efforts to head off a declaration of war. The last week in March, while pacifists besieged Washington in protest, the Socialist party sent final telegrams opposing intervention to Wilson and all members of Congress. They declared that American intervention, if it came, would be in the interest of financial "freebooters" only. The party demanded a referendum on war and asked, "Are you willing to take responsibility for spilling the blood of thousands?" The several socialists serving in the Wisconsin legislature managed to pass an anti-war resolution and that, too, was sent to the President and Congress.[10]

Although Victor Berger participated in all of these last-minute efforts, by late March he was resigned to defeat. The *Leader* had maintained a strong anti-interventionist posture, acting as spokesman for that sentiment and criticizing allied and American pressures toward United States involvement. But on 3 April, the *Leader* published a socialist war program that could be followed within the existing capitalist system. The program included the operation by the government of railroads, telegraphs, telephones, mines and oil wells, coal storage plants and grain elevators, the food supply, passenger and freight vessels, and all industrial monopolies. In addition, the government must guarantee an eight-hour day at a just wage, a 100 percent tax on incomes over $10,000, an inheritance tax to provide funds for pensions for the aged, widows and orphans, and the maintenance of all civil liberties.[11] Many of these demands were framed in the light of the European war experience.

The efforts of Berger and the Socialist party had shifted now from opposition to intervention to confrontation with war policies. But the party's ability to meet the new and even greater challenge was handicapped severely by the splintering of the right wing leadership. Since its inception, the war had badly damaged the group's solidarity. While all members maintained their hostility to war and their allegiance to international brotherhood, simultaneously they divided into small factions, some favoring the Allies, some the Central Powers, and others insisting that there was no significant difference between the antagonists. Party pronouncements followed the third theme and yet were susceptible to the charge of sympathy to the Germans. Consequently those who outwardly espoused the cause of the allies, such as A. M. Simons, found themselves more and more in positions hostile to party policies.

There was no doubt that Simons leaned toward England from the start, and his sympathies for the British increased as the struggle continued. Simons's untenable position in German Milwaukee was aggravated further by his correspondence with Keir Hardie and Ramsay MacDonald, who warned Simons against the German hegemony over American socialism. As Simons's view evolved from the espousal of disarmament to belief in the need to aid the Allies against the threat of German domination, he gradually eased out of his connections with the socialist movement. In December 1916 he resigned as managing editor of the Milwaukee *Leader* and severed his relations with Berger. In the *New Republic* he struck out at the party, which he accused of abandoning its American perspective in abject imitation of the policy of the German-American Alliance. He charged that the party had lost contact with American conditions and democracy and that it was in retreat from the war when it ought to be exploiting the current opportunities for democratization of industry.[12]

William James Ghent, Berger's former congressional secretary, was convinced that the German Empire represented the "most evil force in the world," and was equally certain that the German-born socialists in the American party had been dazzled by German propaganda. Charles Edward Russell angered many socialists by his implicit support of preparedness, and when he boldly announced in 1916 that the United States must arm because the causes of war had not been removed, he alienated the party leaders and soon found himself expelled from the Socialist party. George D. Herron, writing from Europe, became more and more emotional about the war. He congratulated Simons for his criticism of the party's stance and demanded that the Rand School cease publishing the war statements of the Socialist party.[13]

The condemnation of the party by reformists still attached to it was supported by many former members who had resigned in order to elect Wilson. Gustavus Myers, the historian of American fortunes, took that path along with John Reed and Upton Sinclair, and wrote that the decay of the party had begun even before the war issue. Myers felt that the suppression of party democracy, as exemplified by the anti-sabotage clause, had caused the defection of idealists who had hoped to see the party disseminate a clear understanding of American conditions rather than seek the trappings of political power.[14] Thus the barrage of attacks against the leadership came from many sources.

The culmination occurred on 24 March 1917, when two letters signed by prominent party leaders appeared in the major socialist dailies, the Milwaukee *Leader* and the New York *Call*. Such public display of policy differences precluded the possibility of minimizing the discussions. Not only the membership but the public at large was aware of the chaos within the party.

In the *Leader,* a socialist program for democratic defense appeared over the signatures of Ghent, Russell, Sinclair, Graham Phelps Stokes, William English Walling, and the widow of Jack London; in the *Call,* a strongly worded statement of opposition to party policies was published accompanied by the same signatures and a few others. It began:

> We, the undersigned, being socialists, and strongly opposed to the attitude of the Socialist Party with reference to war and national defense, desire to express our opposition publicly and to invite other socialists who may feel as we do to communicate with us. We feel that the present opposition of the Socialist Party to national defense is contrary to the interests of democracy and contrary to the hitherto accepted views of the International Socialist movement.

The statement charged that the American party had strayed from its recognition that existing conditions required a posture of self-defense:

> We feel that the present contrary attitude of the Socialist Party . . . is unsound from the standpoint of Socialist theory, and a betrayal of democracy, and we believe that there are many in the party who . . . do not wish to be identified with that false position. We are for peace, but not at any cost; and believe that the sacrifice of integrity and of general public and private self-respect is too high a price to pay for it. We abhor bloodshed, but see clearly that blood had better be shed than saved by cowardice to decay in bondage. . . . We are anti-militarists and fear both professional and volunteer class armies and believe that people who educate and govern themselves should be prepared to defend themselves against all who would interfere with their rights to liberty and self-government.

After ambiguously stating their abhorrence of militarism while endorsing an unstipulated form of military preparedness, the writers concluded with a reminder of the need to assume responsibilities in the world:

> To refuse to resist international crime is to be unworthy of the name of Socialist. It is our present duty to the cause of Internationalism to support our government in any sacrifice it requires in defense of those principles of international law and order which are essential alike to Socialism and civilization.[15]

The intensity of the statement and its appeal for a mutiny by the rank and file against the party leadership portended an upheaval of the gravest dimensions. The *Call* claimed editorially that the party consistently had maintained the principle of national self-defense, and therefore the current dispute was groundless. But the overwhelming fact was that the issue of the nation's sanctity in the crisis of war had destroyed completely the traditional solidarity of the party leadership. No matter what the *Call* or individual old-line reformists might say publicly, the faction was experiencing internal upheaval. Hitherto, through fifteen years of party bickering, the right had retained sufficient unity to control the Socialist party. Now that unity was gone and the control was endangered.

An explanation of the destruction of the faction's cohesiveness must focus first on its leadership problem. Possibly it was the inherent inability to accept leadership that impaired right wing effectiveness. Clearly there was never one figure who pretended to be the spokesman for all his reformist comrades. Had those who dominated the National Executive Committee been able to agree and submit to one outstanding figure among them, the cohesiveness of the group might have been assured. But there was no one with the charisma, the theoretical and tactical ability of a Lenin.

The most likely candidate was Berger because of his local power base and fame in the party and the country. His claim to the mantle of leadership lay in his ability to build a well-functioning, disciplined, and effective organization in Milwaukee, but he was unable to achieve the type of control in the party which he needed in order to mold it to his wishes. His failure there lay in the difference between the composition of the local and the national parties. In Milwaukee Berger dealt with a homogenous situation, ethnically and occupationally, which led to an easy agreement on fundamentals. Because of the harmony on means and ends, the Milwaukee socialists were able to tolerate Berger's egocentricity and aggressiveness, and readily submitted to his skill as a leader and tactician.

But the diversity of the national party and especially the independence of the policy-makers made consistent acceptance of any dictation out of the question. The very heterogeneity of the party militated against the emergence of one leader, and especially of Berger. Those same idiosyncrasies which Milwaukee accepted galled his comrades in the national leadership, and Berger was never really popular among them. Indeed, Berger's aggressive tones won him the acute dislike of some of those with whom he worked closely. Unable to submit to any one of their members, the reformist clique surely could not defer to the ubiquitous Berger. But the analysis of the group's fragmentation can not lie only in its lack of allegiance to one particular figure, for then the faction would not have endured as long as it did.

A detailed examination of the group suggests an answer. Fundamental differences in background and experience existed between those who clung to the party and those who revolted against policy and defected. A biographical inventory reveals a pattern in the defections which has often been overlooked or misinterpreted.

The defectors had been either clergymen or journalists. George D. Herron, Carl D. Thompson, and Winfield R. Gaylord were former ministers. Herron had entered the Socialist party from the Christian Socialist movement, and eventually left his ministerial position as a result of his own efforts to resolve the antagonisms between Christianity and Marxism. During his deepening estrangement from the party, he wrote, "I was put out of the church because I believed in Christ. . . . I shall probably be put out of the socialist movement for believing in socialism."[16]

Carl D. Thompson, too, was a Congregational minister who became a Christian Socialist. He soon found that his greatest commitment was to the Wisconsin Social Democratic organization, which he served in the State Legislature.[17] The materialist aspect of the socialist philosophy had no appeal for him, and he stressed class cooperation and brotherhood rather than the class struggle. His energies as director of the party's Information Department were devoted to social reform through parliamentary action and cooperation with progressive non-socialist groups. He finally left the party for the Public Ownership League and the collectivist possibilities of public utilities.

Winfield R. Gaylord's path was similar, from Congregational minister to Wisconsin State Senator. He was often Berger's campaign companion, seeking election in the Wisconsin Fourth Congressional District while Berger ran in the Fifth. Gaylord was well known for his eccentricity and volatile temperament which, following American entry into World War I, were illustrated by his extreme, even paranoiac, hostility toward the Socialist party.[18]

Charles Edward Russell, William James Ghent, Allan L. Benson, A. M. Simons, and John Spargo were journalists; all but Ghent, whose socialist writings tended to the theoretical, participated in electioneering. Russell joined the party a half-dozen years after its formation, and as he was a famous, muckraking journalist, he was warmly welcomed into the ranks and nominated in every New York State and national election. But Russell later claimed that he had never been quite at home in a party that had seemed to him essentially a foreign organization. With the opening of the European war, he began to turn away and became the first socialist to commit himself publicly to preparedness; with the American declaration of war, he at once wrote to President Wilson, a not dissimilar crusader, offering his support. He maintained, however, that socialist doctrine did not preclude participation in war and was amused when Berger attacked him in the *Leader* for being influenced by his English descent.[19]

William James Ghent became a socialist in 1893 and even before joining the party in 1904 made two theoretical contributions to the movement, *Our Benevolent Feudalism* and *Mass and Class*. His theoretical bent was matched by organizational skill and he was selected to be the first director of the Rand School of Social Science, and subsequently Berger's aide in Congress. His socialist activities in New York and Washington ended early in 1913 when he contracted tuberculosis. From Arizona he wrote commentary for the socialist press until his resignation from the Socialist party in 1917.]

Allan L. Benson was a Michigan journalist who worked for Detroit and Washington newspapers. With his conversion to socialism of the English Fabian stripe, he became a columnist on *The Appeal to Reason*. Although his popularity with the membership stemmed more from his pacifist than his socialist stance, Benson abandoned the Socialist party in order to support the American war effort.[21] Since he had never been a force within the party, his loss had no effect upon policy-making, but because he had been the party's presidential candidate only a few months earlier, his defection appeared significant to outside observers.

A. M. Simons's odyssey, from the left of the party to the right and beyond to the various progressive reform movements, exemplifies the path of many radicals.[22] Throughout his journalistic career, which saw him edit almost a half-dozen socialist newspapers, Simons participated in almost every phase of the movement. His stress on the necessity of Americanizing Marx led him to revisionism, and finally, as argued by his biographers, to nationalism. "For years he had written . . . about the desperate necessity of making socialism into an American political faith." Simons's socialism had been pervaded by a belief in Anglo-Saxon virtue, and he quickly made an overt transition from socialism to nationalism as his primary loyalty. Because of the intensity of his original commitment to the movement—indeed, the mutual interest in the party formed the very fabric of his marriage to May Wood—and his involvement in policy-making, editing, and lecturing, his departure from the Socialist party left him with deep scars and explain the furious hostility which he demonstrated afterward in his attacks upon positions he had previously held.[23]

John Spargo, a prolific writer on socialism, emigrated to the United States as an evolutionary socialist the year the party was founded, and he quickly took his place in the party hierarchy as a fixture on the National Executive Committee. Unlike Simons's, his views did not fluctuate widely during his socialist career and no fundamental disagreements in policy appeared between Spargo and his reformist comrades. It was only the war which alienated him, and he suddenly noticed what had never occurred to him earlier, that "American socialism has so often spoken with a German accent."[24]

William English Walling and J. G. Phelps Stokes, who spearheaded the assault of the left on the right in 1910, nevertheless must be considered among those who defected from the reformist wing. Walling, a wealthy writer of humanitarian bent who supported such causes as the advancement of labor, blacks, and women, made no effort to enter into high party office, choosing instead to agitate in the socialist press for absolute adherence to principle. From 1914 to 1917, his line of criticism steadily moved him into a more moderate party position. In 1916, Walling argued that the criterion for socialist commitment in war must be the advancement of internationalism, and by March 1917, Walling favored American intervention in that light.[25]

Stokes's path paralleled Walling's. While he lacked the capacity of leadership or literary ability, his wealth, made in railroads, was capable of supporting the Socialist party, and the party happily welcomed him. He viewed the war as one between progress and reaction, and in 1916 voiced support for any anti-tyrannical effort. Even an aggressive war was permissible when liberty was at stake.[26]

The departure of these ten individuals reduced the number of reformist spokesmen. However, a similarly impressive list of names can be drawn of members of the right wing faction who remained loyal to the Socialist party in the interventionist crisis. Besides Berger and Hillquit, there were James H. Maurer, the Pennsylvania labor leader; J. Mahlon Barnes, a leader of the Philadelphia cigarmakers and former Executive Secretary of the party; Julius Gerber, the New York socialist functionary and union activist; and Adolph Germer, currently Executive Secretary of the party and formerly an official of the United Mine Workers.[27] Among other loyalists there were Job Harriman, the

Los Angeles attorney and one-time running mate of Debs, who had been the socialist candidate for mayor during the McNamara imbroglio and was currently immersed in the establishment of a cooperative colony in Louisiana; and Seymour Stedman, a Chicago attorney who handled many of the party's litigations and later ran on the 1920 socialist ticket with Debs.

These eighteen individuals fall into four major occupational categories—ministers, journalists, trade unionists, and lawyers. Those who remained in the Socialist party were involved in labor organizations and in legal practices. In the main they were activists who knew the labor and the socialist movements from the inside, and were representative of those who formed both movements. They were men of practical politics, while those who fled the party were generally, despite their political experiences, men of thought rather than of deed. The party's intellectuals departed but the workers remained.

Another difference found between the two groups is that of national origin: the Anglo-Saxons left and the Europeans stayed. Thus, through the defections of 1916 and early 1917, the party took on a markedly alien accent.[28] While often the Socialist party has been misinterpreted as largely foreign in composition, the party, in fact, had maintained a native cast of characters until the last pre-war winter.

At the time, the national press stressed the disintegration of the fledgling third party. Historian Daniel Bell thinks it significant that all the "names" left the party, and David Shannon believes those departing took with them the party's respectability.[29] However, not all the prominent figures left, and certainly party respectability did not disappear with the refugees. The only concrete loss was certain personnel. No mass exodus occurred. The reformist leaders who remained were as well-known and prestigious to the membership as were those who walked out, and there was no want of policy-making ability.

What has become clear is that the fragmentation of the right wing was actually a division of two segments which had never been cemented into a whole. The groups had cooperated because of their shared framework of belief in political action, but a vast difference in perspective and, as it turned out, in priorities had always existed.

Those reformist leaders who remained, however, believed themselves diminished in strength. They were affected by the experience more than were the rank and file of the party, for they felt keenly that there had been an amputation. A languor, even a defeatist complex, overwhelmed them. Whereas the party was not enfeebled by the actual defections, as outsiders have held, the leadership's attitude in fact created an internal weakness. External opinions eventually were validated. The NEC, too depressed to formulate and effect policy, soon saw the initiative assumed by others.

A comparison of the reaction to war of the Socialist party of America with that of most of the European parties reveals a striking difference. In the United States those who supported the national war effort left the party, while in Europe the parties supported the war and the defectors did not. However, it would be a serious error to identify the defecting groups with each other or to imagine that the parties had differing reactions to the war. The bulk of European socialists supported the war effort because they had developed a political and economic stake in the existing societies. The parties in Central and Western Europe, with the exception of Italy, had become politically successful and confident and were supported by an increasingly prosperous working class. Both the parties and the workers felt themselves tied to and dependent upon the well-being and prosperity of their respective nations, and therefore nationalism triumphed over internationalism.

In the United States the position of the Socialist party in politics and its relationship with the working class was wholly different. The party had been growing confident of future political success, but it did not yet have a firm stake in the existing system. While the American working class was improving its standard of living,[30] the Socialist party did not recognize this adequately, and moreover, because of the party's failure to win the support of the working class, it was not yet dependent upon it. For these reasons the American party was free to choose its policy as the European socialists were not. The Socialist party felt free to oppose the system and the war and call the latter a capitalist adventure rather than a war for democracy, and the membership was able to favor expulsion of any elected public official who supported a war, an action which the European parties had avoided.

Nonetheless, some of the leading intellectuals in the party rushed to the support of the United States, not in terms of the workers' relationship to the system but in terms of the sanctity of the nation-state. The United States was viewed as a force for progress and democracy—the best yet produced—threatened by barbaric hordes. These intellectuals concluded, in the name of self-defense, that preparedness and even war itself were permissible and, indeed, mandatory.

Thus, the Socialist party followed the analysis developed by the

Europeans when confronted with the agonizing decision of war, and the defectors, who were of the right wing reinforced by a few from the pre-1914 left, deviated from the socialist pattern. For them socialism had become a secondary consideration, even for the few for whom the defamation of the party leadership for lack of socialist principle had been an earlier delight. The sanctity of the nation had assumed major significance for them as with the European socialists, but here nationalism conquered internationalism for vastly different reasons.

The American socialist defectors had proved not to be genuine challengers of fundamentals in the system but rather indigenous radicals following a tradition of protest. They exploited the Socialist party as a means to the solution of existing problems and the improvement of American society in accordance with their own views. When the crisis came, they chose to go along with the system. In contrast to democratic socialists like Adolph Germer and Job Harriman, to name only two, they chose to accept capitalism and war without trying to alter essentials. In 1917 the Socialist party had outlived its usefulness to them and they abandoned it in order to proceed to public ownership leagues, progressive parties, industrial management, and other ameliorative efforts within the existing political and economic framework. Those who remained in the party had a more intimate and penetrating understanding of the ideology of socialism and its stake in the United States due to their backgrounds of labor and political activism.

But if the American Socialist party succeeded in adhering to a socialist standard which was national in analysis and international in ideology, what of Victor Berger and his unique role of fitting socialism to the American scene? As measured against his own standards, this was the one great blunder of Berger's career. To be responsive to the existing situation within the framework of socialist principles required that the Socialist party accept the reality of war and the national war effort. For Berger to fulfill the definition of Weber's genuine man with the calling for politics, he had to try to bring together the ethics of responsibility and of ultimate ends at this crucial moment. It was vital that he make the proper series of choices if he were to continue to be the moral man wending his way through the politics of immoral society. But Berger violated his own beliefs in constructiveness and immediacy; he went along with a war policy which reflected the Marxist position of transcending an issue of transitionary society. Berger assumed the posture he had always abhorred and opposed.

He should have insisted upon the recognition and exploitation of the war for whatever advantages the party could achieve. That he and his party had a freedom of choice denied to the SPD did not mean that the German choice was inappropriate for Berger. Nevertheless, Berger used his free choice to follow doctrine rather than principled pragmatism. Thus he invited the devastation that typically results from opposing a national war, in his case most poignant since he thought opposition unwise, unnecessary, and inopportune.

To suggest that if Berger and the Socialist party had moved with national developments, the essentials of the party would have been compromised, is to narrow possibilities. The choice was not simply between blind acceptance or blind opposition to war. Another path was open: the party's consideration of American public opinion (by which it would remain a part of American society) and working for the maintenance and advancement of democracy within a nation at war. But the party, with Berger's concurrence, chose opposition to war at the expense of the party's existence, for it ultimately turned itself into a paper tiger.

Berger's momentous blunder led to the party's complete alienation from the American public and to its own political failure. While earlier the Socialist party had played a viable role in the political dialogue and the voter could turn to it and register an honorable protest, the overwhelming majority of voters could never regard the party sympathetically after its war stance.

But Berger does not bear as much responsibility as this analysis seems to suggest. His responsibility is somewhat limited in that policy decisions were not his to the extent that they had been earlier. His error was one of omission more than commission. He did not dictate a disastrous policy, but he failed to oppose it strenuously. Perhaps even greater responsibility rests on the shoulders of those Anglo-Saxon, native-born intellectuals who virtually abandoned the reformists to the increasingly militant revolutionists.

Berger's dream collapsed in the spring of 1917 without his wholly realizing it. It would take the duration of the war and its aftermath to point up the reality of failure to him and to everyone else.

NOTES

1. Richard W. Leopold, *The Growth of American Foreign Policy* (New York: Alfred A. Knopf, 1962), pp. 310-313; Frederic L. Paxson, *American Democracy and the World War* (Boston: Houghton Mifflin Co., 1936), I, 166, 178, 286.

2. *American Socialist Official Business Supplement,* 16 December 1916.

3. Ibid., 13 January 1917, 27 January 1917.

4. Adolph Germer to NEC, 9 March 1917, Berger Col., MCHS; John M. Work, "The First World War," *Wisconsin Magazine of History* 41 (Autumn 1957): 33; Victor Berger telegram to Claude Kitchin, 2 March 1917, Berger telegram to Robert La Follette, 2 March 1917, Berger Col., MCHS.

5. John M. Work, "Autobiography," II, chap. 5, 39, typescript, John M. Work Collection, SHSW, "The First World War," p. 32; John Spargo, *Americanism and Social Democracy* (New York: Harper and Bros., Pub., 1918), pp. 260-263; Milwaukee *Leader,* 17 February 1917.

6. John Spargo, *Americanism and Social Democracy,* p. 263.

7. Milwaukee *Leader,* 27 February 1917, 28 February 1917; Berger telegram to House Committee on Expenditures, 27 February 1917, Berger Col., MCHS.

8. Clifton Child, *The German-Americans in Politics, 1914-1917* (Madison: University of Wisconsin Press, 1939), p. 162; Karen Falk, "Public Opinion in Wisconsin during World War I," *Wisconsin Magazine of History* 25: 295.

9. *American Socialist,* 17 March 1917; Work, "The First World War," p. 33. Spargo was not present.

10. Work, "The First World War," p. 34; *American Socialist,* 17 April 1917; SP Emergency Committee telegram to President Wilson, 26 March 1917, Berger Col., MCHS; Milwaukee *Leader,* 16 February 1917.

11. Milwaukee *Leader,* 3 April 1917.

12. Ramsay MacDonald to A. M. Simons, 15 December 1916, May Wood Simons, "Diary," 1 December 1916, Simons Col., SHSW. Algie M. Simons, "The Future of the So-

cialist Party," *New Republic* 11 (2 December 1916): 118-119; Simons, "Pacifism vs. Revolution," *New Republic* 10 (24 March 1917): 221.

13. William James Ghent to Algernon Lee, 30 April 1916, Algernon Lee Collection, Tamiment Institute; Milwaukee *Leader,* 5 February 1916; Ghent, "The Collapse of Socialism in the United States," *Current History* 24 (May 1926): 245; "Report on the Intercollegiate Socialist Society Seventh Annual Convention," *Intercollegiate Socialist Review* 4 (February-March 1916): 13; George D. Herron to Simons, 7 June 1915, Simons Col., SHSW; Herron to Hillquit, 7 August 1917, Hillquit Col., SHSW.

14. Gustavus Myers, "Why Idealists Quit the Socialist Party," *Nation* 104 (15 February 1917): 181-182.

15. Milwaukee *Leader,* 24 March 1917; New York *Call,* 24 March 1917.

16. Herron to Simons, 7 June 1915, Simons Col., SHSW.

17. Solon De Leon, ed., *American Labor Who's Who* (New York: Hanford Press, 1925), p. 228.

18. Marvin Wachman, *The History of the Social-Democratic Party of Milwaukee, 1897-1910* (Urbana: University of Illinois Press, 1945), pp. 44, 55.

19. Charles Edward Russell, *Bare Hands and Stone Walls: Some Recollections of a Side-Line Reformer* (New York: Charles Scribner's Sons, 1933), pp. 200, 293-296.

20. Harold Sherburn Smith, "William James Ghent, Reformer and Historian" (Ph.D. diss., University of Wisconsin, 1957), pp. 165, 336.

21. Harold W. Currie, "Allan L. Benson," *Labor History* 11 (Summer 1970): 286-287. See also Harold W. Currie, "A Socialist Edits the Detroit Times," *Michigan History* 52 (Spring 1968): 1-11.

22. An early and therefore surprisingly cogent analysis of the party by sociologist Robert F. Hoxie concludes that the average socialist travels from near impossibilism to constructive opportunism; see "The Rising Tide of Socialism," *Journal of Political Economy* 19 (October 1911): 631.

23. William A. Glaser, "Algie M. Simons and Marxism in America," *Mississippi Valley Historical Review* 41: 421; see Diary of May Wood Simons, Simons Col., SHSW; Kent and Gretchen Kreuter, *An American Dissenter: The Life of*

Algie Martin Simons (Lexington: University of Kentucky Press, 1969), pp. 161, 170-172.

24. Spargo, *Americanism and Social Democracy*, pp. 166-167.

25. *American Labor Year Book (1916)*, p. 239; "Intercollegiate Socialist Society Conference on Defensive War," *Intercollegiate Socialist Review* 5 (October-November 1916): 14. Walling had been pushed to the far left by his interest in the Russian Revolution of 1905, and the upheaval of the world war returned him to a moderate position. See Jack Stuart, "William English Walling and the American Federation of Labor," paper read to the American Historical Association, Washington, D.C., 30 December 1969, p. 8.

26. "Intercollegiate Socialist Society Conference on Defensive War," p. 14.

27. For their pre-war work, see brief biographies in Solon De Leon, *American Labor Who's Who*. Their wartime activities will be found here in Chapters 8-9.

28. Kenneth McNaught, "American Progressives and the Great Society," *Journal of American History* 53 (December 1966): 516-517.

29. Daniel Bell, *Marxian Socialism in the United States* (Princeton: Princeton University Press, 1967), p. 99; David A. Shannon, *The Socialist Party of America: A History* (New York, Macmillan Co., 1955), p. 100.

30. By checking the percentage of the average family budget that was spent on food in 1901 against the figures in 1918, Paul Douglas proved that the real wages and the standard of living improved for the average worker in this period. Paul Douglas, *Real Wages in the United States, 1890-1926* (New York: Houghton Mifflin Co., 1930), p. 499. On the rise in the standard of living, see also John R. Commons, ed., *History of Labor in the United States,* Vol. 3, Don D. Lesochier and Elizabeth Brandeis, *Working Conditions: Labor Legislation* (New York: Macmillan and Co., 1935), p. 51.

8

The Isolation of the Right Wing

The delegates to the Emergency Convention of the Socialist party assembling in St. Louis at the Planters Hotel on 7 April 1917, confronted a complex task. Much like the National Committee meeting of May 1915, which sought to produce a peace program acceptable to the majority of the party, the Emergency Convention hoped to write a manifesto on war which the various factions of the party would support. Unlike the 1915 meeting, the 1917 gathering faced an aroused nation beginning to rally to the Congressional declaration of war of the day before, and any socialist statement which failed to support the American war stance would be met with deep hostility. This background served to charge the air with tension and lent a sense of drama which did not leave the delegates unaffected. Indeed the militancy which pervaded the week-long convention was surely bolstered by the national spirit against which the delegates claimed to be reacting.

The right-wing leaders limped to the convention, their numbers decreased, their energy sapped, and their spirits dim. They were in no position to take on the left wing in combat, for they dealt from a position of weakness that they had never before known in the history of the Socialist party. Victor Berger, whose original inclination was to oppose a convention, would have been even more opposed had he realized to what extent the right would exhaust itself in those few weeks before 7 April.

The opening day of the convention confirmed Berger's worst fears of the revived militancy of the left. The convention agreed to elect a Committee on War and Militarism to draft a statement of the party's position. While it was generally understood that the party would go on record as opposed to the war, the intensity of the statement depended on the personnel elected to the committee. With both factions anxious to dominate this committee, the left moved that each of the thirty-five nominees for the fifteen positions answer one question: "Are you opposed to all militarism and to all war, either offensive or defensive, except the war of the working class against the capitalist class?"[1]

A heated discussion erupted as the surprised right found itself at once on the defensive. Morris Hillquit insisted that the question was untenable because it did not permit an unqualified response. He condemned the intent behind the question as one of moral terrorism. John Spargo, attending his last Socialist party convention, pointed out that there had never been a test for committee membership and argued that Marx and Engels could not have responded affirmatively to the question. Moreover, he said, such a question precluded party debate on the attitude to war which was the purpose of the committee. Berger, his spirits even lower after this initial offensive, tried halfheartedly to speak but was not recognized by the chair.[2]

The motion to poll the nominees before the vote failed. The election produced an unusually well-balanced committee. The left had marshaled its votes and concentrated on the election of certain individuals instead of voting for fifteen candidates. By this method it elected four members while the right elected five, including Berger and Hillquit. The remaining six members of the committee were not closely tied to either faction.[3]

The election results, however, were shocking to the right, which now had concrete evidence that its domination of the party had ended. While the left had elected only a representative number, the right interpreted the results to mean leftist control of the committee.[4] That defeatist attitude served only to strengthen the bellicose mood of the others and led to the militancy of the committee. An indication of the spirit that prevailed at St. Louis was Berger's lack of voter appeal: he was fourteenth of the fifteen elected.

The committee focused on three issues: the party position on war and militarism in general, the attitude to American involvement in the world war, and a program for socialist activity for the duration. To determine the degree of agreement that existed among the members, discussion was opened with each one briefly expressing his own position. Berger reiterated his view on the significant role of the nation as the basis of internationalism and compared anti-nationalism with an-archism. His statement immediately created a dispute. Leftists replied that the state was only a passing form of civilization and added that the illusory issue of nationalism had wrecked the Second International. Rightists defended Berger's position and argued that although the class struggle was paramount, the issue of nationalism was too significant to be ignored.[5]

There was no chance that Berger's views on nationalism might pre-vail. His skillful balancing of the principle of national self-defense and acceptance of war with the promulgation of a socialist program to meet the crisis was irrelevant to the moment. Berger recognized that in the war-charged atmosphere of the convention, his non-doctrinaire ap-proach was out of place, but he was not entirely resigned to his fate. He was agitated and upset throughout the week in St. Louis and stayed away from some of the sessions of the Committee on War and Militarism, angrily sulking in his hotel room. There he composed his own program, but in his depression, destroyed it without presenting it to the committee. His views were fully aired only when John Work ap-peared before the committee and presented the program advocated by the *Leader*.[6]

The committee of fifteen produced three reports. The majority report was signed by eleven members and was composed by the unlikely team of Morris Hillquit and the left wing's Charles E. Ruthenberg. Its proclamation reaffirmed the party's allegiance to the principle of in-ternationalism and working-class solidarity and declared its unalterable opposition to the capitalists' increased accumulation of wealth.

> The Socialist Party of the United States is unalterably op-posed to the system of exploitation and class rule which is upheld and strengthened by military power and sham national patriotism. We, therefore, call upon the workers of all coun-tries to refuse support to their governments in their wars. The wars of the contending national groups of capitalists are not the concern of the workers. The only struggle which would justify the workers in taking up arms is the great struggle of the working class of the world to free itself from economic ex-ploitation and political oppression, and we particularly warn the workers against the snare and delusion of so-called defen-sive warfare.

After an analysis of the economic causes of the European war and the successful efforts of American capitalists to involve the United States, the proclamation continued: "In all modern history there has been no war more unjustifiable than the war in which we are about to engage. No greater dishonor had ever been forced upon a people. . . .[7]

A more vigorous prosecution of the class struggle through a multipoint program was endorsed: continuous manifestation of opposition to the war; opposition to military or industrial conscription and to taxation for war purposes; resistance to encroachments on civil liberties or to compulsory arbitration of labor disputes; consistent propaganda against military training and teaching; expansion of educational and organizational work among workers; and the restriction of food exports and the socialization of major industries and natural resources.

A second report, supported by three committee members, agreed substantially with the majority report. A third report was submitted by Spargo alone. Spargo accepted the national war effort while demonstrating the same concern for nationalization, conscription, and civil liberties as had the majority. Berger had urged him to submit a program for the sake of those socialists who were not opposed to supporting the war, but Berger himself refrained from accepting what seemed to be an overly eager embrace of the war and he signed the majority report.[8]

The Hillquit-Ruthenberg report won acceptance easily, but it was clear that the overwhelming anti-war sentiment was not all of one piece. During the debate on the majority report, some members on the left offered three amendments which expanded the report's condemnation of the current war to that of all wars of the ruling classes; all amendments were defeated. Hillquit successfully argued that such a modification would actually weaken the report, for no war would ever be recognized officially as capitalistic. He convinced the delegates that it was the present war which had to be faced.

The tired delegates instructed the National Executive Committee to initiate a vigorous anti-war campaign. Top level representation was expanded by enlarging the NEC from five to fifteen, and the National Committee was abolished because of its ineffectiveness. As a last gesture, a subcommittee of four, including Berger, issued an address to the socialists of the belligerent countries. Two addresses were drafted, but in order to avoid another struggle, Berger passively withdrew his and the other was adopted unanimously.[9]

The convention ended with the party united in its opposition to the war and within two months, the membership, in referendum, ratified the majority report. However, it is erroneous to assume that the overt unity indicated that the war issue had actually minimized the differences within the party.[10] Although widespread agreement existed on the necessity of opposing war even after American intervention, there were still vast differences in interpretations of the causes of the war, in evaluation of the St. Louis Proclamation (as the majority report was called), and in opinions on the shape opposition should take. The St. Louis meeting itself was a rough-and-tumble affair in which the more boisterous prevailed, but the implementation of the program could assume various forms, and whether the party leadership carried out the intent of St. Louis was a source of controversy in the months ahead.

Berger's role at St. Louis had been an enigmatic and painful one. For once his voice was not clearly heard above the din of a party convention. He was caught in his own conflicting emotions and found himself linked with a report with which he was in basic disagreement, and which had been produced by a committee which he later admitted was not congenial to his tastes. The youthful militancy of its members was too much for the now aging Berger, but he could not force himself to acquiesce in the minority report which accepted the war with a resignation bordering on outright endorsement. Berger, the only member of the Committee on War and Militarism born in an enemy nation, signed the majority report with reluctance. Drained by the daily pressures of party responsibilities prior to the convention, and denied the support of departed comrades, he had virtually succumbed to exhaustion by the date of his signature.[11]

However in the *Leader,* Berger praised the convention for its adoption of a sane and socialist war statement.

A cool, scientific Marxist declaration on war and militarism was surely the best thing that could be gotten under the circumstances from that convention and we got it. In a way this probably was the most turbulent convention ever held by the Socialist party. The jingoism of the militaristic war advocates . . . had bred among Socialists an intense fervor of opposition to war that I did not imagine possible. This intensity of feeling was . . . shown in all . . . proceedings. It reminded one very much of an old-time American revival meeting. . . .

He did indicate that "the impossibilist element" had been vocal but concluded that a reasonable stand was taken which unified the party and precluded the possibility of a split. Publicly he was pleased with the convention.

But in his personal correspondence he revealed a less sanguine attitude. He described the delegates as wild-eyed and raucous and told Hillquit of his dissatisfaction with what he called a lack of constructiveness. He acknowledged that the proclamation of principles followed the socialist tradition of opposition to war, but he believed that an anti-war policy would play into the hands of the party's enemies. Nevertheless, he was resigned and planned to stand by the entire document.[12]

John Work, who was also steadfast in his determination to support the party, had the last, albeit bitter, laugh. He credited himself with the vision to oppose an emergency convention. He later wrote that had his position been accepted by the other members of the NEC, no concessions would have been necessary to the left: "While the proclamation certainly would have been couched in strong language, and we doubtless would have been persecuted, some of the language in the St. Louis anti-war proclamation that got our members into the most trouble with the authorities . . . would not have been there. It was put in to appease the impossibleists [sic] and to come as near unanimity as possible."[13]

Job Harriman, from the platform, had condemned the majority report as a grave error and, like Work, thought that the declaration was an immoderate one resulting from the need to compromise with the left wing's extremism. He later argued that a split at that convention would have been desirable; the inevitable was merely postponed and in the wake of that postponement the Socialist party proceeded to alienate the American public and the labor movement as well.[14]

The *Leader*, a spokesman for what would be a right wing holding action, managed to approve the strikingly militant pacifist tone of the convention. It summarized the convention as challenging the members "to decide whether the American Socialist party was to lead the world for the emancipation of the proletariat—or whether our party was to be drowned in the swamp of patriotic nationalism—or whether our movement was to lose itself in the desert of narrow sectarianism. We have chosen the middle road—undoubtedly the right road."[15]

Spokesmen for the left were more forthright in their criticism of the convention and its results. The *International Socialist Review* condemned the war statement as a compromise. In attempting to appease a German nationalist like Berger, wrote an editorialist, the statement had failed to oppose all wars. The old guard had been found wanting in the moment of truth.[16]

Louis C. Fraina endorsed the majority report during the referendum but denounced what he called its equivocation on principles. The party bureaucrats were excoriated for manipulations which prevented the convention from taking a firmer stand on the issues. The result, according to Fraina's journal, *The Class Struggle,* was a circumspect program that avoided condemnation of the European socialists.[17]

Thus, both factions felt themselves saddled with an unwanted St. Louis Proclamation. In previous years, Berger's dilemma, and that of his fellow reformists, could have been more easily solved. The old Berger would have devised a report which, while accepting a war in which the country had become involved, would have opposed national excesses and attempted social changes within the legal framework of dissent. The old Berger would have recognized American reality—as he had in his congressional service—and worked with it to promote positive evolution. But now he lacked the strength and will to bring together a realistic proclamation and a program of constructive dissent.

The leftists, like L. E. Katterfeld and Fraina, also did not get the proclamation they wanted. To them, a document which did not reject all capitalist wars was unworthy of Marxism. These revolutionists wanted to bypass the possibilities of specific criticisms. Since they felt no relationship to the existing system, they need not respond to its crisis. Thus, with responsibility only to the ultimate goal, they saw no need to assume a viable posture within the framework. Absolute hostility was the only meaningful gesture for them.

The quarreling between the right and left in the months after the convention was accompanied by a wholesale defection of most of the remaining right wing intellectuals. Bitter at the party's failure to stand by the American government in its moment of need, the defectors walked out of the Socialist party while proclaiming their loyalty to the principles of socialism and internationalism.

A. M. Simons, who even before the convention had broadcast widely his opinion of the party's disloyalty to both socialist and American principles, attempted to influence public opinion, through an association designed to exploit the collectivism that war promoted. A particular goal was to give pro-war socialists a home, and reorient the American socialist movement. In July the Social Democratic League was organized in a futile effort to bind together progressives from various minor party movements in the name of social and industrial democracy. The League produced "A Program of Social Reconstruction after the War" and a letterhead which claimed such erstwhile Socialist party luminaries as Simons, Russell, Spargo, Stokes, Walling, Thompson, Benson, Ghent, and Gaylord.[18] The League, however, never germinated support and served only as a slight annoyance to the Socialist party.

But Simons's ability to antagonize the Socialist party was not insignificant. With the cheerful cooperation of Winfield Gaylord, he notified Senator Paul O. Husting of Wisconsin of the "disloyalty" of Victor Berger, thereby hoping to prevent Berger's rumored appointment to the federal commission to Russia. Senator Husting promptly passed the information along to the Justice Department and comforted Simons with the knowledge that Berger had never been seriously considered.[19]

In Wisconsin, Simons embodied the state's Defense League and its successor, the Wisconsin Loyalty League. The major goals of both organizations were the encouragement of loyalty to the war effort and the exposure of treasonable domestic activity. Berger and the *Leader* were the special targets of Simons' efforts.[20]

William English Walling, assuming his now traditional role, set out to expose the remaining Socialist party leadership before the American public. He wrote a blistering letter to the New York *Globe* in which he linked the party to the German war effort. "The view I represent, that the Socialist Party, under its present control is directed from Berlin, is also held by A. M. Simons, Winfield Gaylord, John Spargo . . . and others of the most popular of the Socialist leaders. . . . None of these are working men . . . but they have a far better right to speak for the American working people than Berger, who was born in Austria, and Hillquit, who was born in the German town of Riga. . . ."[21] Using the background of some of the party leaders to suggest active German ties, Walling and his friends were as willing to smear the Socialist party with suggestions of treason as were more openly capitalist American patriots—indeed, even more willing.

Charles Edward Russell became the socialist representative on the American mission to the Russian government in May. A cry of anger

went up in the ranks of the party that a man who had virtually abandoned the organization should have the temerity to pose as its representative on a capitalist-conceived mission headed by the Republican conservative Elihu Root. This contemptuousness resulted in his expulsion
from the party simultaneously with that of Simons and Gaylord.[22]

John Spargo did not wait for his expulsion. His criticism of the
convention to a certain extent echoed those of the leftists. He charged
that an unconstitutional rump convention had refrained from a forthright discussion of socialist principles. But Spargo also declared that
the war resolution proved that the party was out of touch with the country, arguing that internationalism presupposed nationalism and
therefore in the present state of the world, it was a perversion of socialist principle to insist that the only relevant war was the class struggle. In an open letter of resignation Spargo condemned the majority
report as a betrayal of international socialism, declaring that it would
destroy the socialist movement in the United States, and denouncing the
party as an obstacle to socialism.[23] His resignation on 30 May 1917
created a vacancy on the NEC which the committee filled by appointing
Seymour Stedman.

The culmination of the defectors' opposition to the Socialist party
was reached in June 1918, with President Wilson's appointment of the
American Socialist Pro-War Mission to Europe. The group was chaired
by Simons and included Spargo and Herron, in addition to Russell. Its
purpose was to contact and convince European socialists that their
American comrades supported the allied efforts, despite the protesta-
tions of the crippled party. The members visited various socialist and
labor leaders of allied and neutral countries and represented the
American Socialist movement at a labor conference in London. The
mission also attempted to encourage interest in a new socialist International.[24]

The defecting socialists who turned against the party with intense
hostility are not anomalous in the history of radicalism. A traditional
pattern exists in which a traumatic experience may transform a radical
into a staunch conservative bent on atoning for his errant past through
the exposure and punishment of his former colleagues. Prototypes of
such psychological evolution may be seen, for example, in the respective odysseys of Max Eastman from *The Masses* to the *National Review*,
of Jay Lovestone from the American Communist party to the most conservative faction in the hierarchy of the American Federation of Labor.

Only through this phenomenon can be understood the contrast between William English Walling's several pre-war indictments of the party leaders for their feckless betrayal of the class struggle and his total commitment to the prosecution of the war and the chastisement of the Socialist party during that long summer of 1917. It was the trauma of the war that transformed an apparent internationalist into a narrow nationalist.

Those remaining in the right wing were not happy with the policy they found themselves formally supporting in May 1917. Members from Local Oakland and Local Berkeley, California, circularized the leadership, demanding a reevaluation of the party's war position. They declared that the proclamation inevitably identified the party in the public mind with the German cause, and that even some of the membership harbored that suspicion. In order to prevent the wholesale defection of the rank and file, the writers pleaded for a reformulated program, but such dire forebodings were not validated by events. The membership rolls climbed in the succeeding months as the party attracted the attention of pacifists and of others who reacted against the militancy of the American government and its obvious intention of curbing civil liberties. Throughout May, June, and July the membership ranks increased.[25]

The party pursued its policy of dissent. Independence Day was chosen as a day of protest by the National Executive Committee and vast demonstrations were held demanding a clear statement of war aims, a declaration of peace terms, and a referendum on conscription. Petitions were also circulated against the conscription of men into the armed forces, but because of its traditional principle of observance of the law, the party refrained from encouraging draft-dodging. Any draftee who asked the advice of the National Office or the Young People's Socialist League was always told to follow the dictates of his own conscience.[26]

Meyer London's role as the representative of the party in the United States Congress was not an easy one. He voted against the declaration of war and the Espionage Act, but he found constant opposition of the government to be unfeasible. As the only socialist in the national government he assumed the initiative and cabled the new Russian regime, advising against making a separate peace with the Central Powers. As a result, he drew the condemnation of both wings of the party. The left called London a failure for not properly exploiting opportunities for socialist propaganda. On the right, the *Leader* chose to ignore London, while Hillquit wired the Russian government that London's cable was not authorized by the Socialist party.[27]

The *Leader* carefully selected its line of opposition to the war. Berger's editorials and the occasional columns by other socialist leaders concentrated upon safeguarding the rights and interests of the public during the war. Berger described the American socialists as loyal to the highest interests of the nation; he stressed the need to retain adequate food supplies at home under government control, and demanded the preservation of civil liberties. In order to free himself from some of the heavy responsibilities as editor-in-chief of a daily, on 21 May Berger hired John M. Work as the chief editorial writer. Berger then had more time to participate in party activities and to cooperate with other anti-war groups.[28]

The party could do little beyond demonstrating and petitioning against the war, for it found itself in the position of an outlaw in American society. The efforts of the right wing leaders were reduced to a defense against government initiatives and the reformists lacked energy for the further formulation of policy or for meeting the attacks from the left. They could do no more than watch external events affect them.

The March Revolution did not have a significant effect on the American Socialist party. The news reached the socialists at the end of March when attention was focused on the probability of American intervention, and their reaction, like that of non-socialist Americans, emphasized the effect the revolution might have on the war. The *Leader* commented that with the prospective Russian withdrawal from the war, the allies would redouble their efforts to involve the United States.[29] The revolution, however, did stimulate the morale of the party, which had continually expressed the hope that the war would bolster socialism. There was considerable rejoicing among the many New York socialists, and on the Lower East Side the news was celebrated with a mass gathering at the building of the *Jewish Daily Forward.*

One offshoot of the Russian experience was the formation of the People's Council of America for Democracy and Peace in June 1917. Its goals were to oppose conscription and the suppression of civil liberties and to encourage a negotiated peace. While the People's Council included pacifists and progressives, it was dominated by socialists and was actually a bald imitation of the Russian institution. There was no hope, of course, that such American *soviets* would lead a revolution,[30] but the councils seemed to be a useful gimmick for capturing the support of non-socialists.

Morris Hillquit was one of the organizers of the People's Council, and while Berger agreed that his own name might be used as a founder, and while he spoke at its opening rally at Madison Square Garden, he was not active in the national organization. He concentrated his efforts on the Milwaukee branch where his wife, Meta, served on the executive board and an adopted nephew, Carl Haesseler, was the state organizer. The *Leader* publicized the activities of the People's Council, both nationally and locally. Emil Seidel, the former mayor, was active in the local organization as was the Reverend Irwin St. John Tucker, who worked in the National Office of the party and was a founder of the Chicago branch of the Council.[31]

The Council's path was not a smooth one. The AFL organized the American Alliance for Labor and Decmocracy in order to limit the success of the Council, and A. M. Simons was one of the Alliance's most enthusiastic supporters.[32] The Gompers organization harassed and smeared the socialist Council and ultimately prevented the meeting of a convention scheduled for Minneapolis on 1 September.

The Socialist party threw its support behind the proposed convention. Berger was delegated by the Wisconsin State Executive Committee of the party to represent it, and an NEC meeting was scheduled for 31 August in Minneapolis to insure the attendance of leading party figures. James H. Maurer was the most ardent supporter of the Council among the party leadership, and he was to be the temporary chairman at the convention. He had devoted the summer of 1917 to speaking tours for the Council. While on tour, he had noted the hardening war attitude of the public, and was most anxious for the success of the convention. In Maurer's capacity as President of the Pennsylvania Federation of Labor, he challenged Gompers's authority to commit the AFL to support of the war and the American Alliance for Labor and Democracy, and thus caused a breach in their relationship that he had carefully avoided up until then.

Despite the painstaking plans made for the convention by the party, it was not held. The governor of Minnesota insisted at the last minute that they could not meet, while the Gompers group attempted to tie up all possible Minneapolis convention sites. Socialist Mayor Dan Hoan invited the People's Council delegates, stranded in the Twin

Cities, to convene in Milwaukee, but Governor Emanuel L. Philipp over-ruled him and refused to be persuaded by Berger's telephoned pleas. Finally, in a farcical situation in Chicago, where the mayor did not op-pose a convention, thirteen determined delegates met furtively in a member's apartment and conducted the business of the "convention" in only a few hours, hurrying to finish before the arrival of state troopers dispatched by the governor. The harassments to which the People's Council was subject, as a body in opposition to war and as an apparently foreign-oriented organization, illustrate the obstacles thrown into the path of propagandists for peace.[33]

The immediate reaction of American socialists to the November Bolshevik Revolution was one of unsurpassed joy. It appeared to be the culmination of their dreams. Those who had believed in the necessity of a bloody revolution sweeping aside bourgeois and capitalist rejoiced to see it materialize in Russia. Others, like Berger, who had favored a bloodless transition to the socialist system, rationalized that some shed-ding of blood had been inevitable, but in the face of such a triumph it hardly mattered. Hillquit thought that the revolution gave meaning and historical significance to the war. The left wing's enthusiasm was un-bounded and it petitioned the National Executive Committee to endorse each action taken by the Bolshevik government. Local Kings County in Brooklyn and Local Boston requested that the NEC ask locals to demonstrate for the Russian armistice proposal, and both were angry when the committee deferred action until the scheduled policy discus-sions.[34]

The Class Struggle blasted the NEC for its tardiness in responding formally to the Bolshevik conquest of Russia. It accused the entire com-mittee—Berger, Hillquit, Stedman, Work, and Anna A. Maley—of waiting cautiously to see whether or not the Bolsheviks stayed in power before they lined up with them. This was the first serious denunciation issued by the left against the right in the struggle over the relationship of the American socialists to the Russians. *The Class Struggle* charged that actual distaste for Bolshevik tactics was responsible for the committee's silence, which was in contrast to the messages of solidarity sent by European socialists to the Bolsheviks. The Russians, it said, were too "uncompromisingly revolutionary, so little respectable, so ridiculously proletarian." Unlike so many charges hurled at one side by the other, this one turned out to be more fact than fiction. Only in mid-Febru-ary 1918, did the NEC align itself with the Russian government in telegrams to President Wilson and members of Congress urging adherence to its peace program.[35]

Soon after the change of government in Russia, President Wilson enunciated his war aims and peace plan. The aims were not vastly different from the socialists' conception of a just peace. Indeed, except for the latter's goal of democratic socialism, the differences were of degree, not of kind.

By early 1918, the Socialist party was in the anomalous position of supporting, at least *de jure,* a proclamation which did not apply to a situation now wholly altered: Wilson's Fourteen Points and the demise of the czarist ally gave the war involvement a new cast. And yet there was no enthusiasm among the right wing leaders for rushing into a second statement. Because of its experience of harassment by state and federal officials and the party's growing identification in the public mind with subversion, if not treason, the leadership was cautious about attempting policy shifts. In the face of government persecution (See Ch. 9), the bravado shared by even a few of the reformists at the St. Louis convention had disappeared. In addition, the growing spirit of the left wing made the reformist leaders circumspect in their actions. The left drew vicarious sustenance from the successes of the Russian comrades, and their new boldness troubled the right. The more the left clamored for imitation of Russian means and ends, the more tempered became the right wing's enthusiasm for the Russian example. Only five months after the revolution, Hillquit admitted to a sense of skepticism regarding chances of Bolshevik success and acknowledged his disagreement with some of their policies.[36]

The reformist camp was caught in a kind of schizophrenia in which it feared to move to the left or to the right. And so, after its brief enthusiasm of November, the NEC continued upholding the status quo despite its recognition of the changed national and international situations. Men like Berger who believed in adaptability as a principle of growth found themselves involved in an inevitably self-defeating holding action.

Berger favored selectivity in the party's observance of the St. Louis program. He argued that policy must be flexible, and therefore certain measures enunciated in April might yet be supported while the now superfluous ones should be ignored. He assured members that no principle would be sacrificed and stressed that the valid clauses were those endorsing the nationalization of giant industries, the socialization of natural resources, the continued striving for peace, and the resistance to reactionary governmental measures.[37]

Most of the party leaders remained fearful of holding a policy-making convention because the hectic and emotional atmosphere would render calm and reasonable discussion even less attainable than in 1917. Moreover, the stringency with which the socialist press was censored by the postal authorities would prevent a meaningful preliminary discussion in the party newspaper.[38]

Nevertheless, the demands for a convention to reformulate the war program came from all sides. Adolph Germer, the Executive Secretary, favored a new socialist initiative to end the war. A rumor appeared briefly that 95 percent of all Jewish socialists denounced the party position after the German invasion of socialist-led Russia. *The Liberator,* socialist successor to *The Masses,* had endorsed Wilson's war aims and now demanded the overhaul of the party program, arguing that it was not related to the current situation. The existence of a soviet republic in urgent need of assistance and of reasonable American war aims made mandatory an updated socialist platform. Allan L. Benson, who was three months away from his resignation from the party, strongly favored Wilson's announced aims and wrote that the party rank and file supported its government. In demanding a convention where socialist loyalty to the government could be expressed, Benson said the official toleration of profiteering—severely denounced by the party—was an irrelevant issue. After all, he pointed out, Marx favored Lincoln despite the more serious profiteering of that day.[39]

The New Appeal whose change in name marked the paper's change of policy, vociferously denounced the NEC's failure to endorse American war aims. It called the party leaders un-American and anti-socialist and charged the hierarchy with preventing the party from joining an international fight against autocracy: "Very, very few Socialists, who are not pro-German at heart, can be confused about the great issues involved in this war." In a later issue, Carl D. Thompson, still on the fringes of the party, noted what he called the constructive program of the Inter-Allied Socialists in contrast to the American socialists' program. He argued that the latter stance violated the socialist principle of obedience to law and also the principle of majority rule since most socialists favored the war effort. It was only a matter of time before *The New Appeal* cut its remaining ties to the party. That fall in the congressional elections it campaigned against socialists whom it considered disloyal to the American government.[40]

As the conflict raged, Debs joined the fray and issued a personal statement in which he affirmed his support for the anti-war St. Louis Proclamation but insisted that new conditions required new responses. He pleaded for a special convention in order to hear the voice of the rank and file. But Debs insisted that he was in no sense calling for support of the American government and he reiterated his condemnation of nationalistic German Social Democrats.[41]

The National Executive Committee refused to be moved by the tumult and insisted that current conditions within the country made full and frank discussion impossible.[42] Yet the sequence of events led to violations and alterations of the program by reformist leaders. Congressman London worked within the government in an effort to soften domestic policies. While he was a maverick in Congress—his was the only vote against the declaration of war on Austria-Hungary—he was criticized within the party for failure to maintain what London termed "unreasonable opposition." He believed the socialists must participate in guiding the forces released in wartime, and the only party restriction which he accepted on his activities was the prohibition against voting for military measures. The heavy criticism to which he was subject from his party comrades led to rumors of his expulsion. His local demanded that he defend his actions before it and finally asked the NEC to insist that London observe the party position in Congress. London's unpopularity with the New York left wingers led to a campaign against him and to his defeat in the congressional election of 1918.[43]

Meyer London was not the only socialist who sought a viable relationship to the nation at war. The socialist aldermen in New York City supported the third Liberty Loan drive of April 1918. Victor Berger also endorsed that drive. During Berger's trial late in 1918, the prosecution was to charge that his support of the drive represented a last minute effort to curry favor with federal authorities. However, Berger believed that resistance to the bond drive invited financial and physical reprisals because of the excited, even hysterical, state of public opinion in 1918. Therefore, he encouraged readers of the Milwaukee *Leader* and party members to look upon the bonds as a tax that could not be avoided and to purchase all that they could afford. He tried to explain that he did not seek to encourage the sale of bonds but to invite broad compliance with

the law. Dan Hoan, as mayor of Milwaukee, was in an awkward situation. Berger advised him to carry out those provisions of the draft
which fell to his office,[44] but the difficulties in coordinating mayoralty duties with responsibilities to the Socialist party would eventually
lead Hoan into conflict with the party and with Berger himself. The
anomalous position of those socialists attempting to adapt policy to individual roles invited attack by the left whether or not they had compromised on principles, and the leftists consistently exploited their vulnerability.

Even before the reformists had an opportunity to demonstrate
fidelity or infidelity to the St. Louis Proclamation, the left wing assumed
the offensive. Following the St. Louis convention, Berger, Hillquit, and
Algernon Lee were chosen by the NEC to represent the party at the
Russian-inspired Stockholm peace conference. A protest was at once
registered with the still-extant National Committee that all three were
German imperialists. The leftists charged that in choosing the delegates,
the hierarchy was running the party in a high-handed manner and exploiting the reluctance of the members to charge the leaders with German leanings. A referendum on the international delegates was
demanded.[45]

The National Committee was exasperated and Berger was furious,
particularly over the charge that the *Leader*'s editorial policy had been
pro-German ever since August 1914. Berger complained that such attacks on party members under cover of radical phraseology could be as
damaging to the organization as actions of others under the guise of
patriotism.[46]

From this experience the party leadership learned to be more
cautious. At the end of the year a referendum was conducted to choose
three delegates to any international socialist conference that might be
called. Berger, Hillquit, and George R. Kirkpatrick, the party's 1916
candidate for the vice-presidency, were elected despite the left.[47] In
response, *The Class Struggle* initiated a campaign to discredit Berger
and to remove him from the delegation. Berger's presence, it charged,
would lend color to the inevitable accusations that a socialist peace conference had a German bias. After all, Berger favored every German initiative and defended each German excess, in repudiation of principles
of international socialism as well as the anti-war position of the party.
"A born jingo," the article continued, "he has been a German jingo and
an American jingo by turns—contriving a synthesis of the two which

has become familiar under the name of Hearstism, an attempt to put American jingoism at the service of German imperialism.'' Those locals which wished to be represented at an international conference by an international socialist rather than ''a Hindenberg Socialist'' were invited to demand Berger's recall.[48] The plea fell on deaf ears. This one time, at least, Berger escaped the harassment of a recall motion.

Morris Hillquit was another reformist to experience the wrath of the left. Hillquit and the Socialist Campaign Committee of Greater New York were charged with modifying the position of absolute opposition to the war. Hillquit, *The Class Struggle* maintained, approached the war from the point of view of expediency rather than principle and advised that each war situation had its own exigencies, thus freeing members from party policy.

The journal surveyed the activities of various party members and declared that the Socialist party was in chaos. An indeterminate number of members were ignoring the war policy and with the refusal of the leadership to call a convention, there was no way to formulate a satisfactory position. *The Class Struggle* pleaded against equivocation as potentially destructive and demanded that a national convention be held.[49]

The issue had become explosive and it was no longer possible to avoid it. Adolph Germer suggested to the NEC that its conference, with the state secretaries on the congressional elections, scheduled for August, be held as early as June so that a new war statement might be considered at once. He urged that both a declaration of democratic war aims and a constructive economic program without endorsement of the war itself be issued.

The meeting date was not changed, but it was publicized as an opportunity for the rank and file to be heard and war policy re-evaluated. Critics loudly predicted a machine-controlled conference run by the bosses of the party.[50]

The conference met in Chicago from 10 to 12 August. The delegates were welcomed by a fiery address from the recently indicted Gene Debs, who came to the meeting because of anxiety over party wavering. It was not his custom to participate in policy meetings and usually he was unavailable during a convention. During the war, Debs had floundered in his search for a policy much as had the reformist leaders in the months after the St. Louis convention. His infrequent pronouncements attacked the capitalist class in the same tone as his pre-

war excoriations. But with the *de facto* dilution of party policy by socialist officials, Debs became aroused and saw clearly the path he must
follow.[51] He chose the August conference of party officials as his opportunity to energize the members as a whole to a reinvigorated opposition to the capitalist war.

Debs received the ovation due a visiting celebrity. His plea that
there be no modification of the party's attitude toward the war was
answered with tumultuous cheers and shouts. He stressed that workingmen had no place in the capitalist war then raging, that the only
struggle of interest to them was that between the classes. He mentioned
governmental harassment of the party and said that it was a bloody ordeal costing the party only its non-socialist adherents. He ended with
the statement that ''All my life I have never been so proud of being a Socialist as I am today.''[52]

Debs set the tone for the conference and denied the National Executive Committee the initiative. Even if the reformists had desired to
alter the party's war program formally—and there is no evidence that
they were in substantial enough agreement to do so—they had been
disarmed by their presidential nominee emeritus. The reformists were
strongly dissatisfied with the existing program, as illustrated by their
many violations of it, but the modification of that program would have
involved great tact and skill due to the emotionalism rampant in the
country and the party. There probably was no interest in going on
record a second time and opening wider the possibilities of attack from
both the government and the party left wing. Ultimately Debs's speech
terminated any fleeting inclination to fashion a new policy—particularly since the state secretaries represented both factions.

The three-day meeting involved a series of arguments. Every issue,
no matter now insignificant, was thrashed out in great detail, from the
proper length of articles in the congressional platform to the shaping of
that platform. The members of the NEC played a conspicuously minor
role in the debates, permitting the less controversial right wingers to
carry on the fight for them. Instead of a formal restatement of war
policy, the right led the conference into enunciation of a constructive
position on the problems created by war, softening the St. Louis tone of
opposition. The congressional platform dwelt upon the party's peace
aims, reconstruction, and the guarantee of civil liberties. The conference endorsed the Bolshevik regime in merely a restatement of the
NEC stance of the previous winter.[53]

The revolutionist wing left the conference in a state of high agitation. Joseph M. Coldwell, the state secretary of Rhode Island and a leftist spokesman, remarked bitterly that a conference without legislative power should never again be held. He argued that the delegates gathered there represented the heart of the socialist movement and should have had the authority to act. Coldwell's role as a leader of the left against the reformist hierarchy was prophetic, for it was shortly to be enhanced.[54]

That the conference accomplished anything more than formal preparations for the November congressional campaign is doubtful. The confrontation between the two factions had indicated only that the right was too insecure to permit a policy-making role to any group outside of the NEC, and that the left was bitter and rebellious. The conference proved that the party was thoroughly divided and unable to respond to events in the outside world. It remained thus frozen for the duration of the war.

The right wingers bore heavy responsibilities for the party's wartime failure. Had they been prepared to confront the left wingers directly at St. Louis, the party might have followed its traditional path of acting in response to national developments. Instead, Berger and his comrades were immobilized by the threat they saw in the left wing revival. At St. Louis they were innocents, unprepared to meet intrigue with intrigue and found themselves lamely following a policy stimulated by the exuberance of the left wingers.

It was the responsibility of the reformists, since they manned the national offices, to implement the party position, but in good conscience they could not since they lacked faith in it. In the meantime they had lost trusted allies as a result of the proclamation, and those remaining found their ability to manipulate and maneuver limited. They were increasingly isolated and attacked until the leaders were reduced to passivity. They initiated no new policy, not even the formulation of a more congenial program. Instead, they mouthed their loyalty to the existing one while many simultaneously dodged its provisions.

The pattern of the dilemma was exemplified by Berger's actions. He was so badly jolted by the weak position of the right wing at St. Louis that he was unable to throw himself into the proceedings with his accustomed vigor. He withdrew and barely participated in policy-making, and that withdrawal continued so that he might as well have been absent from the Chicago conference in August for all he contributed. His inability to pursue his cherished principle of molding party policy to American exigencies at the time of the interventionist crisis helped move the party toward self-inflicted destruction. Berger's own failure in the face of admittedly inauspicious conditions was partially responsible for the demise of the party as he had known it. Indeed, by 1918 Berger had become a stranger in his own party. He reaped the results of the wartime errors of the socialists more than any other individual, as government persecution of the Milwaukee socialist occurred on three levels. He became the most persecuted leader of the Socialist party, and out of his despair over the party's route and his concern for his own position, continually challenged by the federal government, his withdrawal from national activities became complete in fact, if not in name. In 1918 he was one of the fifteen party members elected to the expanded National Executive Committee which was still dominated by the right but which now contained vocal elements of the left. But Berger's attention was centered upon his personal ordeal and party contingencies became of marginal importance to him. He had not defected from the party as had, for example, John Spargo, but if Berger were asked, he would be likely to reply that the party had abandoned its traditions and principles, and had even abandoned Berger himself as the staunchest defender of those traditions.

NOTES

1. Socialist Party, *Proceedings of the 1917 Emergency Convention*, I, First Day, 106. (System of organization in the two volumes is hopeless; all pagination in footnotes should be viewed skeptically.)
2. Ibid., I, 116, 122-123.
3. The right was represented by Berger, Hillquit, Job Harriman, Algernon Lee, and John Spargo, while the left was represented by Kate Richards O'Hare, Kate Sadler, Charles E. Ruthenberg, and Louis B. Boudin, the latter a prominent left-wing lawyer from New York. The other members were Patrick Quinlan of New Jersey, Dan Hogan of Arkansas, Maynard Shipley of Maryland, Frank Midney of Ohio, Walter P. Dillon of New Mexico and George Spiess of Connecticut.

4. John M. Work, "The First World War," *Wisconsin Magazine of History* 41: 34.

5. Milwaukee *Leader,* 9 April 1917, 10 April 1917.

6. *Berger Trial,* IV, 3117; Work, "The First World War," p. 34.

7. New York, Senate, Report of the Joint Legislative Committee Investigating Seditious Activities, *Revolutionary Radicalism* (Albany, 1920), I, 613-618. This four-volume report reprints many scarce radical documents of the period and the commentary provides insight into the atmosphere prevalent during the Red Scare. The report was popularly called the Lusk Report (hereafter cited as *Revolutionary Radicalism*).

8. John Spargo, *Americanism and Social Democracy* (New York: Harper and Bros., Pubs., 1918), p. 282; Louis B. Boudin, "The Emergency National Convention," *The Class Struggle* 1 (May-June 1917): 46; Spargo's report is found in his *Americanism and Social Democracy,* pp. 283-292.

9. Boudin, "The Emergency National Convention," p. 50.

10. Selig Perlman and Philip Taft argue that the war caused a rebirth of the radical tone in the Socialist party as a whole, the drawing of the left and right together and the minimizing of their differences until the Bolshevik Revolution widened them later. John R. Commons, ed., *History of Labor in the United States,* Vol. 4, Selig Perlman and Philip Taft, *Labor Movements, 1896-1932* (New York: Macmillan Co., 1935), p. 422. Shannon endorses this view of temporary peace in the party. See *The Socialist Party of America: A History* (New York: Macmillan Co., 1955), p. 97.

11. *Berger Trial,* IV, 3117; Sally M. Miller, "Socialist Party Decline and World War I," *Science and Society* 34 (Winter 1970): 410-411.

12. Milwaukee *Leader,* 14 April 1917; Berger to Henry Tichenor, 25 April 1917, Berger to Mrs. William Bross Lloyd, 20 April 1917, Berger to Hillquit, 10 May 1917, Berger Col., MCHS; Ernest Untermann to Paul Gauer, 22 January 1954, Untermann to Frederick I. Olson, 1 September 1947, Untermann Col., MCHS.

13. Work, "The First World War," pp. 35-36; John M. Work, "Autobiography," II, Ch. 3, 6-7, typescript, John M. Work Collection, SHSW.

14. Job Harriman to Hillquit, 14 May 1918, 14 June 1920, 27 May 1920, Hillquit Col., SHSW.

15. Milwaukee *Leader,* 16 April 1917.

16. Leslie Marcy, "The Emergency National Convention," *International Socialist Review* 17 (May 1917): 665-666; Frank Bohn, "To the Old Guard," *International Socialist Review* 17 (May 1917): 684-685.

17. Louis B. Boudin, "The National Convention and Its War Resolution," *The Class Struggle* 1 (May-June 1917): 100; "Debate between Louis C. Fraina and Robert R. La Monte," *The Class Struggle* 1 (July-August 1917): 98.

18. Louis F. Post to Simons, 26 March 1917, Simons Col., SHSW.

19. Senator Paul O. Husting to Simons, 15 May 1917, ibid. Simons's original letter is found in the New York *Call* of 11 May 1917 and the *Congressional Record* of that date.

20. Berger to Hillquit, 21 May 1917, 7 June 1917, Berger Col., MCHS; May Wood Simons, Diary, 20 August 1917, 17 November 1917, Simons Col., SHSW; Kent and Gretchen Kreuter, *An American Dissenter: The Life of Algie Martin Simons* (Lexington: University of Kentucky Press, 1969), pp. 174-175; Kenneth E. Hendrickson, Jr., "The Pro-War Socialists and the Drive for Industrial Democracy, 1917-1920," *Labor History* 11 (Summer 1970); 309-311. Hendrickson remarks (pp. 321-322) that "the 'pro-war socialist movement' might be better labeled the 'pro-war, non-socialist movement.' "

21. Walling to New York *Globe,* 3 May 1917, Walling Col., SHSW. Charles Edward Russell credited his former colleagues with sincerity as socialists but said that "when the pinch came, they could not eradicate from the blood and mind the old instinct of the tribe." Thus he also connected the entire party with the German antecedents of a few. Russell, *Bare Hands and Stone Walls: Some Recollections of a Sideline Reformer* (New York: Charles Scribner's Sons, 1933), p. 288.

22. Milwaukee *Leader,* 17 May 1917; *American Socialist,* 12 May 1917, 19 May 1917. Russell, in his memoirs, termed his expulsion ironic because he had done only what the German Social Democrats had done, accepted a position in a capitalist government. Russell, *Bare Hands and Stone Walls,* p. 294. Kreuter, *An American Dissenter,* pp. 165-166.

23. Spargo, *Americanism and Social Democracy,* pp. 298-302, 306, 317-323.

24. Herron to Hyndman, 1 July 1918, Simons Statement to the Associated Press, 15 July 1917, Algie to May Wood Simons, 24 July 1917, Simons Col., SHSW.

25. Thomas Booth, G. B. Manchester, and F. G. Shallenbliger to Meyer London, 14 May 1917, London Col., Tamiment Institute; Milwaukee *Leader*, 14 July 1917, 28 July 1917. The number of new members exceeded the number of defectors.

26. Ibid., 9 June 1917, 19 June 1917; Alexander Trachtenberg, ed., *The American Socialists and the War* (New York: Rand School of Social Science, 1917); *Berger Trial*, III, 2404.

27. London telegram to President W. S. Tacheidse, 17 April 1917, London Col., Tamiment Institute; Ludwig Lore, "Meyer London," *The Class Struggle* 1 (September-October, 1917): 99-100.

28. Milwaukee *Leader*, 6 April 1917; Work, "The First World War," p. 37.

29. Milwaukee *Leader*, 26 March 1917.

30. Ibid., 31 May 1917; Berger to Hillquit, 11 August 1917, Berger Col., MCHS. Berger wrote that the People's Council could not expect to equal the Russians' achievement because there the soviets controlled the unions and the soldiers. Morris Hillquit, *Loose Leaves from a Busy Life* (New York: Macmillan Co., 1934), p. 172.

31. Milwaukee *Leader*, 9 July 1917, 31 July 1917, 1 September 1917.

32. Simons to May Wood Simons, 5 September 1917, Simons Col., SHSW.

33. Milwaukee *Leader*, 8 August 1917, 25 August 1917, 4 September 1917; James H. Maurer, *It Can be Done* (New York: Rand School of Social Science, 1938), pp. 225-228; Work, "The First World War," p. 37; Hillquit, *Loose Leaves from a Busy Life*, p. 179.

34. Hillquit, *Loose Leaves from a Busy Life*, p. 277; Ludwig Lore, "Our NEC," *The Class Struggle* 2 (January-February, 1918): 123.

35. Lore, "Our NEC," pp. 123-125; *The Eye Opener*, 15 February 1918.

36. Hillquit to Harriman, 30 April 1918, Hillquit Col., SHSW. But he thought the revolution was of great service to the socialist movement because of the shock given to the world.

37. Milwaukee *Leader,* 7 January 1918.

38. Hillquit to Harriman, 30 March 1918, Hillquit Col., SHSW; Trachtenberg, "International Labor and Socialist News," *The Liberator* 1 (July 1918): 31. This issue contains the minutes of the NEC meeting of 6 and 7 May.

39. Germer to Hillquit, 4 March 1918, Hillquit Col., SHSW; editorial, *The Liberator* 1 (July 1918): 1; Allan L. Benson, "Benson Scores Proposal to Withdraw United States Army," *The New Appeal,* 6 April 1918.

40. Editorial, *The New Appeal,* 18 May 1918, 26 October 1918; Carl D. Thompson, "Must Rescind S. Louis Platform," *The New Appeal,* 1 June 1918.

41. Debs, "Personal Statement," Spring 1918, typescript, Debs Col., Tamiment Institute.

42. Trachtenberg, *The Liberator* 1 (July 1918): 31; Hillquit to Harriman, 28 June 1918, Hillquit Col., SHSW.

43. Harry Rogoff, *An East Side Epic: The Life and Work of Meyer London* (New York: Vanguard Press, 1930), pp. 104-105, 108, 159.

44. Milwaukee *Leader,* 20 April 1918, 28 September 1918; Robert C. Reinders, "Daniel W. Hoan and the Milwaukee Socialist Party during the First World War," *Wisconsin Magazine of History* 36 (Autumn 1952): 49.

45. Louis B. Boudin to National Committee, 23 June 1917, Boudin to Germer, 4 June 1917, Berger Col., MCHS. The three were denied passports by the federal government and never left the country.

46. Berger to Germer, 4 June 1917, to Hillquit, 7 June 1917, Berger Col., MCHS.

47. *The Eye Opener,* 12 January 1918.

48. "Recall Berger," *The Class Struggle* 2 (March-April 1918): 229-232.

49. Boudin, "Act Not Withdraw," *The Class Struggle* 1 (November-December 1917): 106-107; "St. Louis and After," *The Class Struggle* 2 (January-February 1918): 126-128; Boudin, "St. Louis—One Year After," *The Class Struggle* 2 (May-June 1918): 338-340.

50. Germer to NEC, 6 May 1918, Berger Col., MCHS; editorial, *The New Appeal,* 18 May 1918.

51. See his biographer on his wartime confusion, Ray Ginger, *Eugene V. Debs: A Biography* (New York: Collier Books, 1962), especially pp. 364-365, 368.

52. Socialist Party, *Minutes* of the Joint Conference of

the National Executive Committee and State Executive Committee and State Secretaries, August 1918, pp. 17-21.

53. The Congressional Platform of 1918 is found in the SP *Congressional Manual* of that year, in *The Eye Opener* of August 1918, and in *The Liberator* of 18 October 1918.

54. SP *Minutes* of the Joint Conference, pp. 358-359. It would be Coldwell who would lead a considerable number of leftists out of the September 1919 Emergency Convention over contested seats.

9
The Crucifixion of Berger

When the United States finally made its commitment to intervention, the successful prosecution of the war became an all-consuming interest. For the government and for most of the nation nothing mattered other than victory and to the achievement of that victory everything was sacrificed. The prosecution of the war occurred not only on the battlefields of Europe and on the seas but on the home front as well—in churches, schools, and public forums. It became mandatory that each citizen pledge the same total commitment to victory as had the government. Any whose dedication differed in pattern or degree were, in turn, suspect, persecuted, and prosecuted. And for those who questioned the causes or purposes of the war, there was no sanctuary.

In order to ensure considerable enthusiasm for the war among the citizenry, the federal government organized the Committee on Public Information. The committee's task, in the words of its chairman, George Creel, was the eradication of pacifist and pro-German opinion—which the government noted particularly in the middle west —and the development of an understanding of national ideals.[1] Patriotism was preached to the public by every means available— newspapers, pamphlets, films, posters. "The public press had followed . . . the pattern and the net result had been an indoctrination of hate, prejudice, and 100 per cent Americanism on a colossal scale." As historian Robert K. Murray remarks, the government conscripted and mobilized public opinion as it did men and money. The predictable result was the termination of the free play of opinion.

A number of private, subsidiary helpmates for the Committee on Public Information arose. The National Security League, the American Defense Society, various state loyalty leagues, and the government-sponsored American Protective League all strove to instill patriotism by spreading propaganda exaggerating the dangers of domestic sabotage and sedition. These organizations were complemented by several associations of employers, such as the National Association of Manufacturers, which also sought to inculcate patriotism and expose disloyalty, with their particular sphere of activity the organized labor movement. These groups became the repositories of elements whose concern for healthy nationalism was smothered by an overwhelming interest in strengthening economic and political conservatism. The overlapping personnel of the patriotic societies and employer organizations implicitly revealed the close connection seen by these groups between patriotism and the security of private property and the major goal of the maintenance of economic conservatism.

The tendencies fostered by these groups—support for the conservative, distrust of the radical—were immeasurably stimulated during the course of the war by the emergence of bolshevism.[2] Bolshevism aroused intense animosity in the United States because of the separate peace its leaders signed, thus depriving the nation of an ally, and because of its ideologically frightening and aggressive appeals. When that same ideology was echoed within the United States, the wrath of the populace turned upon those related in any vague manner to the new threat, inevitably the very same individuals and groups already suspect because of their attitudes to the war.

Therefore, the American government and public turned against the Socialist party and other radical organizations as alien and subversive. Whereas the party had hitherto been tolerated by the public, as the result of government-led hysteria it now found itself treated as an illegal organization and an intolerable threat in American politics. Diversity, earlier permissible, became perverse in wartime. The pathological intensity with which the war was pursued allowed for no individualism, and the Socialist party lost its hopes, appeal, and indeed its constitutional right of free speech. The tragedy the United States experienced during World War I, apart from the battlefield itself, was "the suppression of debate and inquiry so important to the democratic process."[3]

The first amendment to the constitution became a major casualty of the war. As the Espionage Act and its successors revealed, the government preferred saving the country without the constitution to saving the constitution but possibly losing the country. That the war could be won only at the cost of free speech and free press was an assumption the government and the badgered public refused to question. The prevailing notion appeared to be that the Bill of Rights was a peacetime luxury.

The national press was attuned to the danger of government censorship at the opening of congressional discussion on the Espionage Act, and it successfully opposed a clause which provided punishment for inaccurate reporting. After this victory, however, the press abandoned its concern for the first amendment and supported restrictive legislation and also exercised self-censorship.

The Espionage Act of 15 June 1917 made it a crime to report inexact news which sought to interfere with the armed forces, to cause military insubordination, or to obstruct conscription; such offenses were subject to fines of $10,000 or twenty years imprisonment, or both. The act prohibited from the mails any matter that violated the provisions. A Trading-with-the-Enemy Act, passed 6 October 1917, reinforced the censorship provisions of the Espionage Act and resulted in the first government censorship board. Despite their wide scope, the two acts were deemed inadequate by federal authorities because they did not reach individual and impulsive actions. To rectify the omissions of the earlier legislation, on 16 May 1918 the popularly known Sedition Act was passed which specified nine further offenses, including *attempts* to obstruct the draft, publication of disloyal matter, and interference with the sale of government bonds. The net had been cast wide enough to catch anyone committing an unacceptable action. Little distinction existed in public opinion "between a person who really threatened the country's security and one who opposed war in principle or who demanded a statement of peace objectives."[4]

The Socialist party quickly collided with the restrictive legislation. Berger, Hillquit, and Algernon Lee, the delegates to the socialist peace conference at Stockholm, were denied passports by the American government on the grounds that in their non-official capacity they could not negotiate for the government, which of course they did not intend to do. Berger confessed to considerable embarrassment that the Russian Council of Workingmen had to cable Washington to plead for passports for the three delegates.[5]

By the middle of July, issues of fifteen major socialist publications had been excluded from the mails on accusations of violations of the Espionage Act. These publications included *The Masses*, the *International Socialist Review*, *The Appeal to Reason*, the *American Socialist*, the New York *Call*, and the Milwaukee *Leader*. The publications were aided in their efforts to regain their mailing privileges by the National Civil Liberties Union, which had evolved from the pre-war American Union Against Militarism. On 13 July, the Union held an emergency conference with editors of suppressed papers and sent several prominent attorneys, including Clarence Darrow, a perennial ally of the Socialist party who endorsed the war effort, Frank P. Walsh, a progressive who had chaired the pre-war federal Commission on Industrial Relations, and Socialist attorneys Morris Hillquit and Seymour Stedman, to see Postmaster General Albert S. Burleson in order to obtain a clear statement of censorship policy.[6] The delegation was not successful.

Max Eastman of *The Masses* wrote to President Wilson after the August issue was declared unmailable and asked bluntly if the President's authority was behind the Post Office's destruction of socialist journals. Wilson's reply candidly stated his position that "a time of war must be regarded as wholly exceptional and [that] it is legitimate to regard things which would in ordinary circumstances be innocent as very dangerous to the public welfare. . . . A line must be drawn and . . . we are trying . . . to draw it without fear or favor or prejudice." On the whole Wilson's interest was at best cursory and the problem of censorship was left to the postal authorities who delegated power to subordinates lacking in enthusiasm for constitutional rights.[7]

With the suppression of radical publications in wholesale numbers, a cry of alarm went up in left of center circles. Even some who had already cut their ties with radical organizations spoke up in their behalf. Upton Sinclair wrote to Wilson to call to his attention the acts of minor officials which, Sinclair said, contradicted Wilson's appeal for democracy. He supported the suppression of alien-edited socialist papers, but pleaded for the rights of American citizens to offer criticisms. Debs insisted, in a newspaper immediately suppressed, that the socialists must hold their ground. He wrote that the sacrifice of individuals and periodicals was of minor concern when measured against the principles of the entire movement. Norman Thomas, then a Presbyterian minister, was led by the wartime injustices to the realization of his own socialist proclivities. He admired the party's struggle for freedom of speech and, by the end of the war, despite some personal reservations, applied for membership in order to encourage unity among radicals.[8]

Morris Hillquit actively defended the suppressed publications in the courts and at public rallies. He told a meeting at Madison Square Garden that the federal government was seeking to destroy the Socialist party. He described the censorship apparatus of the government and explained how an assistant to the Postmaster General "never elected by the people and totally unknown to the people is the sole accuser, judge and executioner of the people's organs of public expression. He is a prolific accuser, a merciless judge and prompt executioner."[9]

But the popular press saw no cause for alarm. Outside of a number of former radicals, current radicals, and those still suffering the birth pangs of radicalism, few defended the constitution. Meyer London's voice was nearly the only one heard in Congress demanding the absolute right of freedom of expression.[10]

In addition to the suppression of socialist newspapers, including the *American Socialist,* individual party members were involved in constant litigation. Indeed, the party ultimately issued a legal reference book for those indicted under the various restrictive acts. Of the approximately one hundred and fifty convictions under the Espionage Act, most involved German-Americans and radicals, such as members of the Socialist party, the Industrial Workers of the World, or the Non-Partisan League.[11]

The Executive Secretary of the party, Adolph Germer, was tried in October 1917 with members of Local Grand Rapids, Michigan, for the distribution of anti-war literature and won acquittal. The Rand School of Social Science was indicted for the publication of a book about the war entitled *The Great Madness.* Interestingly, the author, Professor Scott Nearing, was acquitted while the school was found guilty of violating the Espionage Act.[12]

Many socialists were indicted for specific acts of war opposition. Charles Ruthenberg and Alfred Wagenknecht were each sentenced to one year for inducing men not to register for the draft, while Louis C. Fraina was sentenced to thirty days for conspiracy to violate the Draft Act through his public remarks on conscientious objection. Kate Richards O'Hare was convicted and imprisoned for five years for a speech in which she discouraged enlistment, while Rose Pastor Stokes, wife of the millionaire Socialist party defector Graham Phelps Stokes, received a sentence of ten years for a letter she wrote to the Kansas City *Star* in reference to her own speech on war profiteering. The intention to cause insubordination or to obstruct recruitment was the test of guilt.

That there were no practical means to establish intent, no definite standards for a jury to consider, stimulated little comment. Indeed, the already excited public serving in court offered no protection to freedom of speech. Moreover, the typically unrepresentative character of juries was exacerbated during the war; members tended to be financially secure, conservative, and prejudiced against the radicals they tried. Some trial judges revealed their personal sentiments, some even lecturing the jury on their responsibilities in a time of national crisis. [13]

Indictments occurred with increasing momentum throughout 1917 and 1918. In February 1918, five Socialist party leaders, all having some connection with the National Office, were indicted for conspiracy. There was, however, no common denominator among the five either in position or philosophy other than their membership in the party. These indictments confirmed the previously expressed belief among socialists that the federal government was after the party itself rather than subversive individuals. Debs wrote that their only crime was disloyalty to profiteering interests, "and if this be sufficient warrant of their indictment then I appeal to the grand-jury to pay me the same compliment and include me in their number."[14] Debs had to wait only until the following June for his own indictment.

Most of the cases against socialists involved members of the reformist wing of the party, which convinced that group that the federal government was also encouraging the left wing ferment in order to divide and destroy the party. As evidence, the right cited the suppression of almost all its papers, while many on the left were allowed to function.[15] The government may well have enjoyed the growing divergence within the party and abetted it when possible; the fact that more reformists were prosecuted may have been due to their prominent hold on the party machinery, thus inviting attack.

The expenses which government harassment forced on the party were prodigious. On the three most publicized cases involving socialists, the party spent over $14,000—$8,000 on the defense of the five national officers, $5,600 on the Debs trial, and $1,000 for the *Masses* case.[16] These massive expenditures during a time of internal upheaval placed an immense strain on the party. All of the socialist attorneys had to confine their work to the espionage trials, to the exclusion of other party matters. Perhaps the unkindest blow at this time was the loss of Hillquit in the summer of 1918 to a tuberculosis sanitarium. For well over a year, during the greatest crisis in the life of the Socialist party, Hillquit could do nothing but watch events from remote Saranac Lake, New York.

Despite the burdens, the party continued to function. Socialists participated in elections throughout 1917 and 1918 and campaigned more diligently than even before in the face of prosecution and mob persecutions. The November 1917 elections were seen by the party as an opportunity to demonstrate that American sentiment was not pro-war; Berger in fact announced prior to the election that the vote gleaned by the Socialist party would be an indication of peace sentiment. [17]

The most important race was for the mayoralty of New York City. Hillquit registered a 145 percent gain over the socialist total in the previous campaign for that office. Six socialist aldermen were elected for the first time, and the number of assemblymen elected increased from two to eight. The popular press emphasized Hillquit's defeat, and yet his capture of 21.7 percent of the vote in contrast to the socialist total of 5.1 percent in 1913 was striking. The official party paper claimed a great triumph and maintained that the fusion ticket presented by old line parties in New York was a last attempt to defeat socialist candidates. Berger wrote that Hillquit's impressive vote was a defeat for Woodrow Wilson and a mandate for peace negotiations.

Throughout the country, the socialist vote of November 1917 registered marked gains. In Chicago the vote was five times its previous total. The Cleveland vote increased more than fourfold. Party leaders, pleased by the rising numbers, did not delude themselves that the new socialist voters were doctrinal converts. Peace was recognized as the major concern. In addition to attracting the support of the pacifists and the peace-minded, the socialists also won votes from others who resented the abrogation of free speech and even from those who were protesting rising prices with their ballots. The usual lack of accord among socialists ensued, however, as the left wing admonished the reformists for their claims of progress. The campaign was successful, it advised, only if it had created more class-conscious workers who understood the essence of socialism. [18]

Thus during the war, the party leaders continued to hear the same criticisms as before. While faced with severe harassment on all sides, the growing voice of internal discontent consistently resounded. The party officers fought off the government, and simultaneously engaged in a rear-guard action against the perennial left. But the familiar antagonist was bolder than ever and its ultimate triumph over the now weakened party hierarchy became assured after the war ended.

Victor Berger, more than any other party leader, experienced the full wrath of government persecution. From the time of the passage of the Espionage Act until 1920 he was a prime government target in the war on radicalism. In September 1917 Berger was informed by the Post Office Department that the *Leader* was in violation of the Espionage Act. He was invited at once to a private hearing in Washington to show cause why the *Leader* should not be excluded from the mail.

Berger immediately wrote to Postmaster General Burleson, with whom he had served in the Sixty-second Congress. He tried to convince the Texas politician that the destruction of the socialist press would serve only to unbalance the movement, for it would strengthen those who deprecated orderly and evolutionary tactics. He warned that suppression could only produce Russian-like extremism. Berger's arguments went unheeded. Burleson, who remembered his former colleague, would not be brought into a dialogue on the issue of censorship. The Postmaster General explained to a journalist that "the instant you print anything calculated to dishearten the boys in the army or to make them think this is not a just or righteous war—that instant you will be suppressed and no amount of influence will save you."[19] This was his answer to requests for guidance on publishable matter. When pressed further, he would only advise that a paper ignore the war entirely.

Despite Burleson's warning that influence would not avail, Berger turned to his powerful contacts. To everyone he insisted that the *Leader* had never advocated resistance to war measures, never hindered the military, and had no connection with Germany. He appealed to Arthur Brisbane, the Hearst columnist who had helped Berger in organizing the *Leader,* and begged him to talk to friends in Washington on behalf of the paper. Brisbane spoke to Burleson, who insisted that Berger incited rebellion by calling the draft illegal.

When Berger visited Washington for his informal hearing, he managed to get an appointment with Colonel Edward M. House, President Wilson's special assistant. House was cordial to him. He promised to try to speak to both Wilson and Burleson about the *Leader,* and subsequently Berger, in response to a request, sent House a statement on the necessity of a free press. He added a notation that it would be bad politics to embitter a growing political party which had given Wilson 350,000 votes in his 1916 campaign.

He was convinced that the Wilson administration wanted to destroy the paper as an effective socialist voice, and when Burleson told him that he would suppress any newspaper that maintained that the war was a phenomenon of the capitalist system, Berger despaired. Nothing came of Colonel House's promised intervention, and Berger frantically forwarded copies of the editorials cited as unmailable to influential and respected public figures such as Amos Pinchot in an effort to find support outside the movement.[20]

Berger's hearing on 22 September 1917 took place before the Third Assistant Postmaster General, who charged that the *Leader* had violated the Espionage Act in its tendencies. Several editorials from the *Leader* were read to illustrate those illegal tendencies, but the official refused to specify which comments had actually violated the law. No judicial procedure was followed. A few weeks after the perfunctory hearing, the *Leader* lost its second-class mailing privileges.[21]

The loss of privileges was a serious threat to the paper's circulation. While rates within Milwaukee would not be affected by the ruling, readers outside the city would be required to pay twice as much for their subscriptions as previously. Berger's fears materialized when only one of every six out-of-town readers continued to subscribe. At once he planned to issue a weekly in order to reach former *Leader* readers. He hoped that a socialist paper of theoretical propaganda would escape government attention.[22]

Berger was not, however, resigned to abandoning the *Leader* without a full legal battle. Attorney Stedman advised him that he was in a favorable position for an appeal to the Supreme Court due to his loss of fundamental rights without a formal legal hearing. Berger filed suit to compel the return of the second-class mailing permit, arguing the invalidity of a statute that destroyed the freedom of the press, but his usually buoyant spirits began to fall. A legal suit would take years, he realized, and he lacked the tenacity to continue the daily grind of publication in the face of mounting obstruction. It was only the enthusiasm and resourcefulness of his friend Oscar Ameringer, that kept Berger and the *Leader* struggling. Ameringer insisted that publication must not be interrupted, and when Berger despondently replied that the readers might not be loyal, Ameringer proposed that they find out by calling a mass meeting to save the *Leader*.[23]

On 13 October 1917, an overflowing crowd of 5,000 filled the Milwaukee Auditorium. The audience gave Berger a fifteen-minute ovation and listened intently to his account of the *Leader*'s tribulations.

> This is the time when our rulers are . . . afraid of the great revolution that will come right after the war—the time that [is seen as] . . . the right time to suppress the Socialist papers in order to prevent the revolution from coming. . . . The men in power are making a great mistake because they will never be able to stave off the revolution in that manner. What they may accomplish is the suppression of the sane, constitutional and conservative Socialist papers. In their place they will get a secret press. Instead of mass action, as the Socialists propose . . . they will get the opposite—they will get direct action. They will not make the revolution impossible, but they will make the revolution impossibilistic. . . .

Berger's not inaccurate prognostications were applauded by the crowd which contributed hundreds of dollars in order to save the *Leader* and "sane socialism." Washtubs were passed around and returned to the stage filled with money, Liberty bonds, war-savings stamps, and jewelry.[24]

With renewed hope—and economy measures—the publication of the daily continued. The paper's national edition was abolished, its size reduced from twelve to six pages, and it was sent out of town in bundles as fourth-class mail to be distributed by local socialists. Further complications arose, however, as advertisers withdrew, some willingly, others under threat from the Fuel and Food Administrations. The *Leader*'s increased city circulation held some advertisers until pressure from the Loyalty League caused them to sever their connections with Berger. All the major department stores cancelled their advertisements.[25]

The government continued its harassment, and the *Leader* lost its right to send first-class letters and to receive mail deliveries. Some of the staff, including Mrs. Berger, drove through the city each day with outgoing mail in plain envelopes, dropping some in each post box.

Mayor Hoan's office sometimes received *Leader* mail and passed it on to Berger.

The newspaper's defense fund grew through contributions from individuals and labor organizations. The unsolicited receipt of Liberty bonds from those forced into purchases encouraged Ameringer to visit disgruntled victims of the various patriotic organizations throughout the state. Through his efforts, Ameringer later claimed, the *Leader* gained $150,000 in bonds.[26]

Understandably, Berger was keenly sensitive to the government's censorship policies, and in August 1918 he issued to his staff new directives regarding the editorial policy of the paper. Berger said that the task of the newspaper was to educate the readers to draw their own conclusions. He insisted that there be no explicit editorial criticism of the administration and he stressed that great tact was required. Editorials must always be checked by two staff members, he announced, and he indicated that fewer editorials would be published. He concluded by declaring, "We will say nothing we don't think, although we think a great deal that we can't say."[27]

None of Berger's modifications softened the government's attitude and he was left with the Supreme Court as his only hope. The decision in *Milwaukee Social Democratic Publishing Co.* v. *Burleson,* handed down two years after the termination of the war, was far-reaching. The Supreme Court, in a seven-to-two decision on 7 March 1921, upheld Burleson's denial of the *Leader*'s second-class mailing privileges. This action has been termed the most sweeping decision in sustaining governmental powers over the press. "Although the case arose under the Espionage Act, its most important effect will probably be in extending the power of the Postmaster General to penalize discussion in time of peace," an authority on constitutional law predicted. The Court had recognized earlier the power of the Post Office to declare matter nonmailable, and only in this case was that power extended to the type of mailing privilege. A second-class rate was deemed not a right but a privilege and therefore revocable.[28]

In the case of *The Masses,* the Supreme Court had approved the doctrine of remote bad tendency by which conviction was possible for statements which might indirectly have a harmful effect, for example, statements which might discourage enlistment. Therefore, intention rather than clear and present danger had become the critical issue. The *Leader* was found guilty of violating the Espionage Act in its tendency and the Court allowed the Post Office its assumption of the power of previous restraint. By revoking its mailing privileges, the Post Office penalized future issues, which amounted to deprivation of property—unusual punishment—and the abridgement of freedom of speech —in effect, the silencing of the press. Civil libertarians have called the decision the low ebb in an eternal struggle.[29]

Somehow the *Leader* survived its severest crisis. The fact that the newspaper's circulation within Milwaukee climbed at a time when the government charged the paper with disloyalty was indicative of the mood of the city. Milwaukee was a small battleground in the world war, with a backdrop of conflict in domestic politics and rivalries among ethnic groups. It was described as 70 percent below par in loyalty by the National Security League, a self-appointed judge in such matters, and yet the city and the state consistently oversubscribed in bond drives and draft quotas, and it was the state of Wisconsin that initiated the practice of meatless and wheatless days for the nation.

Such an ambiguous position should be understood in terms of the active discord raging within the community. Milwaukee entered the war in a defensive posture; because of the high percentage of German-Americans, the city was suspect from the start. Therefore, the Milwaukee press and business leaders were acutely sensitive to her national reputation and worked diligently to achieve full participation in various federal drives. The state loyalty league was one of the most active in the country. All types of lawful pressure were applied to insure overt support for the war, and this pressure was supplemented, especially in the rural areas, by mob persuasion. To such an extent were Wisconsin residents subject to extralegal stress that a popular magazine wrote of the "prussianizing" of Wisconsin.

As a result of these pressures upon the Milwaukee Germans and the open hostility that flared between them and the Poles and Czechs of the city, Milwaukee's German image began to be muted. By the eve of American intervention, campaigns to assist the Central Powers had ceased and soon the respected German theater was disrupted, the Deutscher Club became the Wisconsin Club, and some German names became Americanized.

While the German ethos was experiencing dilution, a concurrent drive for Americanization was undertaken—spearheaded by the Milwaukee County Council of Defense, whose Americanization program was supervised by May Wood Simons. Prior to the war, the various nationalities in the city had stymied efforts to promote Americanization through preparedness or other devices, but for the duration, schools and factories became blatant instruments of Americanization. By the end of the war, a rapid pace of assimilation was under way in Milwaukee.

The anomalous position of the Milwaukee socialist organization was recognized by its members. Despite stable membership rolls, the quandary of the party position led to a slackening of activities. The loss of Gaylord, who had been very popular among the socialists, hurt the local party, as did Simons's series of articles in the Milwaukee *Journal* on the un-American complexion of the Socialist party. The leadership of each in the Wisconsin Loyalty League was a boon to Wisconsin conservatives.

The local party was weakened also by some defections among its labor supporters. The FTC maintained its formal alliance with the party, however. It was aligned to the People's Council rather than to Gompers's pro-war Alliance, it assisted the *Leader,* and it supported socialist candidates for local office. Nevertheless, it stepped cautiously and refused to declare its opposition to the war; its caution served to sway the local socialists into modifying their position of unalterable opposition to the war. While Berger spoke of the war as seldom as possible and restricted himself to non-controversial aspects, the party's course of action revealed its distance from the St. Louis stand. The Socialist party of Milwaukee—the name Social Democrats having been dropped after the United States entered the war—urged support for the Red Cross and concentrated on developing peace programs.[30]

The most vulnerable of Milwaukee socialists was Mayor Hoan. As Berger had been out on a limb in Congress because of the need to take a position on every issue, so Dan Hoan had to declare himself and take action on all significant matters. Hoan had declined to attend the St. Louis convention, to the disgust of some members. He alienated others by his participation in Milwaukee's war programs, although the party's County Central Committee had approved of that course. He chaired, for example, the Bureau of Food Control of the Milwaukee Council of Defense. When he refused to state his own position on the St. Louis Proclamation in public debate in December 1917, a party split threatened as Berger flung out a barely veiled challenge in an editorial entitled "The Party Will Stand No Wobbling."

Though Berger felt trapped by the platform, he believed party unity and dignity required that it be supported in public and so he declared: "Plain notice to all party members, and especially to those who are seeking office. . . . Of all times this is the poorest time to hedge, to wobble or to try 'a seat on the fence' when a question of vital principle is asked—as, for instance, a question about the St. Louis platform —be that man a mayor or a constable—[he] must get out of the party in justice to himself and the party. . . ." There was some feeling in the party that Berger had been too ruthless, and the Milwaukee *Journal* hailed a break in the Berger machine. However, the breach was formally mended, the County Central Committee of the party revealed its endorsement of Hoan's position, and Berger and Hoan were appointed to draft the local party's platform for the April election. Berger wrote it, and, with Hoan's public approval, reaffirmed the local organization's support of the St. Louis program. The platform, however, stressed immediate issues of the war and the home front.[31] The challenge to Berger's local authority subsided and Hoan stepped into line, supporting the local platform undoubtedly with the same limited enthusiasm that Berger inwardly felt toward the national platform.

In March, Berger conducted his most exciting campaign to date as he ran for the United States Senate seat vacated by the death of Senator Husting. Berger ran on a peace platform in which he tried to differentiate the administration from the government in order to argue the feasibility of criticising the Wilson administration. He maintained that the latter was planning five more years of war which, he said, would not be defensive but in actuality an invasion of European countries. Berger stressed that the election of a socialist would be an appropriate refutation of the claim that the people favored war.

In this campaign, he was aided at the polls by his own German image. Unlike his campaigns of 1914 and 1916, in which he had lost to blatant appeals for German votes, now, perhaps despite himself, he was the German candidate. While Milwaukee was undergoing assimilation under pressure, his race for the Senate offered a possibility to cast a pro-German vote for those who chose to do so.

Berger also had the support of all the local socialists and of those voters who were seeking a means to express their disapproval of the loss of civil liberties. He was opposed by Joseph E. Davies, an enthusiastic pro-war Democrat who had active campaign support from President Wilson, and by Irvine L. Lenroot, a progressive Republican who had broken with La Follette over the war. The Loyalty League vainly attempted to convince Davies and Lenroot to join efforts in a fusionist campaign against Berger. Members of the League disrupted Berger's speeches and, in one instance, prevented a meeting which Seidel was scheduled to address. Berger angrily wrote Governor Emanuel L. Philipp in protest, but to no avail. In Milwaukee, and especially in rural areas, his posters were destroyed and his advertising refused.[32]

Nevertheless, Berger felt optimistic about his chances for election. He was convinced that there existed a sizeable but unheard bloc of opinion in favor of a prompt cessation of hostilities, and consequently he played down his socialism and emphasized peace.[33] If he could capture the peace vote, he reasoned, then a voice for peace and socialism would at last be heard in the United States Senate. He campaigned full time and paid little attention to his other responsibilities. While the problems of the *Leader* were significant to him, a victory would surely indicate to the administration grassroots support for his stand on freedom of speech. He told Germer that he would prefer not to run for the next NEC unless the party needed him there.[34] He wanted every moment for his Senate campaign.

Without warning, on March 11, only ten days before the Wisconsin primary, the federal government announced that in February it had indicted Victor L. Berger and four other national party officers for conspiracy to violate the Espionage Act. Berger was furious. Convinced that the indictment, and particularly the timing of its announcement, was a political move by a frightened opposition, he declared flatly that the Socialist party was to be tried. "Without going out of existence," he said, "our party could not have changed [its] position even to please President Woodrow Wilson. . . ." The *Leader* began a series of first-page editorials in support of the newly threatened Berger. To the charges, it wrote, "There is only one answer free men can give." Berger must be sent to the Senate.

Berger did not win the election, but he received 110,487 votes out of the 423,343 cast, the largest number of votes ever won by a socialist in Wisconsin and 27,000 more than Benson polled there in 1916. Berger termed the results not disappointing considering the persecution he endured and the lack of adequate funds even for postage. He claimed that he had won at least 10,000 additional votes which had been stolen by those he called the "paytriots." He predicted more time and better organization might mean socialist victory in the November election in Wisconsin.

Berger had outpolled his rivals by two to one in the heavily German areas of the state. This fact prompted him to editorialize later that he did not want German nationalist votes. He sought to disassociate himself from pro-Germanism publicly in view of his federal indictment and his up-coming campaign for the House of Representatives, only a few months away. He claimed publicly that his increased vote was in the main due to recent converts to socialism who had been won over by the party's war stance and by those who realized that the socialists were the only trustworthy advocates of a democratic peace.[35]

One week before the November election, Berger was indicted again for conspiracy along with the other socialist candidates for major Wisconsin offices, including Oscar Ameringer, who was campaigning for the governor's chair. This blatant political move by the government received full publicity in the *Leader* and outright contempt from the candidates. Again Berger protested that "We are not charged with any crime; we are on trial for having written and spoken in favor of peace."[36] The attention that Berger had attracted the previous spring through his one-man fight against the federal government strengthened him in his campaign. On 6 November 1918, he was returned by the voters of the Fifth Congressional District of Wisconsin to the House of Representatives after three fruitless campaigns to regain his seat. The sweetness of the victory over the opposition of the government must have been increased for Berger by the fact that his triumph was at the expense of Representative Stafford, his perennial rival who, despite the support of the German-American Alliance, had come in a poor third behind the Democrat, Joseph Carney.

Berger's victory apparently resulted from a combination of factors, the least important of which may have been the conversion of a few voters to class-conscious socialism. One factor was the support of German nationalists, some of whom had turned away from Stafford and voted for Berger because of his opposition to the war. But it seems likely that his major support from non-socialist sources came from men who longed for peace and others who protested against unreasonable and unjust pressures of the war-induced hysteria.

While many national newspapers were reflecting sadly on the disloyalty of Wisconsin, and the Milwaukee press was trying desperately to rationalize the voters' behavior, newly elected Senator Lenroot embarrassedly insisted that the state which had chosen him for such high honors was loyal to the nation. He protested that there were only a few "bad spots" and that most of the Berger vote came from

Wisconsin citizens who favored full freedom of opinion. A freelance journalist who resided in Wisconsin stated that the socialist victory was a pro-American vote registered by those with a healthy affection for disappearing internal freedoms.[37]

There was little time for Berger to gloat over his election and the prospect of returning to the congressional life which he had found so congenial. That December and January, the trial of the five Socialist party leaders was a major news story throughout the country. The socialists had hoped that the case would not come up before the November election so that Berger's electoral chances would not be further prejudiced.[38] In this regard, their hopes were gratified, but in little else. On 27 April, the five indicted socialists had asked for dismissal of the charges on several counts, the strongest being Germer's plea that he had been found innocent on the same charges in Grand Rapids, Michigan. After the denial, a petition for a change of venue was filed in May on twenty-one different counts, the most significant of which rested on the open prejudice of the judge who was to preside at the trial.

The petition quoted Judge Kenesaw Mountain Landis's words to a German-American defendant at a recent trial: "One must have a very judicial mind, indeed, not to be prejudiced against German Americans in this country. Their hearts are reeking with disloyalty. . . . I know a safe blower, he is a friend of mine, who is making a good soldier in France. He was a bank robber for nine years, that was his business in peace time, and now he is a good soldier, and as between him and the defendant, I prefer the safe blower." It was Judge Landis who ruled on the petition and he found no reason to disqualify himself from presiding.[39]

The indictment of Victor L. Berger, Adolph Germer, J. Louis Engdahl, editor of the party newspapers, William F. Kruse, director of the Young People's Socialist League, and Rev. Irwin St. John Tucker, until recently responsible for the Literature Department in the National Office, charged them with conspiracy to violate the Espionage Act through personal solicitations, public speeches, and writings. The several overt acts cited were five editorials from the *Leader,* two pamphlets by Tucker, the publication of the St. Louis Proclamation and War Program for which Germer was held responsible, items in the *American Socialist* which Engdahl had edited, and two private letters written by Kruse on conscription.[40]

The five were a strange combination to be found in the dock

together. Berger and Germer were well-known leaders of the reformist wing of the party who had had long experience in its inner councils. Tucker, as a minister, favored a type of socialism not congenial to the others, and he had worked only briefly in the National Office and was not a member of the party's highest circles. His commitment to pacifism, seen in his writings and his active participation in the People's Council, was perhaps stronger than his commitment to socialism, although he had opposed the St. Louis Proclamation as not scientific enough. Engdahl and Kruse were not readily identified with either wing of the party but both were en route to the left. There was no cohesion among the five. Indeed, except for Berger and Germer, none of them could be described as close friends.

The common denominator they shared was their party membership and high office. Evidently, with the exception of Berger, they had been selected at random, and the government just as easily could have chosen other leaders in its effort to discredit the Socialist party. The identity of the particular men or their specific activities were of little consequence, except that it was helpful to select men of German descent (only Tucker was not). Morris Hillquit, still recuperating from tuberculosis, expected an indictment for the major part he had played in the formulation of the St. Louis Proclamation, but he never received one. He assumed that the government decided against his inclusion because of the great following he had won in New York City in the November 1917 election. John M. Work, whose American ancestry was pre-Revolutionary, looked forward to an indictment as the author of three-and-a-half of the five editorials for which Berger was prosecuted, but he was not charged.[41]

The trial lasted twenty-three days. Landis, fresh from the mass trial which had broken the IWW, presided with relish. John Reed described Landis as "A wasted man with untidy white hair, an emaciated face in which two burning eyes are set like jewels, parchment skin split by a crack for a mouth; the face of Andrew Jackson three years dead."[42] Landis enjoyed the attention that a major trial brought him. His courtroom in the old Cook County Courthouse of Chicago was crowded with spectators and reporters from all the national magazines and there was about it an almost festive air as the proceedings opened.

The defendants' interest and reactions to the trial varied. Berger and Germer followed the proceedings intensely, often conferring with one of their three attorneys over specific points. The others, however, seemed to take the trial less seriously. Tucker sometimes read throughout the day.[43]

Berger was not only interested in the trial. He was, in turn, angry, indignant, frightened, and self-righteous. He resented the notoriety the indictment brought to him and to the party, and he was furious that he had to stand trial in Chicago rather than in his home city. The atmosphere of the trial reminded him of the persecution of witches in seventeenth-century Salem. So much was assumed and allowed, he later said, that the case did not belong in a court of law at all. He thought that the jury of elderly and conservative business men might as well have been handpicked by the National Security League, while its lack of knowledge of socialism meant certain conviction for any one the government sent before it. Berger felt confident only about the imminent demise of the Democratic party as the result of its persecution of radicals. He freely predicted that it would collapse as had the Federalist party after its passage of the Alien and Sedition Acts of 1798.

Berger's hot temper worried his comrades, who feared that he would be "lashed into a fury" when grilled by the prosecuting attorneys. John Work cautioned him that the District Attorney wanted to anger him and he must not fall into the trap. As it happened, he did lose his temper three or four times, became red in the face and pounded his fist on the table before him to emphasize his words. Attorney Stedman was of little help, for he needed calming himself. Adolph Germer wished that Hillquit were there to control both Berger and Stedman.[44]

The trial proceeded slowly as the prosecution paraded to the stand a number of witnesses who testified to the radical and pacifist positions of the defendants through their activities in the Socialist party and other organizations. After proving those connections, often by extraneous, irrelevant, and dated testimony, the prosecution tried to demonstrate the disloyalty of the five. The effort to show a conspiracy among them, the favorite form of prosecution under the Espionage Act, could only be attempted by the most circuitous route. As Hillquit later described the proceedings: "Everything said or done by any of them is admissible against everybody else on the ground that they are responsible for each other as fellow conspirators, and the alleged conspiracy is established by combining the individual acts and statements of the different defendants."[45] The defense acknowledged all connections with the Socialist party and peace organizations, while differentiating the defendants from the Soviet Bolsheviks abroad and the direct actionist Wobblies at home.

It did, however, try to prevent the admission of extraneous evidence, but its many objections were usually overruled. The defense argued that the accused were not parties to a conspiracy, that a conspiracy did not in fact exist, that the Socialist party never favored the violation of the law, and even that individual defendants had actually offered some support for the war effort. It tried to maintain that the principle of free speech was on trial but, unlike the prosecution, the defense was limited to the narrowly germane.

Berger took the stand only after the character witnesses and his co-defendants had testified. He spent two full days and two half days on the witness stand and his testimony, eagerly awaited, since he was the major defendant, was the highlight of the trial. Seymour Stedman led him through his autobiography, his socialist philosophy, and socialist and wartime activities, all the while unsuccessfully attempting to weld his rambling and loquacious testimony into a cohesive whole. Berger showed all of his many faces to the courtroom. He demonstrated his ample knowledge of history and profound familiarity with scientific socialism through his explanations of various party positions. On the other hand, he also displayed his aggressive temperament, the ease with which he could be exasperated even by his own attorneys, and his propensity for boasting.

Berger explained that socialists traditionally opposed militarism and war and he quoted the anti-war resolution passed by the Stuttgart International Congress of 1907. He described efforts by socialists, including members of the Socialist party of America, to prevent outbreaks of war prior to April 1917, and stated that the intent of the St. Louis Proclamation was to express the socialist view rather than to interfere with American participation in the war. Berger denied that the program recommended violations of the law. However, he admitted that the convention and its proceedings were not to his taste. He blamed the crisis atmosphere of the time with enabling the radical faction to dominate the party. "When I got to the convention," he said, "I hardly knew the convention." To illustrate the minor role he played at St. Louis he mentioned that "this was one of the few conventions that I never made a speech at." He testified, however, that he supported the majority report.

Berger had no compunctions about his work in the party and on the newspaper, in each case assuming responsibility for his own deeds and explaining them in terms of the historical and factual frames of reference. He readily accepted liability for the five editorials cited in the indictment, although his contact with them was little more than formal. Only the first editorial was Berger's, but in his capacity as editor-in-chief of the *Leader,* he freely acknowledged responsibility for all of them, as well as for the many other editorials mentioned as objectionable.[46]

Throughout the first half of his testimony Berger appeared to be a principled figure standing by his party, his paper, and his peers. He was aware of the favorable response which so many—despite themselves—had felt towards Debs at his trial and, out of his determination to be the most celebrated, respected, and popular socialist leader, Berger hoped to make as powerful an impact as had Debs.[47] But his deep desire for fame was balanced by an even more profound fear of the imprisonment which could follow a verdict of guilty. Unlike many socialist agitators, Berger had never been in jail and he admitted that he had no taste for martyrdom. Indeed, a Milwaukee comrade related that Berger often questioned him with morbid fascination about life as a political prisoner in Europe.[48]

In his later testimony Berger proudly related to the court the outstanding record that Milwaukee had made in various war drives and claimed, "I kept the population there exceeding [*sic*] law abiding, and we had less trouble there than in any other city, and . . . I promulgated a philosophy in that town which is probably not represented in any other city in the United States." With this self-inflating statement he destroyed any chance he might have had to emerge with a pure, Debsian image. Rather, he invited the active derision of his comrades.

The longer he spoke, the more his fear of imprisonment shaped his remarks. Berger pointed to the successful bond drives in Milwaukee and the comparatively few draft-dodgers there. He emphasized his membership in the Red Cross, his purchase of Liberty bonds and war savings stamps. Berger claimed to have several nephews in the United States armed forces and then referred to his adopted nephew, Carl Haessler, who was serving five years in Leavenworth Federal Penitentiary as a conscientious objector, and told how zealously he had tried to convince the young man to accept the draft call (confirmed by both Haessler and his wife). He also took credit for advising Mayor Hoan to comply with the law.[49]

The trial ended on 8 January, with Judge Landis' lengthy and objective charge to the jury. Berger was not without hope as he watched the jury file out of the courtroom. He and Germer had assiduously studied the twelve men and concluded that two or three of them had begun to empathize with the defendants' position. An acquittal seemed unlikely but they hoped for disagreement. The defense had recognized that the question of conspiracy was a vicious circle impervious to logical argument, and it had consequently emphasized constitutional aspects. In Stedman's conclusion he insisted that Congress lacked the power to abridge freedom of speech.[50]

The jury deliberated only six hours and found the defendants guilty of conspiracy to violate the Espionage Act. At once the defense planned to appeal the decision to the Circuit Court of Appeals and thereafter, if necessary, to the Supreme Court. The Socialist party was ready to spend every cent required. Berger, however, was very gloomy and melodramatic. When he returned to Chicago from Milwaukee for the sentencing he brought with him a few parcels containing a small library. "He was all prepared for his twenty year stay,"[51] Germer wrote Hillquit.

Before the sentencing, each of the defendants made a lengthy statement to the court. All of them stressed principles of socialism, Christianity, or democracy, each with one eye on posterity, apparently, and the other on Debs's speech to the court.

Berger's voice shook with emotion as he read a prepared five-page statement. He declared that the defendants were no more guilty of conspiracy than was the judge himself. He spoke of the teachings of socialism and announced that if such a philosophy "is a crime, then we are all criminals." He charged that reactionaries sought to exploit the existence of bolshevism and the war hysteria in order to destroy the Socialist party. "This is the reason why . . . [we] were indicted. This was a political trial. The Socialist party was on trial." While the district attorney had specifically denied that charge, Berger quoted his post-trial remark that the verdict was a blow against radicalism.

Berger warned of the rising spirit of resistance and of revolution and reiterated his view, expressed ever since government harassment began, that a secretive and dangerous political opposition would replace the constructive and legitimate Socialist party. He closed with his original theme:

If I am guilty, if my comrades here are guilty, then every member of the Socialist Party is guilty. Every man who voted the Socialist ticket is guilty. Every man who has criticized the administration on war is guilty. And if the Socialist party is a conspiracy against capitalism, then the Republican and Democratic parties are conspiracies against human progress and human welfare. If I am to be punished for having told the truth as I saw it—I ask no mercy.[52]

And Berger and the others received no mercy. Judge Landis, before pronouncing sentence, said that the several writings of the five defendants attempted to obstruct the draft, ample evidence of violation of the Espionage Act. He waved aside the affidavit presented by one of the jurors that a bailiff had denounced a defendant in the presence of the jury, and sentenced the five men to the maximum prison term, twenty years in Leavenworth.[53]

Berger commented bitterly that the United States had replaced czarist Russia as the bulwark of reactionary and tyrannical autocracy. Germer said that he preferred the maximum sentence to one of only two or three years because it proved the defendants' contention that Landis was prejudiced against them and not qualified to preside at the case. He believed that the stringency of the sentence strengthened the chances of winning an appeal.

Judge Landis denied the defendants' request that he set bond. Anxious to avoid a night in jail, they managed to be heard that afternoon in the District Court of Appeals, where bond was set at $100,000 each, the highest bond in any socialist case. The group was momentarily stunned but within five hours socialists throughout Chicago were contacted and more than enough money was raised, with millionaire William Bross Lloyd making the largest contribution. That night at ten o'clock the convicted men and their friends celebrated their bail in a Chicago restaurant.[54] At least for the immediate future prison would wait.

It took two years for the case to be settled by the Supreme Court. Seymour Stedman appeared before the Court for the plaintiffs and argued that Judge Landis lacked the legal right to rule on the change of venue because of his prejudice against the defendants. By a six-to-three decision, the conviction was reversed in January 1921.[55] For more than two years after the Armistice the defendants had lived in the shadow of the penitentiary with Berger prohibited from participating in policy-making or editorial writing for the *Leader* under terms of his bail. The war for him had lasted an incredibly long time.

Berger was not able to concentrate exclusively upon the lengthy legal proceedings because he was simultaneously involved in a struggle with his congressional colleagues over his seat in the House of Representatives. It was an uneven contest in which Berger was the inevitable loser. The hearings involved a duplication of his Chicago trial and thus history repeated itself, but it would be erroneous to term the first trial a tragedy and the second a farce. Rather, the first approached a travesty on justice and the second exposed an hysteria-ridden Congress mirroring national reactions. The two proceedings were inherent parts of the post-war atmosphere.

The sixty-sixth Congress was scheduled to convene late in May 1919. Prior to its opening the press excitedly discussed the possibility of Congress using its power as sole judge of elections to declare null and void the results in the Fifth Congressional District of Wisconsin. Almost unanimously, the national press applauded any intent to deprive the Milwaukee socialist of the seat to which he had been legally elected. Only one respected non-radical journal reminded its readers that there were no grounds for exclusion and that Congress would be wise to avoid impinging on judicial functions.[56]

On the first day of the session, Representative Frederick W. Dallinger of Massachusetts objected to the swearing-in of Berger as a member of Congress on the grounds of his conviction for a federal offense. Without granting Berger's request to make a statement on a question of highest privilege, the House unanimously resolved to investigate Berger's right to his seat and meanwhile suspended him from his position.[57]

A committee of nine was appointed, chaired by Dallinger, to conduct hearings which lasted for most of the opening session of the sixty-sixth Congress. The material examined by the investigators was much the same that had been explored at the trial, even though it was maintained that the hearings were divorced from the latter. However, the committee reviewed a copy of the trial proceedings and then explored Berger's position and political philosophy in somewhat greater depth than had occurred at the trial. The defense, handled by Henry F. Cochems, one of Berger's non-socialist attorneys at his trial and once his opponent in a congressional election, argued in vain that the Fourteenth Amendment of the Constitution did not apply to the case. The committee held that clause three, barring from Congress anyone who had given aid and comfort to the enemy, was indeed germane.[58]

Much time was lost in debate over the legality of exclusion. When this approach proved ineffectual, Cochems followed the main line of argument utilized at the trial. He maintained that Berger was a loyal American citizen who happened also to be a socialist believing in the traditional, international philosophy of that ideology. Cochems' major witness was Berger, whose testimony was highlighted by serious flareups with members of the committee. Supporting testimony was offered by other socialists who verified Berger's "Americanism" and internationalism.

In an attempt to reach the particular audience whom he was addressing, Berger turned to history to demonstrate that his wartime activities were consistent with American tradition. He argued that the Socialist party was the one political organization that sought to follow the advice of early American statesmen to avoid European entanglements. Berger linked himself and the party with earlier denunciations of foreign policy by the loyal opposition, such as Abraham Lincoln's hostility to the administration during the Mexican War. Berger cited the names of men who had opposed Wilson's policies and yet were still serving honorably in the House, such as James R. Mann, Claude Kitchin, and Champ Clark. Feigning confidence, the socialist told the committee that he had no doubt that Congress would eventually seat him. "They know that I am no more guilty of a conspiracy in connection with this war than is Woodrow Wilson."[59]

As usual, Berger did not limit himself in his choice of weapons. He appealed for assistance to influential friends and linked his own struggle to a fundamental principle. For example, he wrote to Republican Representative John Jacob Esch of Wisconsin explaining the basic issue in the case: "The question whether I should be forbidden to take my seat in the House after having been regularly elected by a plurality of 5,560 votes—which is not disputed—is of vital importance to representative government and deserves your closest attention."

Appeal to principle made no difference in the outcome of the hearings. Neither Berger's insistence upon the inapplicability of the Fourteenth Amendment nor upon the inability of Congress to exclude a legally elected and certified representative was persuasive to the committee. Its prejudice was evident and the result inevitable.[60]

The committee reported on 24 October 1919, that Victor Berger was ineligible to serve in the United States Congress because of his hindrance, obstruction, and embarrassment of the government in its pursuit of the war effort, thereby giving comfort to the enemy. The report was signed by eight of the nine committee members, with one abstaining in favor of a delay until Berger's conviction was settled by the courts.

Berger was permitted to make a lengthy statement. He reviewed his own and the party's position once more, and if Berger were somewhat weary and even bored by this time, it was understandable. He called his exclusion a result of the hysteria of those in power who saw bolshevism everywhere. He insisted again that he was being punished because of his membership in the Socialist party rather than for his specific acts. He maintained that he would never retract anything, and that indeed, some of his predictions were already materializing. Finally he concluded: "Remember, Gentlemen, you may exclude me once, you may exclude me twice. But the Fifth district of Wisconsin cannot permit you to dictate what kind of man is to represent it. If representative government shall survive, you will see me or a man of my kind . . . in the nation's legislature."[61]

The vote for exclusion was nearly unanimous, with only one Congressman, Edward Voigt, progressive Republican from Wisconsin, opposed. It was not long, however, before Berger's parting words began to haunt Congress. The Wisconsin socialists at once nominated Berger as their candidate in the December election to fill his seat. He was opposed by Henry H. Bodenstab, a German-American and fusionist, and through him the old parties hoped to settle the Berger issue finally. Bodenstab's slogan, and entire platform, was "Protect your home from Bolshevism."

Berger, on the other hand, dealt with all the usual issues, bragged about his twenty-year sentence, and exploited his exclusion. In an interview with the Milwaukee *Journal*, Berger warned of the serious consequences of overruling legal elections: "It is fundamentally a question whether representative government and political action . . . are to be thrown to the scrapheap as inadequate. . . . My rejection by Congress will bring home the great question of whether, after all, the advocates of 'direct action' and of the 'Dictatorship' of the 'proletariat' have not the logic of facts in their favor."[62]

Berger's campaign efforts were buttressed by support from his close colleagues in the Socialist party, such as Oscar Ameringer and Morris Hillquit. The still inactive Hillquit appealed for funds for Berger and, using a word that was unfamiliar to socialist ears, he mentioned sentiment as a reason for aiding the much persecuted Berger.[63]

The non-socialist Milwaukee press called the campaign one be-tween "Bergerism" and "Americanism" and warned that Berger's elec-tion would mean Milwaukee's disgrace before the nation. Nevertheless Berger easily won re-election, with 13,892 votes to 9,273 for his op-ponent.[64] His support came once again not only from socialists but from German-Americans and miscellaneous protest voters and others who admired his spirit.

There was even less doubt than before that Congress would not allow Berger to assume the seat to which he had been legally elected, but he was not as isolated as he had been in his earlier struggle. He was the focus of greater publicity now and various progressive journals and individuals came to his defense. Oswald Garrison Villard stressed that Congress was increasing the current political unrest by overturning legal election results. Such congressional action, he said, indicated to the voters that the government was "not willing to give a square deal to those who voice, wisely or mistakenly, the rising tide of popular discon-tent and dissent from present-day government policy." Others noted the beneficial results Berger's arbitrary bouncing in and out of Congress might have for his cause.[65]

In Congress, Representative Voigt was now joined by a few others who favored seating Berger. One old Wisconsin Progressive and erst-while rival of Berger's circulated a letter among the representatives which tried to place the Berger case in perspective.[66] On 10 January 1920, the Milwaukee socialist was once more denied his seat in the House of Representatives, this time with six votes in opposition to his exclusion. For a second time Congress ousted the legally elected Berger and strengthened the dangerous precedent it had set a few months earlier. With the war now sinking further into the past, the only basis upon which the exclusion stood was hysteria.

Throughout the years of struggle to salvage his reputation with the public and the government, Berger seethed over the insufficient support accorded to him by the socialists. The Socialist party spent more money on his trial than on any other case and the party newspaper gave wide publicity to his fight for his congressional seat, so the party's official support could not be questioned; but on a less formal level it was ob-vious to Berger that the socialists as a whole were not behind him. He did not receive the socialist press coverage that he thought his activities warranted nor did he receive personal encouragement from other than his immediate circle.

Because his stand at his trial, especially his patriotic façade, was not one that invited full admiration from socialists, their papers did not applaud him as they had others. In accusing the New York *Call* and other papers of neglecting his case, Berger complained to Hillquit, "the Socialist press has made a lot of Gene Debs and Kate Richards O'Hare, who got only five and ten years respectively—but nobody seems to think much of the twenty years the rest of us received—in fact some so-called radicals tacitly seem to approve the sentence." Hillquit agreed that Berger had a valid grievance against the socialist press, particularly for its nearly total lack of interest in his exclusion from Congress, but he was unable to aid him.[67]

Berger had failed to capture the imagination of socialists as had Mrs. O'Hare, who was separated from four young children by the prison doors. Nor had he held as impressive a position as Debs or the pacifist Roger Baldwin, head of the National Civil Liberties Union, who admitted their beliefs boldly and invited the government's punishment. But more than individual courage was at issue in this matter. Support for the indicted socialists had become a source of dissension among the party factions. Some of the radical wing of the party were indeed indifferent to the sentence Berger received, as he suspected.

The Liberator published observations on the Berger trial by William Bross Lloyd, still friendly to Berger but flirting ominously with the left wing, which termed the proceedings "largely trivial." The editor, Max Eastman, who believed in supporting the administration in time of war and the party during a crisis, apologized to Berger for the Lloyd article.[68]

But for many it was the boastful and aggressive Berger who was beset by difficulties, and there was no desire to support him. The lack of popularity of the man and his positions was markedly clear. For many there was the hope that Berger would be ruined, and with him step-at-a-time socialism.

The days in which Victor Berger had been a prominent leader of a growing political movement in the United States were over. He would again assume the role of an unchallenged leader of the Socialist party, but by then it would be the same party in name only and its position in American political life would be less than marginal. His resumption of leadership, then, would be of little significance. He would return in triumph to Congress only a short two years after his repudiation by that body, but his role there would be even less notable than it had been during his long-ago first term. Rather than enjoying the limelight as a unique representative of a fledgling political party, Berger would take on the color of just another of the handful of American progressives in the House and Senate.

The *Leader* survived the war apparently unscarred, but it was no longer a young daily with a potentially exciting future as a labor newspaper in the middle-west. It was clear that the *Leader* was no more than a tired metropolitan newspaper seeking attention in the loudest Hearst-like manner. Berger still had the Milwaukee movement but that, too, was growing weary and losing its vigor. Dan Hoan continued to occupy City Hall and made no effort to overrule Berger's authority, but the daily decisions required of a mayor more and more diluted the remaining socialist stance of the local party.

Thus, by the early 1920s Berger, the only socialist to experience triple jeopardy during the war, had lost everything but his now baseless dreams. Crucifixion had cost him the promise he had seen in the party, the paper, and the country. It was a sadder though still buoyant Berger who lived beyond the promise of American socialism into the era of normalcy. He never abandoned his socialism or the party, but the struggles fought over its declining patrimony undoubtedly left unhealed wounds within him.

NOTES

1. George Creel, *The War, The World and Wilson* (New York: Harper and Bros. Pubs., 1920), pp. 48-49, 53.

2. Robert K. Murray, *Red Scare: A Study in National Hysteria, 1919-1920* (New York: McGraw-Hill Book Co., 1964), pp. 12-13, 33, 85, 92.

3. H. C. Peterson and Gilbert C. Fite, *Opponents of War, 1917-1918* (Madison: University of Wisconsin Press, 1957), p. 29.

4. James Mock, *Censorship, 1917* (Princeton: Princeton University Press, 1941), pp. 5, 50-53; Zechariah Chafee, Jr., *Free Speech in the United States* (Cambridge: Harvard

University Press, 1942), pp. 8, 38-41; Peterson and Fite, *Opponents of War,* p. 152.

5. Milwaukee *Leader,* 12 July 1917.

6. Donald Johnson, *The Challenge to American Freedoms: World War One and the Rise of the American Civil Liberties Union* (Louisville: University of Kentucky Press, 1963), pp. 22, 57-60; *Berger Trial,* II, 1954.

7. *The Masses* 10 (November-December 1917): 24. For a skeptical view of Wilson's commitment to freedom of speech see Jerold S. Auerbach, "Woodrow Wilson's 'Prediction' to Frank Cobb: Words Historians Should Doubt Ever Got Spoken," *Journal of American History* 54 (December 1967): 608-617.

8. Upton Sinclair to Woodrow Wilson, 22 October 1917, SP Col., Duke; clipping from *Truth,* 17 May 1918, in Debs Col., Tamiment Institute; Norman Thomas to his mother, 2 November 1917, to Alexander Trachtenberg, 18 October 1918, Norman M. Thomas Col., New York Public Library.

9. Morris Hillquit speech, 14 October 1917, typescript, Hillquit Col., SHSW.

10. Meyer London speech, 6 October 1917, typescript, London Col., Tamiment Institute.

11. See SP, *Court Rulings Upon Indictments, Search Warrants, Habeas Corpus, Mailing Privileges: Growing Out of Alleged Offences Against Draft and Espionage Acts* (Chicago: Socialist Party, 1918), copy found in World War I Dissenters Collection, University of Chicago; National Civil Liberties Bureau, *War-Time Prosecutions and Mob Violence* (New York: National Civil Liberties Bureau, 1919), pp. 3-4 (hereafter cited as NCLB).

12. Adolph Germer to Hillquit, 23 October 1918, Hillquit Col., SHSW; NCLB, p. 25; *The Trial of Scott Nearing and the American Socialist Society* (New York: Rand School of Social Science, 1919), p. 249.

13. NCLB, pp. 19, 25; Chafee, *Free Speech in the United States,* pp. 76-77.

14. Debs, "The Indictment of Our Leaders," April 1918, newspaper clipping in the Debs Col., Tamiment Institute.

15. Germer to Hillquit, 17 April 1919, Hillquit Col.,

SHSW; Germer to David A. Shannon, 14 July 1950, Germer Col., SHSW.

16. Report of the Executive Secretary to the NEC, 18 January 1919, SP Col., National Office File, 1896-1922, Duke.

17. Milwaukee *Leader,* 6 November 1917.

18. Election figures are found in SP Col., MCHS; Paul H. Douglas, "The Socialist Vote in the Municipal Elections of 1917," *National Municipal Review* 7 (March 1918): 133, 138; *The Eye Opener,* 17 November 1917; Milwaukee *Leader,* 7 November 1917; Berger to New York *Call*, 9 November 1917, Berger Col., MCHS; "The New York Mayoralty Campaign," *The Class Struggle* I (November-December 1917): 100.

19. Office of Postmaster General to Editor of the Milwaukee *Leader,* 11 September 1917, Berger to Burleson, 17 September 1917, Berger Col., MCHS; George P. West, "A Talk with Mr. Burleson," *International Socialist Review* 18 (November-December 1917): 284.

20. Berger to William Kent, 17 September 1917, to Arthur Brisbane, 17 September 1917, Brisbane to Berger, 27 October 1917, Berger to Colonel Edward M. House, 2 October 1917, Berger Col., MCHS; Germer to Hillquit, 17 October 1918, Hillquit Col., SHSW; Berger to Amos Pinchot, 25 October 1917, Berger Col., MCHS.

21. Berger to Kent, 14 November 1917, Berger Col., MCHS. Failure to issue a publication regularly, in this case as a result of government action, means ineligibility for second-class mailing privileges.

22. Berger to Arthur Brisbane, 23 October 1917, Berger Col., MCHS. He published a weekly called *The Commonwealth* starting 6 July 1918 without interference.

23. Berger to Hillquit, 24 October 1917, Berger Col., MCHS; Eberhard P. Deutsch, "Freedom of the Press and of the Mails," *Michigan Law Review* 36 (March 1938): 743; Oscar Ameringer, *If You Don't Weaken* (New York: Henry Holt and Co., 1940), pp. 315-316.

24. Milwaukee *Leader,* 13 October 1917; Ameringer, *If You Don't Weaken,* p. 316. The *Leader* reported that more than $800 was collected. In 1940 Ameringer recalled that the amount was over $4,000, but he was prone to exaggerate.

25. Berger to Carl D. Thompson, 21 November 1917, to Oscar Ameringer, 23 November 1917, Berger Col., MCHS; Milwaukee *Leader*, 27 October 1917.

26. Robert C. Reinders, "Daniel W. Hoan and the Milwaukee Socialist Party during the First World War," *Wisconsin Magazine of History*, 36: 51; Ameringer, *If You Don't Weaken*, pp. 318-325, 335.

27. Berger Memorandum to Staff, 1 August 1918, Berger Col., MCHS.

28. Chafee, *Free Speech in the United States*, p. 299; Morris E. Cohn, "The Censorship of Radical Materials by the Post Office," *St. Louis Law Review* 17 (February 1932): 105-106. The *New Republic* editorialized that this decision more than any other shook confidence in the judicial process. See "Press Censorship by Judicial Construction," *New Republic* 27 (30 March 1921): 125. The two dissenters to the decision were Louis D. Brandeis and Oliver Wendell Holmes, Jr.

29. Zechariah Chafee, "The Milwaukee *Leader* Case," *Nation* 112 (23 March 1921): 428; Chafee, *Free Speech in the United States*, pp. 299-300; Cohn, "Censorship of Radical Materials," p. 108; G. J. Patterson, *Free Speech and a Free Press* (Boston: Little Brown and Co., 1939), pp. 215-216; Louis Caldwell, "Freedom of Speech and Radio Broadcasting," *Annals of the American Academy of Political and Social Science* 177 (January 1935): 191-192.

30. Karen Falk, "Public Opinion in Wisconsin during World War I," *Wisconsin Magazine of History* 25; 390, 407; Charles D. Stewart, "Prussianizing Wisconsin," *Atlantic Monthly* 123 (January 1919): 103; Frederick I. Olson, "The Milwaukee Socialists, 1897-1941" (Ph.D. diss., Harvard University, 1952), pp. 358, 377; Bayrd Still, *Milwaukee: The History of a City* (Madison: State Historical Society, 1948), pp. 455-463; Gerd Korman, *Industrialization, Immigrants, and Americanizers: The View from Milwaukee, 1866-1921* (Madison: State Historical Society of Wisconsin, 1967), pp. 165, 173; Thomas W. Gavert, *Development of the Labor Movement in Milwaukee* (Madison: University of Wisconsin Press, 1965), pp. 128-131.

31. Reinders, "Daniel W. Hoan and the Milwaukee So-

cialist Party,'' pp. 49-52; Milwaukee *Journal*, 11 January 1918; Milwaukee *Leader*, 28 December 1917, 28 February 1918.

32. *Voice of the People*, 10 March 1918; Milwaukee *Leader*, 25 February 1918; 25 March 1918; Falk, ''Public Opinion in Wisconsin,'' p. 404; Berger to Governor Philipp, 19 February 1918, Berger Col., MCHS; 30 March 1918 Milwaukee newspaper clipping in Victor L. Berger Collection, Milwaukee Public Library. (Hereafter cited as Berger Col., MPL.)

33. Milwaukee *Leader*, 28 March 1918. He told his audience, ''I am for peace and I want your vote only if you are also for peace. Those who are not for peace will make a mistake if they vote for me.'' His platform favored an immediate peace, a congressional resolution directing the President to summon a peace conference, the withdrawal of troops from Europe, and the prohibition of war profiteering. Ibid., 4 March 1918; *Voice of the People*, 10 March 1918.

34. Berger to Germer, 25 February 1918, Berger Col., MCHS. Berger did serve on the NEC, the expanded fifteen-member body.

35. Hillquit to Berger, 12 March 1918, Berger to William Bross Lloyd, 18 April 1918; ibid.; John M. Work, ''The First World War,'' *Wisconsin Magazine of History* 40:41; Milwaukee *Leader*, 11 March 1918, 14 April 1918, 6 November 1918.

36. Milwaukee *Leader*, 28 October 1918, 29 October 1918. These indictments were not pressed.

37. Irvine L. Lenroot, ''War Loyalty of Wisconsin,'' *Forum* 59 (June 1918): 696-699; Stewart, ''Prussianizing Wisconsin,'' p. 105. Berger won 17,920 of 41,053 cast. His closest opponent had 12,450 votes. Wisconsin, *Blue Book*, 1919, 40, 153.

38. Germer to Hillquit, 4 September 1918, Hillquit Col., SHSW. In December Berger was indicted again, this time in La Crosse on sixteen counts; he was never tried.

39. *The Eye Opener*, 27 April 1918, 4 May 1918, November 1918; *Berger Trial*, I. The petition is bound into Volume I of the five volumes of the trial. Landis was also heard to say: ''If anybody has said anything worse about the

Germans than I have I would like to know it so I can use it.''
This was also quoted in the petition.

40. A copy of the indictment may be found in the Berger Col., MPL.

41. Morris Hillquit, *Loose Leaves from a Busy Life* (New York: Macmillan Co., 1934), p. 234. Oswald Garrison Villard, whose *Nation* had one issue held up by the postal authorities, noted that the government avoided harassing the powerful journals of opinion in favor of the powerless foreign-language, rural, and western press. Oswald Garrison Villard, *Fighting Years: Memoirs of a Liberal Editor* (New York: Harcourt, Brace and Co., 1939), p. 327; Work. "The First World War," p. 43.

42. Granville Hicks, *John Reed: The Making of a Revolutionary* (New York: Macmillan Co., 1936), p. 310.

43. Milwaukee *Journal*, 11 December 1918.

44. Berger to Representative James R. Mann, 24 February 1919, Berger to Arthur Brisbane, 29 April 1918, Berger Col., MCHS; Work, "The First World War," p. 43; Germer to Hillquit, 20 December 1918, Hillquit Col., SHSW. The jury consisted of five farmers, two insurance brokers, three small businessmen, a foreman, and an inventor. *The Commonwealth,* 21 December 1918.

45. Hillquit, *Loose Leaves from a Busy Life,* p. 239.

46. *Berger Trial,* IV, 3095, 3116, 3154-3168, 3297, V, 3334-3335. The five editorials, written in July and August 1917, were entitled: "Why We Are in This War," which gave six underlying causes of American intervention; "War and Insanity," which argued for a direct correlation between military service and insanity; "Difference of Opinion," which indicated that the typical young man hoped to avoid the draft; "A Big Business War"; and "Censoring God," which stated that the political and commercial powers had reworded a familiar biblical commandment to "Thou Shalt Kill."

47. William Bross Lloyd reported that the Debs trial reminded him of a Greek drama while the Berger trial was episodic and largely trivial. He claimed that he could recall clearly what Debs said but he could not remember Berger's remarks. William Bross Lloyd, "The Socialist Party on Trial," *The Liberator* 1 (February 1919): 10, 13.

48. Heinrich Bartels to Frederick Olson, in Olson, "The Milwaukee Socialists," p. 337.

49. *Berger Trial*, V, 3551-3553, IV, 3201.

50. Germer to Hillquit, 20 December 1918, Hillquit Col., SHSW; Associated Press dispatch, 7 January 1919, clipping in Berger Col., MPL.

51. Germer to Hillquit, 11 February 1919, Hillquit Col., SHSW.

52. Milwaukee *Journal*, 20 February 1919; *Berger Trial*, V, 5551-5552, 5556-5562.

53. Ibid., V, 5666-5667. The *Nation* noted the contrast with European sentences: in Germany those found guilty of high treason received maximum sentences of eight years while English conscientious objectors were sentenced to two years. "Our Ferocious Sentences," *Nation* 107 (2 November 1918): 504.

54. Milwaukee *Leader*, 21 February 1919; Germer to Hillquit, 24 February 1919, Hillquit Col., SHSW.

55. "Recent Decisions," *Columbia Law Review* 58, Pt. 1 (April 1921): 387; *Motion to Dismiss or Abate Persecution to the Supreme Court* (1920) in *United States of America v. Berger, Germer, Engdahl, Kruse and Tucker*, copy in Berger Col., Tamiment Institute; Chafee, *Free Speech in the United States*, p. 250. Guilt or innocence was not the issue to the Supreme Court, reported the *New Republic*, but whether the trial had been by law or by war passions. "The Berger Decision," *New Republic* 25 (23 February 1921): 360.

56. "Congress and Mr. Berger," *The Public* 22 (24 May 1919): 536.

57. U.S., *Congressional Record*, 66th Cong., 1st sess., 1919, 59, Part 1, 8-9.

58. U.S., Congress, House, *Hearings before the Special Committee Appointed under the Authority of House Resolution No. 6 Concerning the Right of Victor L. Berger to be Sworn in as a Member of the 66th Congress*.

59. Ibid., I, 147-148. Portions of Berger's testimony were issued as a pamphlet entitled "Open Letter from Victor L. Berger to His Colleagues in the Sixty-Sixth Congress," copy in the Berger Col., MPL.

60. Berger to John Jacob Esch, 2 September 1919, John Jacob Esch Col., SHSW; Edward J. Muzik, "Victor L. Berger: Congress and the Red Scare," *Wisconsin Magazine of History* (Summer 1964): 312-313.

61. U.S., Congress, House, Special Committee, *Report,* 66th Cong., 1st sess., 1919, pp. 15-16. The committee's report is bound into Volume I of the *Hearings Before the Special Committee. . . .* ; Berger speech to House of Representatives, 10 November 1919, p. 31, typescript, Berger Col., MCHS. The principles of representative government and freedom of speech are yet to be reconciled in American politics. Similar to the World War I position of Berger and other radicals elected to public office was that of Julian Bond. On 10 January 1966, Representative-elect Bond was excluded from the Georgia House of Representatives, to which he had been legally elected, because of his criticisms of the American government's foreign policy.

62. Milwaukee *Journal* clipping, n.d., Berger Col., MPL. Internal evidence indicates December 1919.

63. Hillquit Statement, December 1919, Speeches and Articles of 1918 to 1927, Hillquit Col., SHSW.

64. Milwaukee *Journal,* 13 December 1919, 17 December 1919; Milwaukee *Leader,* 20 December 1919.

65. Oswald Garrison Villard, "The Berger Victory," *Nation* 109 (27 December 1919): 821; "Why Milwaukee Insists on Berger," *Literary Digest* 64 (3 January 1920): 19.

66. Edward Voigt to Robert Schilling, 8 January 1920, Burton L. French to Schilling, 12 January 1920, Robert Schilling Collection, SHSW. Voigt wrote of Congress; "The Constitutional guaranty of free speech is never referred to around here as it is not considered stylish to do so."

67. Berger to Hillquit, 20 August 1919, Hillquit to Berger, 24 August 1919, Hillquit Col., SHSW.

68. William Bross Lloyd, "The Socialist Party on Trial," *The Liberator* 1 (February 1919): 10; Max Eastman, "Victor Berger," *The Liberator* 2 (May 1919): 7.

10

The Agony of the Party and the Failure of Constructive Socialism

The war and its ramifications changed the nature of the Socialist party. Communication among the factions, never smooth in the pre-war era, deteriorated until party functioning was disrupted, and the organization virtually annihilated. Those who maintained their membership after the St. Louis Proclamation agreed upon the necessity to oppose war, but in the long months that followed, the gulf between those who actively observed the policy and those whose commitment was merely passive widened.

While Victor Berger and his reformist comrades defied the United States government, they were not wedded to proclaimed socialist policy. Indeed, their immobilization in a policy which they never fully accepted handicapped them before both the government and their more radical associates. The leftists were increasingly hostile to the circumspection of the party leadership. Many had entered the war period smoldering silently under leadership they opposed but could not defeat. The unanimity of St. Louis had been a necessity during a crisis, but it was no more than a shoddy imitation of unity, and the following months witnessed a steady pulling apart of the two sides with the more radical group buoyed by war and revolution and angered by the policy of the right. Throughout 1918 the two groups grew farther apart with neither articulating its true position. It was not until after the Armistice in November that the veritable schism wracking the party was exposed.[1]

The composition of the left wing was a mixture of old and new

227

motifs. The leftists frowned upon a political-economic division of spheres between the party and the labor movement, and preferred to emphasize union struggles, utilizing political action only in an auxiliary sense. The efforts of labor itself were viewed in revolutionary and industrial terms, with the AFL anathema. Accordingly, the leftists shunned immediate demands and stood closer to the policy of the Socialist Labor party than to that of the Socialist party, and in their dedication to the class struggle they were spiritually akin to the IWW. The leadership of the left built upon traditional dogma supplemented by new conceptions which evolved from the world war and post-war experiences.

The Bolshevik Revolution disturbed the tenuous balance between the two major factions by reinforcing the leftist perspective and transferring those ideas from the realm of the theoretical to that of the possible. As David Shannon has written, "Their condemnation of gradual evolution into socialism, their disapproval of social reform within capitalism, and their opposition to parliamentary socialist action . . ." now bolstered by the hope of imminent revolution in the United States, meant greater divergency within the party than ever before.

Louis C. Fraina, a pre-war antagonist of the reformists, sparked the leftist renaissance, supplying that faction with its major journalistic ammunition. If any one individual must be cited as the leader of the radical wing in the 1918-1919 schism, it must be Fraina. He was a self-educated intellectual who, by the age of twenty had already "gone through three movements, the Socialist party, the IWW, and the Socialist Labor party." His wartime criticisms of the party leadership went far beyond disputations and distortions, and after the Armistice it was Fraina who controlled the strategy and tactics of the left wing, which culminated in the existence of three separate socialist parties in September 1919.[2]

The radical opposition was joined in the post-war era by a number of socialists who had abandoned the party in order to support Wilson in 1916 and by a smaller group which had left over the war issue in 1917. These apostate socialists were enticed into returning to the party by the government's persecution, by the promise of the Russian Revolution, and by the opportunities for socialist advancement they saw as the war progressed. The most prominent of these returnees was John Reed. His vivid imagination was kindled by the events he witnessed in Russia in November 1917, and upon his return the following April he saw signs of revolution in the United States. An unsympathetic reformist accurately described Reed as a romantic radical who found in the Bolshevik Revolution a basis for intellectual and emotional excitement that more moderate political parties could not offer him.[3] His imaginative and rebellious nature easily transferred the Russian experience to the American environment.

The leftist leaders needed a following in order to mold the Socialist party, and that was supplied by the foreign-language federations of the party. In the year after the Bolshevik Revolution, Slavic immigrants who hitherto had been aloof from the party joined its foreign-language federations as a symbol of their loyalty to and approval of the new Russian government. Since their formation in 1913, the semi-autonomous federations had contained 25 or 30 percent of the membership, but in April 1919 they held 53 percent. That year the party claimed almost a record membership. With 104,822 members, it reached the peak of its numerical strength, with the exception of the 118,000 of 1912. But since the greatest growth occurred in the Russian, Lithuanian, Ukrainian, and south Slavic federations among people who were not American citizens, who typically did not plan to remain in the United States, and who had little interest in its conditions, the reformist leadership was not gratified by the additions. The newcomers' interests lay in Europe, and their membership in the Socialist party only represented their European links and their wish to manipulate the party for the sake of external situations. Because of their perspective, these groups readily responded to charismatic leaders like Reed and Fraina who, while thinking in terms of the American party, attempted to utilize Russian tactics and experience. From the European revolutionary wave they drew the strength that flows from faith but bore the weakness of disorientation.[4]

The first concrete sign of a spirited and ambitious radical challenge to the party leadership appeared with the organization of the Communist Propaganda League in Chicago on the first anniversary of the Bolshevik Revolution. By the close of the year, a League-inspired movement existed in Chicago and in Boston, focused on the Latvian Federation and a newspaper called *The Revolutionary Age,* of which Fraina was the editor-in-chief. The Boston group was the most active and, after capturing the central committee of Local Boston, it forwarded a resolution to the NEC demanding an emergency convention of the party where policy would be formulated in light of the existing international crisis. Local Boston hoped to goad the NEC into action and to embarrass it by publicizing its idleness before the membership.[5]

In January and February of 1919, an organized left wing emerged in New York City. Delegates from Queens and Brooklyn locals, joined by some representatives of Manhattan and the Bronx, bolted a joint meeting of the central committees of the Greater New York locals in protest against the policies of the socialist aldermen of New York City. They formed a city committee which organized a party within the party, constructing its own machinery. The group held a convention on 15 February, passed a manifesto and program, and the Left Wing Section of the Greater New York locals was born.[6]

The policies of the Left Wing Section were debated during February and March as the New York group quickly became the focus of the movement. *The Revolutionary Age,* joined by the *New York Communist*, which John Reed edited, served as the battleground on which tactics and strategy were debated. By the end of March the manifesto and program were modified and accepted by the still loosely organized left wing. The original denial of the possibility of splitting the party was now deleted. The entire program was refined into a revolutionary document which smacked of syndicalism: the capture of the machinery of production and distribution by the workers was endorsed and immediate demands were condemned.

Formulation of policy was accompanied by increased warfare upon the leadership of the Socialist party. Charges of National Executive Committee negligence were intensified. When the NEC called for an amnesty convention to be held jointly with non-socialist organizations, the left charged it with intent to sabotage the demand of the rank and file for an emergency convention. The officials were condemned as reactionaries who did not want a revolution, and *The Revolutionary Age* called for mass action against a leadership which dampened the spirit of the party. It urged that the initial step be the election of revolutionists to the National Executive Committee. Several locals sent resolutions to the NEC in favor of an emergency convention.[7]

The old party leaders, absorbed by numerous government indictments, had not been thoroughly cognizant of the various alterations in mood and membership of the party in 1918. The formal and publicized birth of the Left Wing Section struck at the leadership with more devastating impact than any government indictment. The growth within the party of a strong movement with its own machinery and increasing mass support was seen to be a menace to the Socialist party. While the right wing leaders were aware that their own positions of responsibility and authority were tottering, they were even more agitated over the threatened integrity of the movement they had nourished with their own lives ever since the formation of the party two decades earlier.

The right wing leaders of 1919 were not the same men who led the party a decade earlier, even though there were consistent elements and policies as well as personnel in the leadership of the party. The politics of the schism involved only a few of the earlier dominating figures. By the end of the war, many of the reformist leaders of 1910 had disappeared from the party. Many of the intellectuals, figures as disparate as Simons and Walling, had departed over the war issue. Some, such as Hunter, had retired from the leadership for career or personal reasons. Illness barred Hillquit from direct participation in the monumental post-war socialist power struggle. And Victor L. Berger, always in the forefront in the battles of the right against the left, was absent from the center-stage at the climatic moment because of government persecution.

Thus, old leaders who were responsible for the consistent tenor of party policy were unable to guide the Socialist party in its moment of agony. At a time when the old left merged into a new one, cemented by stimuli that produced its greatest momentum, the right wing found itself fatally crippled and incapable of meeting vigorously the severest internal challenge. That the right wing would not possibly triumph, given the circumstances, should have been obvious to all those involved. That it managed to continue to call the party its own was the most that it could wring from an unequal struggle.

The burden of the battle fell to a few men who had been intimately involved in the reformist faction for many years but who had never occupied the front ranks. The holding action, usually defensive, occasionally unconfidently offensive, was led by Adolph Germer, the unionist who had held party offices since early in the decade and who experienced, as Secretary of the party, the onslaughts of both the left and of the government; James Oneal, a native Indianan who flirted with the left until 1918 when he joined the staff of the New York *Call* and the majority on the National Executive Committee;[8] and Seymour Stedman, one of the founders of the party whose main contribution through the years was the handling of its legal affairs. Other long-time party agitators and organizers who shouldered the responsibility of the struggle were Julius Gerber of New York and George N. Goebel of New Jersey. These men did battle with their party antagonists, encouraged by Berger and Hillquit and their newspapers.

The right wing leaders were quick to conclude that the internal threat to the party was descended from the revolutionist left that periodically challenged the leadership. A different opinion was offered by Hillquit who, far from the scene, argued that the present challenge came from a breed apart from the old "impossibilists." Germer believed that the new faction was not really distinct from the old but was better organized and more determined.[9]

Berger spoke out through the *Leader,* warning the membership against joining the new left. He compared the revolutionists with the German Spartacists who sought to incite a series of turbulent uprisings in order to foster revolution. "We do not say that there will never be any violence used in making the social transition in this country. We do say we hope there will not be any violence used. We say there will not be any violence used if we can help it. . . ." He opposed unnecessary bloodshed and insisted on the probability that such actions would fail and lead to vengeance upon all radical groups by the forces of the status quo. History had taught him that a technologically advanced state had sufficient power to crush would-be revolutionists.

Berger maintained that the left wingers were opposed to political action entirely and, therefore, ought to resign from the party. Bitter because of his own experiences, Berger considered the activities of the leftists treasonous. "The great bulk of the membership of the party . . . had their faces set like flint towards our enemies, when the left wingers began stabbing us in the back."[10]

Since it was more vital than ever before that the reformists maintain their control of the National Executive Committee, the months leading up to the May NEC elections saw aggressive campaigning, with legal and illegal methods employed. The left became increasingly noisy in its propaganda and it was impossible for its opponents to determine the degree of solid support upon which it could actually draw. The reformist leaders began to shift their strategy and to modify their passive, holding tactics. While they continued to plan an amnesty convention in conjunction with non-socialists, they now considered calling a party convention to comply with radical-stimulated requests from the rank and file. Germer's decision to confront the revolutionist movement in convention swung the reformists to that point of view. Germer was in a better position than any of his comrades to watch the leftist maneuvers, and he told Hillquit that the Left Wing Section had succeeded in converting some very active locals into mere debating societies. "The interesting thing about their whole propaganda is that everything they publish is couched in practically the same language, showing that they have sown their seeds throughout the entire movement," he wrote. It was the fear of such a destructive and monolithic force that changed Germer's mind about the advisability of holding a convention. Although he prevailed, not all reformist factions were convinced that a confrontation through a publicized convention would be good policy. The Wisconsin State Executive Committee unanimously voted against it, arguing the still operative Espionage Act would hinder discussion.

Both the right and the left promoted their own slates of candidates for the NEC; in addition, the left tried to block the election of the perennial leaders, signalling out Berger, Hillquit, Work, and Stedman as especially worthy of defeat. The campaign of the left was a well organized attempt to win over district after district for its candidates.[11]

The strategy of the right, which was not peculiar to this specific campaign, was to capture those marginal individuals and groups which belonged to neither the right or the left.[12] But the prospects of the reformists were not bright, as more and more locals endorsed the program passed by the Left Wing Section. The election results confirmed their worst fears as the leftists elected twelve of the fifteen on the committee as well as the international representatives of the party. Berger was elected to the NEC, although his vote was much diminished from previous years; although the third-highest vote-getter, he ranked far behind Louis C. Fraina and Charles E. Ruthenberg in total votes.

But the reformists saw no reason to accept a verdict that they were certain would do the party and their own faction irreparable harm. The resurgence of the left had achieved one of its announced aims: it had prodded the party leadership into action. Gone was the mold in which the war had encased the leaders, and they assumed an offensive that knew no bounds. Irony marked the struggle between the two factions as it was played out between May and September of 1919. The reformists exploited and manipulated party machinery and utilized direct action to insure control of the party, while the Left Wing Section demanded democratic political procedures.[13]

The right wing assembled in Chicago the week of 24 May for the most important meeting that the National Executive Committee ever held. Its two big names were missing—Berger was in Washington, D.C., and Hillquit in Saranac Lake, New York. But all the other major reformist leaders were present and the task before them was clear. They had had to recall Big Bill Haywood in 1913 from the NEC for the danger he represented to the party. That the party constitution did not provide them with power of recall in the Haywood case did not deter them. So, too, in 1919 the leaders were determined to rid the party of those threatening it from within. The cancer had to be excised from the organism and the extent of the surgery, that is, the numbers involved, was of no consequence. A careless reading of the constitution had allowed them to oust Haywood, and they saw little difference between that and the current unpleasant task.

Hillquit's influence was felt through his suggestion of a division of the socialist movement into two distinct groups. He insisted that the antagonisms stirred by the in-fighting were too great for reconciliation. Hillquit condemned the left wing for tactics which, he said "would lead us nowhere." Essentially, he thought, the Left Wing Section was reactionary and emotional, and a split was desirable. "Better a hundred times to have two numerically small Socialist organizations, each homogeneous and harmonious within itself, than to have one big party torn by dissensions and squabbles, an impotent colossus on feet of clay. The time for action is near. Let us clear the decks." The not unsophisticated left wing realized that the right had determined to expel the leftists one way or another while simultaneously placing the onus on them. The left complained of the use of gangster tactics by its opponents and stated that its own aim was not to split the party but to capture it.[14]

The NEC, after several long days of meetings during which the committee heard various charges against the leftists, voted to revoke the charter of the leftist Michigan State organization and to suspend seven foreign-language federations.[15] The committee also reviewed the ballots cast in the recent elections, in which it had been overwhelmingly defeated, and appointed an investigatory commission to examine the election thoroughly. Its own cursory investigation, it stated, revealed that the ballots had been subject to wholesale fraud. Certain locals had cast more votes than they had members, others obviously had been marked by one individual, and, throughout, a "mechanical unanimity" in voting never before seen in the Socialist party prevailed. To justify its suspensions of the foreign-language federations for their suspected illegal conduct of the elections and its expulsion of Michigan for amending its own constitution to exclude political actionists, the NEC maintained that its ability to grant affiliation was accompanied by the power to revoke such grants, and it insisted that the ousters were not related to the proclivity of those organizations for the left wing.[16]

Berger's attitude toward the upheaval within the party was rather philosophical and detached, reflecting his distance from the scene of the action. Despite a number of leftist efforts to take over Milwaukee locals, Berger did not feel his organization threatened. Therefore, he was able to accept the partial responsibility of the reformists for the resurgence of the left wing. "We have always played too much with the revolutionary phrase," he wrote. "In this game of would-be radical phrases the one who can play the game the hardest will naturally win. And the emptier the barrel the louder the sound." All through the eventful summer of 1919 Berger was occupied with the congressional hearings; but with an eye on the party divisions, he told Congress that recent events verified his dire predictions of the extremism that would result from government harassment of patriotic and democratic socialists.[17]

During the next three months, both factions of the party concentrated upon preparations for the 30 August national convention summoned by the National Executive Committee. A farcical series of events ensued as resolutions were submitted and denounced, referenda and election results overturned, and contested offices held only by the mere physical presence of the office holder. The melodrama of right against left was complicated further by the division of the left into two separate groups as a result of a Left Wing policy conference.

The left continued its offensive. It charged the leadership with unnecessarily causing a breach in the party through the suspensions and insisted that its own goal was party unity in revolutionary socialism. It denounced the NEC policies as counter-revolutionary and maintained that the left wing movement was now dominant. Late in May, the Left Wing Section—while arguing that it was not a disruptive organization—announced its determination not to be ousted.[18]

The Ohio State organization, through the governing body of Local Cuyahoga County (Cleveland), submitted a resolution to the National Office which restored to good standing the Michigan State organization and the seven foreign-language federations by reversing the ruling of the NEC. It insisted that the original and legitimate ballots cast in the party elections be recognized as valid. The Ohio branch of the party was one of the most militant. It was dominated by Alfred Wagenknecht, who represented the left wing on the NEC, and by Charles E. Ruthenberg. Their continuous evolution leftward was accompanied by the recruitment of revolutionists who strengthened the trend. Max Hayes, an old right wing leader, resigned from Local Cuyahoga County rather than accept its increasing radicalism.[19]

A conference of the Left Wing Section was scheduled for June in order to unite formally all leftist elements; a second goal was the clarification of policy over continued membership in the Socialist party. Many had read the NEC's earlier actions to mean a parting of the two groups and they came to the conference with the objective of founding a new party.

Ninety-four representatives from twenty states met in New York on 21 June only to find themselves a sorely divided group. The foreign-language delegates and those from Michigan wanted to organize a new revolutionary party at once, while most of the English-speaking delegates favored the capture of the Socialist party. The conference, by a vote of fifty-five to thirty-eight, opposed the immediate organization of a communist party. The disgruntled minority withdrew from the conference and embarked upon the path that led to their own convention on 1 September in Chicago, where the Communist party was born.

The conference elected a National Council of nine, headed by Fraina and Ruthenberg; it also promulgated a national manifesto in amplification of the February manifesto and planned its strategy for the capture of the Socialist party. An attempt was to be made to dominate the socialist convention so that the party could be transformed into a communist party. Failure to gain control would be followed at once by the organization of a new party.

The next month the leftists' National Council declared those who had won the disputed party elections to be the new NEC. It named L. E. Katterfeld temporary party chairman and Alfred Wagenknecht temporary executive secretary, reinstated the ousted organizations, decreed *The Revolutionary Age* to be the official party newspaper, and voted to affiliate with the Communist International.[20] But any chance of capturing the Socialist party lay in the events of the convention.

The party itself changed in structure and membership during the months preceding the 30 August convention. In early spring it claimed 104,822, but from May onward its membership decreased drastically and continuously. Twenty thousand members were expelled by the NEC in May, and subsequently those locals and state organizations which supported the ousted groups and the left wing program were expelled by the old leadership. It conducted a brief investigation of the Massachusetts organization which had given birth to the left wing; the result was its expulsion and the reorganization of the Massachusetts branch around dependable reformist elements.[21]

The motion for a referendum to reverse NEC actions by Local Cuyahoga County was delayed by the National Executive Committee and then dropped on the technicality of editorial content. The motion had received considerable support from left wing locals and others who disapproved of the NEC's arbitrary policies, and the National Office had been flooded with seconds to the referendum on forms prepared by Local Cuyahoga. Indignation erupted when the referendum was prevented from reaching the membership, and the leadership tried to placate outraged members by identifying the left with the threat of violence.[22]

In August the Ohio State organization was expelled by the NEC. Berger voted for the revocation of its charter because of Ohio's "plain and open violation of the National Constitution." This ouster brought the leaders considerable satisfaction, for they saw the Ohioans as capable of more than average chicanery. For example, both Germer and Goebel believed that the Cuyahoga referendum had been worded unconstitutionally in the hope that the NEC's expected condemnation of it might boomerang.[23]

Thereafter the main interest of the party officials was the election of acceptable delegates to the national convention. Berger's *Leader* played up its knowledge of the radicals' plan to pack the convention or withdraw. It warned its readers against electing demogogic radical delegates, and used Berger's old tactic of identifying the left wing with anarchism.

Berger himself, whose opinions were reflected by Mayor Hoan, had one last plan. If, despite all efforts, the so-called anarchists gained control of the party at the convention, the right could bolt. While the reformists were prepared to expel the radicals, loss of leadership to that group would result in the bolt of the right. Schism was not the choice of the old line leaders, but since it was imminent, they began to look forward to the convention as a chance to start anew. "We are confronted with an opportunity for the first time in years to clear the deck for clean-cut political action."

In addition to the welcome chance to separate from the leftists, Berger saw another opportunity in the agony of the party. Not only might the organization henceforth proceed along its chosen path unhindered by direct actionists, but further sanctification of the principle of local autonomy might be forced on the vulnerable party. To Hillquit, he revealed that: "we will insist that the constitution of the national party be changed in such a way as to give us more freedom of action in future, both as to *giving* and *accepting endorsements* and as to making *arrangements* with other *organizations* so long as the *integrity* of our *organization* is made *secure.*" (Italics Berger's.) Since the party was on its knees now, subject to dictation from persons new to the organization, why should not Victor L. Berger exploit the opportunity as well? Who had more right to shape Socialist party policy, he reasoned, than a man who had dedicated his entire adult life to its well-being and success. He had always insisted upon the right of local organizations to guide their own policies so long as they remained within accepted socialist principle, but he had met with only a degree of success. He had also striven unsuccessfully to lead the party into non-entangling alliances with other organizations for the sake of specific and temporary goals. Now he hoped to make both into permanent party principles.[24]

Confiding his plans to Hillquit did him no harm and might well have had beneficial results, for it was the convalescing Hillquit, far from the daily exigencies of politics, who had been invited by the nervous reformist leadership to draft a platform for presentation to the membership. Hillquit worked carefully during the month of August and, ignoring vituperation, finally decided upon a theoretical and tactical statement which could be utilized as a framework upon which to build a platform.[25] The statement he ultimately produced attempted to vindicate the St. Louis Proclamation, for which he bore much responsibility.

Any radical worthy of the name entrained for Chicago the last week in August. The National Executive Committee opened the convention on the morning of 30 August only to face a determined opposition prepared to dominate the proceedings or withdraw, while a mile-and-a-half away the formative convention of the Communist party was set to open.

For the first time in its history, police-enforced order was required so that a convention of the Socialist party might begin. The leftists, led by John Reed, hoped to control the proceedings through sheer numbers and, lacking the proper identification cards held by the elected delegates, arrived early and filled the front seats of the hall. The Chicago police were present because of Wagenknecht's public boasting the day before that the left wing could "take over the convention by storm . . ." if necessary, and the police cleared the hall of the would-be usurpers at the request of Adolph Germer.[26] Once in undisputed possession of the hall, the reformists tried to clear themselves of any taint of leaning upon the capitalist police force, and in the ensuing discussion considered a resolution condemning the police! Berger, who played no role in substantive matters, derided the motion. In remarks which Max Eastman described as the most straightforward heard, he said: "I've never tried to be revolutionary . . . but I've tried to be honest. If the police weren't here, none of you would be, so what's the use of all this hypocrisy?"[27]

The convention had to settle contested delegations, and this resulted in a further loss of members to the other two parties. Half of the contesting left wingers were seated, but when their candidate for convention chairman, Joseph M. Coldwell, lost overwhelmingly to Seymour Stedman, they realized it was hopeless to expect to win over the delegates, and Coldwell led a walkout which was followed by another the next day.

The convention did not turn to the right after the departure of the most vociferous radicals. The Socialist party, despite the hesitation of the reformist-minded leadership to welcome the revolution abroad and its internal implications, was not, after all, content with the status quo in the United States. The members were radicals seeking a more equitable life for the masses they desired to lead. They could not, therefore, remain untouched by the change in atmosphere of the post-war world. Moreover, the withdrawal of the revolutionists from the party was accompanied by the virtual retirement from policy-making of the most tenacious foe of anything suggestive of revolution: Victor Berger. His major interest now centered upon his still-intact Milwaukee organization, and his activity at the Chicago convention was limited to verbal assaults upon the departed communists, née left wingers. His only lengthy speech called them criminals for stabbing the Socialist party in the back, and he successfully opposed a motion which was designed to encourage recalcitrant bolters to return to the party.[28]

Those who picked up the policy-making role which Berger dropped found themselves faced with militant and aroused delegates who did not choose to stand aside from the seething world of political and social revolution. The delegates accepted the NEC report in justification of the suspensions, but berated the leadership for failing to allow the suspended members the opportunity to repudiate their officials and remain in the party. The delegates insisted upon investigating the charges by seceders that the convention was packed and, in this matter, completely exonerated the leaders.[29] But they continued to demonstrate that they were capable of more than rubber-stamping.

Morris Hillquit, *in absentia,* helped set the tone for the convention when his statement was adopted as a preamble to its constitution. Hillquit never condemned the left wingers with the malice shown by some of his comrades, possibly because he did not experience personally their machinations. Uninvolved in the turmoil, he was better able to maintain perspective on the modifications which the radical world was undergoing and to evaluate the opportunities presented by such changes. In his preamble he reaffirmed the existence of the class struggle and committed the party to "every measure which betters the conditions of the working-class and which increases the fighting power of that class within the present system" in order to achieve social ownership and democratic control of production. Echoing Hillquit's tones, the delegates wrote a party manifesto in which they pledged "support to revolutionary workers in Russia, to radical Socialists of Germany, Austria and Hungary in efforts to establish working-class rule."[30]

The party's increased militancy was best evident in its policy on international affiliation. The majority report, which Berger signed despite his announced support for the pre-war International, repudiated European efforts to revive the Second International, ignored the five-month-old Communist International, and proposed the formation of a new international organization to include all parties which subscribed to the principle of the class struggle. Such a dodge was unpalatable to some members of the committee on international relations, and J. Louis Engdahl and William Kruse, who led the remaining leftist forces, submitted a minority report which endorsed the Russian International as a proletarian force genuinely challenging capitalism and imperialism. An indication of the mood of the party's membership was evidenced when, in an almost unique event in the party's history, the membership voted three-to-one to adopt the minority report instead of the majority report. Thereafter, the leadership unwillingly applied to the Russian-based International for admission.[31]

As the ultimate gesture to the remaining membership to prove that the old guard leadership had no interest in dominating machinery or dictating policy, the entire National Executive Committee refused to run for re-election and Adolph Germer resigned as Executive Secretary of the party.[32] To ensure a degree of continuity, however, one of the leaders who had been involved in the war and post-war crisis, James Oneal, was persuaded to serve on the new NEC. But with the change in personnel, the opening era of the Socialist party ended.

The only consistent element was the choice of Debs as presidential candidate, and the nomination was made without any of the rancor which was involved in his previous race. Confined to a federal penitentiary in Atlanta under a ten year sentence for violation of the Espionage Act, Debs, the personification of the amnesty controversy, was the logical selection. His candidacy was agreed upon at the 1919 convention and officially confirmed at the 1920 convention.

The major issue at the convention of 1920 was the question of international affiliation, since the referendum had not settled the issue. Hillquit submitted the majority report which recommended joining the Communist International contingent upon its de-emphasis of its endorsement of the dictatorship of the proletariat, while Engdahl and Kruse again submitted the minority report in favor of unqualified affiliation with the Russian organization. Berger, whose major interest within the national party was the severance of all ties with Moscow and the domestic communist parties, came from Milwaukee to the New York convention determined to stamp out such influences.[33] He warned the convention against trying to unite forces which did not belong together, and denounced any effort to imitate Russian patterns of socialist development as erroneous and harmful. Russia, he argued, was a backward country whose needs were different from nations of the west. In reference to the party platform he said: "We should use as few revolutionary phrases as possible. Let us discard the Marxian verbiage that has become so hackneyed by continuous repetition in the last 30 years. . . . The Socialist Party of America has not bowed down before the American plutocracy and its government in Washington. Let us see whether that party has the courage and the stamina not to bow down before the revolutionary phrase."[34]

He embodied his views in a third report, which he alone of the committee on international relations signed, proposing an International of socialist parties of all western nations. In arguing fervently against any link with the Russians, his voice was at times drowned by a chorus of jeers from some of the delegates. Berger was at his most eloquent as he maintained that he would defend Soviet Russia's right to exist, but that Russia could not provide the Socialist party of America with its principles. American socialists, he said, favored the collective owner- ship of the means of production and distribution, but never collective consumption. Another difference he noted was the socialist preference for complete democracy, including the enfranchisement of non- socialists who might be converted gradually, in contrast to the ter- roristic disenfranchisement in eastern Europe. "The American Socialist Party," he said, ". . . after having gotten rid of its Communists and Anarcho-Syndicalists—has absolutely no reason nor any excuse to join an organization made up of these elements." Berger used his major arguments against the concept of the dictatorship of the proletariat which he knew displeased Hillquit and his other comrades. He said he had no taste for any form of dictatorship or bossism, despite his own reputation. He denounced such a policy as nonsense, adding that a minority could not prevail for long. Chillingly he warned, "The idea of the dictatorship finally means the dictatorship of the small crowd and in the end the dictatorship of one man. . . ."[35] The accuracy of Berger's remarks was revealed in the not too distant future, but for the present, his influence spent, his words went unheeded.

A referendum on the majority and minority reports endorsed the less radical of the two. The leftist mood of the party was receding and, indeed, signs of the old spirit of comradeship were visible at the conven- tion.[36] This was Berger's compensation for his own loss of ef- fectiveness. The shift of the Socialist party to the left had been brief, and the party soon regained its inner equilibrium as it ceased to find its frame of reference outside American conditions.

The agony which the Socialist party experienced in the war-torn world of 1918 and 1919 has been evaluated by some of the participants who suffered through it. James Oneal sees the resurgent left as a revival of the force tendency which periodically characterizes American labor.

The affinity of the new left of this period for mass action and the general strike and its opposition to political reformism connected it to the anarcho-syndicalism that briefly touched the party in the pre-war era. Thus, Oneal ties the nascent Communist party to the American Wobblies, whom he considered to be integrated into a traditional radicalism which lacked patience for political means and endorsed a qualified use of force. For Oneal, while the communists arose from mainly external causes, they were not out of place on the American radical stage. The communists inherently expressed the earlier force tendencies.[37]

Louis Waldman, who was one of the duly elected but expelled New York Assemblymen in 1920, believed that as a result of the ill-advised war policy, the rise of the Communist party and the decline of the Socialist party was inevitable. Waldman found his own comrades, rather than external events, responsible.[38]

William James Ghent had left the reformist faction and the Socialist party over the war policy but, unlike other former members, he never turned on his old comrades. He believed that the socialists had been caught between the forces of war and bolshevism, and through their own errors had compounded the dilemma, resulting in a resurgence of reaction in the country. He held the Socialist party responsible for being swept away by the revolutionary atmosphere. Apologizing for and even justifying the radicals abroad, Ghent said, led to support for a radical course at home. "Striving by elastic formulas, and by new definitions of such words as 'democracy' and 'dictatorship,' to hold to its ranks both the radical extremists and the moderates, it failed."[39] And so, Ghent concluded, the reformists brought the holocaust down upon themselves.

Berger had no overall comment on the post-war events for he did not think the life of the party was spent. While he had withdrawn from an active role, his move was intended to be only temporary. But his role as policy-maker in a growing political organization was behind him. With the end of the second decade of the Socialist party of America, Berger's contribution and that of his close comrades was finished. After the war, the Milwaukee socialist was only a peripheral figure in the momentous events that shook the foundations upon which he had helped build the movement. The war experience had served to drain the party leadership and immobilize it in a policy alien to it; the reformists could not act in accordance with their own judgments, and they lacked the will to break their bonds and react to the exigencies of the war as they perceived them. To compound the agonies suffered by the officials, a great gap developed which eventually fragmented the party completely. Involved as they were with indictments, trials, and appeals, the leadership realized with painful surprise at war's end how immense a gulf divided the party. By the time they could respond, the resurgent left had walked off with some of the most active individuals and locals.

The reformist leaders and Berger himself could no longer fight back with the customary vigor and agility. Berger, weakened by immobilization, indictment, and isolation, had relinquished the burden. The struggle could only be pursued by others less experienced and less tired. Berger's usefulness, and indeed his story, end before the 1919 convention. From that time onward, his movement—its potential and its very being—was no more. External events and internal errors combined to destroy the dream.

NOTES

1. As an example of leftist criticism of the reformists at this time, see "The Crisis and the Socialist Party," *The Revolutionary Age* 1 (30 November 1918): 1.

2. Theodore Draper, *The Roots of American Communism* (New York: Viking Press, 1957), pp. 17-22, 24-28, 60-63; David A. Shannon, *The Socialist Party of America: A History* (New York: Macmillan Co., 1955); pp. 127-128. A few years later (in 1922), Fraina was dropped from the Communist party and became an "unperson" to American communism. Draper offers one of the fullest treatments available of the details of this period; James Oneal and G. A. Warner, *American Communism: A Critical Analysis of its Origins, Development and Programs* (New York: E. P. Dutton and Co., Inc., 1947), is also helpful.

3. Granville Hicks, *John Reed: The Making of a Revolutionary* (New York: Macmillan Co., 1936), p. 324; Louis Waldman, *Labor Lawyer* (New York: E. P. Dutton and Co., Inc., 1944), p. 71.

4. Adolph Germer to Nathan L. Welch, 7 June 1919, SP

Col., Duke; Germer to Morris Hillquit, 17 April 1919, Hillquit Col., SHSW.

5. Draper, *The Roots of American Communism*, p. 144. The documents issued by the Communist Propaganda League of Chicago were signed by J. Louis Engdahl, William Bross Lloyd, Alexander Stoklitsky, and I. Edward Ferguson, its secretary, among others. Edward Lindgren, "What Is the 'Left Wing' Movement and its Purpose?" *The Class Struggle* 3 (February 1919): 114-115; "The Crisis and the Socialist Party," *The Revolutionary Age* 1 (30 November 1918): 1.

6. Maxmilian Cohen, "The Growth of the Left Wing," *The Revolutionary Age* 1 (8 March 1919): 7. The manifesto and program of the Left Wing Section are found in *The Class Struggle* 3 (May 1919): 209-216, and in *The Revolutionary Age* 1 (8 February 1919): 4-5 and, as modified, in *The Revolutionary Age* 1 (22 March 1919), 4. They are also found in *Revolutionary Radicalism*, I, 706-716. The latter contains the inaccurate and simplistic history of the rise of the left wing, by the New York investigatory committee, 676-705.

7. "Our NEC," *The Revolutionary Age* 1 (22 February 1919): 2; "We Must Have a National Emergency Convention," *The Revolutionary Age* 1 (8 March 1919): 1.

8. Solon De Leon, ed., *American Labor Who's Who* (New York: Hanford Press, 1925), p. 179.

9. Germer to Hillquit, 9 April 1919, 22 March 1919, Hillquit Col., SHSW.

10. Milwaukee *Leader*, 28 April 1919; *The Commonwealth*, 3 May 1919.

11. In March Berger moved unsuccessfully that the NEC declare ineligible for office members who had been in the party less than three years and who had been officials of foreign socialist parties. *The Bulletin*, 24 March 1919; *The Commonwealth*, 3 May 1919; Germer to Hillquit, 9 April 1919, 22 March 1919, Hillquit Col., SHSW.

12. Germer to Hillquit, 17 April 1919, Hillquit Col., SHSW. He wrote: "There are two elements in the party that I feel can be harmonized. The one is the so-called 'right-wing' and the other the so-called 'center.' "

13. Draper, *The Roots of American Communism*, pp.

156-157; Lillian Symes and Clement Travers, *Rebel America: The Story of Social Revolt in the United States* (New York: Harper and Bros., Pubs., 1934), p. 327.

14. Morris Hillquit, *The Immediate Issue* (New York: The Socialist, 1919), p. 15; "Split the Party," *The Revolutionary Age* 1 (17 Mary 1919): 2.

15. *The Eye Opener*, May 1919; NEC Statement on Suspensions and Expulsions, 30 May 1919, SP Col., National Office File, 1896-1922, Duke. The seven federations and the Detroit local, nucleus of the Michigan organization, had endorsed the Left Wing Section's program. Only Wagenknecht and Katterfeld opposed the oustings. Those voting in favor were Stedman, Goebel, Hogan, Krafft, Work, Oneal, and A. Shiplacoff. Germer to Glenn H. Pangborn, 12 June 1919, SP Col., Duke.

16. John M. Work, "Autobiography," II, ch. 5, 15, typescript, John M. Work Collection, SHSW; Germer to John Sutton, 18 June 1919, SP Col., Duke. It is unfortunate that the ballots are no longer extant. Draper maintains that the reformists' cry of fraud was based on flimsy evidence. He argues that their actions in May split the party; the later conventions were merely postscripts. Draper, *The Roots of American Communism*, pp. 157-158; Germer to Ethel Tait, 26 June 1919, SP Col., Duke.

17. Berger to Hillquit, 20 August 1919, Hillquit Col., SHSW; Berger speech to House of Representatives, 10 November 1919, p. 23, typescript, Berger Col., MCHS.

18. Ludwig Lore, "Left or Right?", *The Class Struggle* 3 (August 1919): 263; "Split the Party," *The Revolutionary Age* 1 (24 May 1919): 3; "Clear the Decks," *The Revolutionary Age* 1 (31 May 1919): 3.

19. *The Revolutionary Age* 1 (7 June 1919): 1; *The Commonwealth*, 24 May 1919.

20. "Call for a National Conference of the Left Wing," *The Revolutionary Age* 1 (26 April 1919): 1; "Program of the Left Wing Conference," *The Revolutionary Age* 1 (3 May 1919): 1; Ludwig Lore, "The National Convention," *The Class Struggle* 3 (August 1919): 348; Draper, *The Roots of American Communism*, p. 174; Shannon, *The Socialist Party of America*, pp. 140-141; I. E. Ferguson to Left Wing

locals, 11 July 1919, SP Col., Duke. This collection has a typescript of the letter from the National Council detailing its decision.

21. Germer to John Sutton, 8 June 1919, SP Col., Duke.

22. Germer to NEC, 11 July 1919, SP National Office File, 1896-1922, Duke.

23. *The Eye Opener,* June, July 1919; Germer to NEC, 11 July 1919, 20 August 1919, SP National Office File, 1896-1922, Duke; Germer to J. F. Denison, 15 July 1919, SP Col., Duke.

24. Milwaukee *Leader,* 11 July 1919; 29 July 1919, *The Commonwealth,* 6 September 1919; Berger to Hillquit, 20 August 1919, Hillquit Col., SHSW; Daniel W. Hoan to Thomas Van Lear, 5 July 1919, Berger Col., MCHS. Van Lear was the socialist mayor of Minneapolis from 1916 to 1918.

25. Hillquit to Algernon Lee, 24 August 1919, Hillquit Col., SHSW. This letter is also found in the Lee Col., Tamiment Institute.

26. There are many versions of this incident. In Reed's biography, Hicks insists that Germer called the police. Hicks, *John Reed,* p. 359. Reed's group organized the Communist Labor party the next day.

27. Socialist Party, *Proceedings of the 1919 National Convention,* pp. 7, 84-87, 120; Max Eastman, "The Chicago Conventions," *The Liberator* 2 (October 1919): 11.

28. Socialist Party, *Proceedings of the 1919 National Convention,* pp. 317, 551. All of the documents issued by the convention are found in *The Bulletin* of 15 September 1919. The normally eight-page party weekly contained twenty-four pages in order to accommodate the many documents of the convention.

29. *American Labor Yearbook* (1919-1920) (New York: Rand School of Social Science), p. 408; Shannon, *The Socialist Party of America,* p. 151.

30. *American Labor Yearbook* (1919-1920), p. 410; SP, *Manifesto of the Socialist Party* (Chicago: Socialist Party, 1919), p. 4.

31. *American Labor Yearbook* (1919-1920), p. 411. The majority and minority reports are found on pp. 410-411;

Shannon, *The Socialist Party in America,* p. 153. The Socialist party was refused admittance by the Third or Communist International and condemned as bourgeois.

32. Harry W. Laidler, "The Present Status of Socialism
in America," Pt. 2, *The Socialist Review* 8 (January 1920):
113.

33. It was ironical that in the 1930s, after Berger's
death, his widow, a lifelong socialist activist, was persuaded to
join the Communist party secretly and to contribute the re-
mains of Berger's estate to the party. The result of the entry
of the Communist party into Wisconsin was the disruption of
the remnants of the Socialist party there. Benjamin Gitlow,
*The Whole of their Lives: Communism in America—A Per-
sonal History* (New York: Charles Scribner's Sons, 1948), p.
365.

34. Milwaukee *Leader,* 24 April 1920.

35. Socialist Party, *Proceedings of the 1920 National
Convention,* pp. 876-881. The New York *Call* of 17 May
1920, acknowledged that Berger was hated as was no other
socialist by "reactionaries" and communists alike.

36. Laidler, "The National Socialist Party Convention,"
The Socialist Review 9 (June 1920): 24; Shannon, *The Socialist Party of America,* p. 153.

37. Oneal and Werner, *American Communism,* pp. 10,
65, 75.

38. Waldman, *Labor Lawyer,* p. 46.

39. William James Ghent, *The Reds Bring Reaction*
(Princeton: Princeton University Press, 1923), pp. 10, 31.

Epilogue

The Socialist party of the 1920s was a different one from that of its first two decades. Traditional socialist optimism and faith were present but less ardent. The Socialist party and its members had had to face the fact that the possibility of assuming a major role in American life was gone for the present—and perhaps forever.

Americans of many views who favored change in the status quo had been alienated from the Socialist party during World War I. Those who remained committed to socialism were divided thereafter among several parties—the Socialist party, the Communist party, and the Communist Labor party, as well as the moribund SLP. They were at odds over the imminency of revolution, over tactics, and over the relationship to Soviet Russia.

The old Socialist party, putting on the best face possible, pursued its traditional organizational tasks and election campaigns, but its shrunken base denied it validity. Its membership of 26,766 in 1920 was equal to that of its total in 1906. But fourteen years made a vast difference. Membership in the Socialist party in 1920 could not easily elicit belief in the inevitability of a growing national movement gradually reshaping the American system. Rather, membership signified a protest against the present or the past. A vote for the party meant solidarity with a set of ideas and a hope that those ideas would come to permeate and then rearrange American life. But any hope that the party might direct change had evaporated.

The reformist wing surely recognized the disparity between its present situation and its early ambitions. It felt its own failure, for it had held the dominant position in the party during its expansion and after its collapse. Had this group's policies and efforts, geared to constructive socialism, been somehow ill-conceived or misdirected?

The reformist wing attempted to operate within the tenets of democratic socialism and apply them to American politics, and the pragmatist who achieved the greatest success in this area was Victor L. Berger. The major internal difficulty which plagued socialists everywhere was no problem to Berger, who was capable of following a political path to political solutions. Unlike some of his comrades, his was not the dilemma of the moral man in an immoral society who fears to act. His steps were not dogged by an inability to participate in the daily give-and-take of politics. Rather, he was willing to confront the basic issues of capitalist society simply because they existed. That the coming of the socialist millennium, for example, would erase the problem of a fair wage, since workers would own the means of production, did not mean that a fair wage ought not to be a concern in the present. Moreover, Berger had personally settled the revisionist-dogmatist conflict and believed that he knew the limits to which Marxism might be followed. He willingly utilized Marxist theory when appropriate and his own revisions when necessary. He was the outstanding example of the individualist as socialist and of a principled pragmatist in the image of Weber's analysis.

After resolving the socialist moral dilemma for himself, he was prepared to do so for the party. He wanted the Socialist party to act and participate in the existing political system in order to transform the system gradually. He wanted it to strive, on the basis of its fundamental concepts, for positive change, and thus transcend the dilemma which doomed it to irrelevancy. The obvious path for the party, according to Berger, was to maintain a socialist analysis while "accepting" capitalist society in order to alter it. The alternative, that of sworn hostility to existing society, was foolish and futile. Berger's task, and that of his constructive socialism, was twofold—to achieve socialism within the American framework and to guide the Socialist party toward that end. Once the party was led to relate the ethic of responsibility to the ethic of ultimate ends, it could function meaningfully in the achievement of its goals. The party, like Berger himself, would embody Weber's teachings.

Had it not been for Berger's egotism, bossism, and aggressiveness, he might have combined local political strength with national renown to become the acclaimed leader of the reformists. His personal characteristics precluded even the possibility of such a development. But had he held undisputed leadership, he might have been able to solve the party's dilemma.

His frustrations were compounded further when his effectiveness was curtailed during the interventionist crisis. Personal depression overwhelmed him and he allowed the opportunity for initiative to slip away. By April 1917, the party decisions were no longer his to help formulate. Aside from the fact that he had been deserted, Berger clearly failed at a critical moment. Instead of fighting for his own views at the convention, he signed the majority report and thus abnegated responsibility to the ideal of constructive opposition and obliterated all chance of that ideal materializing. Thereafter the revolutionists refused to relinquish the initiative and Berger witnessed the disintegration of the party he had known.

Berger's failure meant the defeat of his efforts to fit the party to American conditions. Americanizing socialism was the nucleus of his constructivism. But when Berger agreed that intervention was unjust and that the war effort was not supportable, he and his party assumed a posture apart from American conditions, thus violating Weber's principled pragmatism. He soon regretted this rejection of his life's work and his regret led him to all sorts of absurdities, such as the boasting over his purchase of Liberty bonds. But the party's direction had shifted and on this fundamental level he failed. He had not resolved the party's moral dilemma.

But Victor Berger himself can not be dismissed as a failure. He personally did much to enlarge the party's potential and to shape its development. As a freshman congressman from 1911 to 1913, he presented the American public with an attractive and palatable image of socialism. His efforts to find meaningful solutions to the problems faced by the workingman, his endorsement of progressive legislation, his appearance of respectability, all tended to persuade the public that socialism was not inconsistent with democracy and the American ethos. Leftists treated Berger's congressional role with contempt, but he provided a genuine service to the Socialist party by demonstrating that the party offered an alternative to the voters. Had he not been hampered by the left's constant criticism and lack of support from his own timid comrades, Berger might have made a still greater impact on the public.

Berger's distinctive and enduring contribution to American socialism may be found in the extent to which he molded the party
through his stress upon the necessity of working within the American
system, his justification of revisionism, and especially his emphasis on
the peaceful evolution of socialism. The Socialist party of America was
marked at its birth by a reputation for violence to the degree that even
its members believed force was unavoidable. Through Berger's constant
preaching and supplications, the evolving reformist faction grew to look
askance at the use of violence. It minimized that possibility in the
transformation of society and grew to cherish its democratic principles.
The democratic heritage became as important to the reformist wing as
did socialization, and when the schism occurred, the reformists realized
that their commitment to democracy was too fundamental to be waved
aside and submerged in a Communist party subservient to an alien
system. Democratic socialism, though crippled and shrunken, yet survived, and Victor L. Berger was its patron saint.

Bibliography

MANUSCRIPTS

Victor L. Berger Collection, 1900-1932. Milwaukee County Historical Society.

Victor L. Berger Collection. Milwaukee Public Library.

Victor L. Berger Collection. Tamiment Institute. New York.

Eugene V. Debs Collection. Tamiment Institute. New York.

John Jacob Esch Collection. State Historical Society of Wisconsin, Madison, Wisconsin.

Adolph Germer Collection, 1898-1958. State Historical Society of Wisconsin, Madison, Wisconsin.

Frederic Heath Collection. Milwaukee County Historical Society.

Morris Hillquit Collection. Tamiment Institute. New York.

Morris Hillquit Collection. State Historical Society of Wisconsin, Madison, Wisconsin.

Algernon Lee Collection. Tamiment Institute. New York.

Meyer London Collection. Tamiment Institute. New York.

Robert Schilling Collection, 1852-1922. State Historical Society of Wisconsin, Madison, Wisconsin.

Emil Seidel Collection. Milwaukee County Historical Society, Milwaukee, Wisconsin.

Algie M. and May Wood Simons Collection. State Historical Society of Wisconsin, Madison, Wisconsin.

Socialist Party Collection, 1900- . Duke University Library, Durham, North Carolina.

Socialist Party Collection. Municipal File. Duke University Library, Durham, North Carolina.

Socialist Party Collection. National Office File, 1896-1922. Duke University Library, Durham, North Carolina.

Socialist Party Collection. State and Local. Wisconsin, 1898-1920. Duke University Library, Durham, North Carolina.

Socialist Party Collection. Milwaukee County Historical Society.

Socialist Party Collection. Milwaukee Public Library.

Socialist Party Collection. Tamiment Institute. New York.

Norman M. Thomas Collection. New York Public Library.

B. C. Vladeck Collection. Tamiment Institute. New York.

Ernest Untermann Collection. Milwaukee County Historical Society.

William English Walling Collection. State Historical Society of Wisconsin, Madison, Wisconsin.

John M. Work Collection. Milwaukee Public Library.

John M. Work Collection. State Historical Society of Wisconsin, Madison, Wisconsin.

World War One Dissenters Collection. University of Chicago Library, Chicago, Illinois.

GOVERNMENT DOCUMENTS

New York. Senate. Report of the Joint Legislative Committee Investigating Seditious Activities, *Revolutionary Radicalism.* 4 vols. Albany, 1920.

U.S. Congress. House. Committee on Immigration. *Hearings on Dillingham Bill, S. 3175, to Regulate the Immigration of Aliens to and the Residence of Aliens in the United States.* 62d Cong., 2d sess., 1912.

———. Committee on Rules. *Hearings on House Concurrent Resolution No. 6 for the Appointment of a Committee of Investigation.* 62d Cong., 1st sess., 1911.

———. Committee on Rules. *Hearings on House Resolutions 409 and 433: The Strike at Lawrence.* 62d Cong., 2d sess., 1912.

———. *Hearings before the Special Committee Appointed under the Authority of House Resolution No. 6 Concerning the Right of Vic-*

tor L. Berger to be Sworn in as a Member of the Sixty-Sixth Congress. 2 vols. Washington, D.C., 1919.

U.S. *Congressional Record.* Vols. 47-49, Vol. 59.

United States of America v. *Victor L. Berger, Adolph Germer, J. Louis Engdahl, William F. Kruse and Irwin St. John Tucker.* District Court of the United States, Northern District of Illinois, Eastern Division (1918-1919). 5 vols. (Stenographic typescript.)

Wisconsin, *Blue Book.* Vols. 36-40.

NEWSPAPERS AND PERIODICALS

American Socialist, 1914-1917.
American Socialist Official Business Supplement, 1914-1917.
The Bulletin, 1917-1919.
The Class Struggle, 1917-1919.
The Commonwealth, 1918-1920.
The Eye Opener, 1917-1919.
Intercollegiate Socialist Review, 1913-1920 (became *The Socialist Review* in 1919).
International Socialist Review, 1900-1918.
The Liberator, 1918-1920.
The Masses, 1913-1917.
Milwaukee *Free Press,* 1910.
Milwaukee *Journal,* 1910, 1918-1919.
Milwaukee *Leader,* 1911-1920.
The New Appeal, 1918-1920.
The New Review, 1913-1916.
New York *Call,* 1910-1912, 1917-1919.
The Party Builder, 1912-1914.
Political Action, 1910-1911.
The Revolutionary Age, 1918-1919.
Social-Democratic Herald, 1900-1913.
Socialist Party Official Bulletin, 1910-1913.
Voice of the People, 1910-1920 (published during the Milwaukee election campaigns only).

PROCEEDINGS AND MINUTES

Socialist Party. *Minutes* of the Joint Conference of the National Executive Committee and State Secretaries, August, 1918.
————. *Minutes* of the National Committee, 1914.
————. *Proceedings* of the National Congress, 1910.
————. *Proceedings* of the National Conventions, 1901-1920.

PAMPHLETS AND REPORTS

Berger, Victor L. *Madam, How Will You Feed Your Family?* Chicago: Socialist Party, 1910.
————. *What Should We Do to be Saved.* Milwaukee: Social-Democratic Pub., 1910.
Hillquit, Morris. *The American Socialists and the War.* New York: Rand School of Social Science, 1917.
————. *The Immediate Issue.* New York: The Socialist: 1919.
————, and Augustus P. Gardner. *Must We Arm?* New York: Rand School of Social Science, 1915.
Mills, Ethelwyn, ed. *Legislative Program of the Socialist Party: Record of the Work of the Socialist Representatives in State Legislatures, 1899-1913.* Chicago: Socialist Party, 1914.
Social Democracy. *Red Book.* Terre Haute: Debs Publishing Co., 1900.
Social Democratic Party, Milwaukee County. *Campaign Manual,* 1912.
Socialist Party. *Campaign Book,* 1908-1920.
————. *Congressional Manual,* 1904-1920.
————. *Constitution,* 1901-1920.
————. *Court Rulings upon Indictments, Search Warrants, Habeas Corpus, Mailing Privileges: Growing Out of Alleged Offences Against Draft and Espionage Acts.* Chicago: Socialist Party, 1918.
————. *Manifesto of the Socialist Party.* Chicago: Socialist Party, 1919.
————. *Report of the Socialist Party of the United States to the International Socialist Congress at Copenhagen,* 1910.
————. *Socialism in the United States Congress: The Work of Victor L. Berger.* Chicago: Socialist Party, 1912.

The Trial of Scott Nearing and the American Socialist Society. New York: Rand School of Social Science, 1919.

National Civil Liberties Bureau. *War-Time Prosecutions and Mob Violence*. New York: National Civil Liberties Bureau, March, 1919.

CONTEMPORARY WORKS

The *American Labor Year Book*. New York: Rand School of Social Science, 1916-1919.

Berger, Victor L. *Broadsides*. Milwaukee: Social-Democratic Pub. Co., 1912.

———. *Voice and Pen of Victor L. Berger*. Edited by Elizabeth H. Thomas and Meta Berger. Milwaukee: Milwaukee *Leader*, 1929.

Bourne, Randolph. *The War and the Intellectuals*. New York: American Union Against Militarism, June 1917.

De Leon, Daniel. *Berger's Hits and Misses*. New York: New York Labor News Co., 1917.

De Leon, Solon, ed. *American Labor Who's Who*. New York: Hanford Press, 1925.

Ghent, William James. *The Reds Bring Reaction*. Princeton: Princeton University Press, 1923.

Howe, Frederic. *Wisconsin: An Experiment in Democracy*. New York: Charles Scribner's Sons, 1912.

Hunter, Robert. *Violence and the Labor Movement*. New York: Macmillan Co., 1914.

St. John, Vincent. *The I.W.W.: Its History, Structure, and Methods*. Rev. ed. Chicago: The Industrial Workers of World, 1919.

Some Anti-Socialist Voices of the Press on Victor L. Berger and His Work in Congress. Milwaukee: Social-Democratic Pub. Co., 1912.

Spargo, John. *Americanism and Social Democracy*. New York: Harper and Bros., Pubs., 1918.

Trachtenberg, Alexander, ed. *The American Socialists and the War*. New York: Rand School of Social Science, 1917.

Walling, William English, ed. *The Socialists and the War: a Documentary Statement of the Position of the Socialists of all Countries, with Special Reference to their Peace Policy*. New York: Henry Holt and Co., 1915.

————. *Socialism as It Is: A Survey of the World-Wide Revolutionary Movement*. New York: Macmillan Co., 1912.

AUTOBIOGRAPHIES AND MEMOIRS

Ameringer, Oscar. *If You Don't Weaken*. New York: Henry Holt and Co., 1940.

Bruce, William G. "Memories of William G. Bruce," *Wisconsin Magazine of History* 28 (September 1934): 42-65.

Creel, George. *The War the World and Wilson*. New York: Harper and Bros., Pubs., 1920.

Cross, Leslie. "The Milwaukee *Leader,* an Unusual Newspaper," *Historical Messenger* (Milwaukee) 17 (December 1961): 11-16.

Gitlow, Benjamin. *The Whole of their Lives: Communism in America—A Personal History*. New York: Charles Scribner's Sons, 1948.

Gompers, Samuel. *Seventy Years of Life and Labour*. 2 vols. London: Hurst and Blackett, Ltd., 1925.

Haywood, William D. *Bill Haywood's Book*. New York: International Publishers, 1929.

Hillquit, Morris. *Loose Leaves from a Busy Life*. New York: Macmillan Co., 1934.

Maurer, James Hudson. *It Can Be Done*. New York: Rand School of Social Science, 1938.

Poor, Gilbert H. *Interesting Sketches: Blazing a Trail, The Story of a Pioneer Socialist Agitator*, 1911.

Russell, Charles Edward. *Bare Hands and Stone Walls: Some Recollections of a Sideline Reformer*. New York: Charles Scribner's Sons, 1933.

Spargo, John. "Memoir." New York: Oral Research Office, Columbia University, 1950.

Villard, Oswald Garrison. *Fighting Years: Memoirs of a Liberal Editor*. New York: Harcourt, Brace and Co., 1939.

Waldman, Louis. *Labor Lawyer*. New York: E. P. Dutton and Co., Inc., 1944.

Work, John M. "The First World War," *Wisconsin Magazine of History* 41 (Autumn 1957): 32-44.

CONTEMPORARY ARTICLES

"A Neat Minority," *Saturday Evening Post* 183 (31 December 1910): 23.

"Advance of Socialism in the United States," *Chatauquan* 64 (September 1911): 18-19.

"The Berger Decision," *New Republic* 25 (23 February 1921): 360-361.

Berger, Victor L. "Socialism, the Logical Outcome of Progressivism," *American Magazine* 75 (November 1912): 19-21.

———. "What is the Matter with Milwaukee," *The Independent,* 68 (21 April 1910): 840-843.

"The Bouncing of Berger," *Literary Digest* 63 (8 November 1919): 20.

Brown, Rome G. "The Disloyalty of Socialism," *American Law Review* 53 (September-October 1919): 681-710.

Brunchen, Ernest. "Germans in America," *Annual Report of the American Historical Association for 1898.* Washington: Government Printing Office, 1899.

Carroll, Thomas F. "Freedom of Speech and Press in War Time: The Espionage Act," *Michigan Law Review* 17 (June 1919): 621-665.

Casson, Herbert N. "Socialism, its Growth and its Leaders," *Muncy's Magazine* 33 (June 1905): 290-298.

Chafee, Zechariah, Jr. "The Milwaukee *Leader* Case," *Nation* 112 (23 March 1921): 428-429.

"Cheerful Destroyers," *Nation* 88 (27 May 1909): 527-528.

Collier, John. "Experiment in Milwaukee," *Harper's Weekly* 55 (12 August 1911): 11.

"Congress and Mr. Berger," *The Public* 22 (24 May 1919): 536.

"Currents in American Socialism," *Nation* 92 (15 June 1911): 594-595.

Debs, Eugene V. "How I Became a Socialist," *The Comrade* 1 (April 1902): 146-148.

"Debs, Seidel and the Socialist Dissensions," *Current Literature* 53 (July 1912): 35-38.

Douglas, Paul H. "The Socialist Vote in the Municipal Elections of 1917," *National Municipal Review* 7 (March 1918): 131-139.

England, George A. "Milwaukee Socialists and Government," *American Review of Reviews* 42 (November 1910): 445-455.

Ghent, W. J. "The Collapse of Socialism in the United States," *Current History* 24 (May 1926): 242-246.

Grendon, Felix. "In Defense of Socialism," *New Republic* 10 (7 April 1917): 297-298.

Hackett, Francis. "How Milwaukee Takes the War," *New Republic* 6 (17 July 1915): 272-273.

Heath, Frederic. "How I Became a Socialist," *The Comrade* 2 (April 1903): 154-155.

"Hillquit Memorial Issue," *New Leader,* 6 October 1934.

Holmes, Fred L. "Socialist Legislators at Work," *The Independent* 70 (23 March 1911): 592-594.

Howe, Frederick C. "Milwaukee: A Socialist City," *The Outlook* 95 (25 June 1910): 411-421.

Hoxie, Robert F. "The Rising Tide of Socialism: A Study," *Journal of Political Economy* 19 (October 1911): 609-631.

"International League of Peace," *Survey* 34 (8 August 1915): 293.

Karsner, David. "Passing of American Socialism," *Current History* 20 (June 1924): 402-407.

"Larger Bearings of the McNamara Case, a Symposium," *Survey* 27 (29 December 1911): 1422.

Lenroot, I. L. "War Loyalty of Wisconsin," *Forum* 59 (June 1918): 695-702.

"Milwaukee," *The Independent* 68 (14 April 1910): 819.

"Milwaukee Deserves Better Luck," *Wilshire's* 16 (April 1912): 6-7.

"Mr. Burleson to Rule the Press," *Literary Digest* 60 (6 October 1917): 12.

Myers, Gustavus. "Why Idealists Quit the Socialist Party," *Nation* 104 (15 February 1917): 181-182.

Nock, Albert J. "Socialism in Milwaukee," *The Outlook* 107 (11 July 1914): 608-612.

Oneal, James. "Changing Fortunes of American Socialism," *Current History* 20 (April 1924): 92-97.

"Our Ferocious Sentences," *Nation* 107 (2 November 1918): 504.

"Plans of the First Socialist in Congress," *Survey* 26 (27 May 1911): 331.

"Press Censorship by Judicial Construction," *New Republic* 27 (30 March 1921): 123-125.

"Recent Decisions," *Columbia Law Review* 21, pt. 1 (April 1921): 387.

Simons, Algie M. "The Future of the Socialist Party," *New Republic* 9 (2 December 1916): 18-20.

————. "Pacifism vs. Revolution," *New Republic* 10 (24 March 1917): 220-221.

"The Socialist Vote in Wisconsin," *Wilshire's* 16 (December 1912): 3.

Spargo, John. "Victor Berger: First Socialist Congressman," *Survey* 25 (3 December 1910): 337-339.

Steffens, Lincoln. "Eugene V. Debs on What the Matter is in America and What to Do About It," *Everybody's Magazine* 19 (October 1908): 455-469.

Stewart, Charles D. "Prussianizing Wisconsin," *Atlantic Monthly* 123 (January 1919): 99-105.

"Tide of Socialism," *World's Work* 23 (January 1912): 252-253.

"Victor Berger Reproaches his German Friends for Inconsistency," *Current Opinion* 59 (August 1915): 80.

"Victor Berger, the Organizer of the Socialist Victory in Milwaukee," *Current Literature* 49 (September 1910): 265-269.

"Victor L. Berger," *American Magazine* 70 (May 1910): 41-43.

Villard, Oswald Garrison. "The Berger Victory," *Nation* 109 (27 December 1919): 820-821.

Walling, William English. "Crisis in the Socialist Party," *The Independent* 72 (16 May 1912): 1047-1051.

Watkins, Gordon. "The Present Status of Socialism in the United States," *Atlantic Monthly* 124 (December 1919): 821-830.

"Why Milwaukee Insists on Berger," *Literary Digest* 64 (3 January 1920): 19-20.

Yarros, Victor S. "Chicago Socialist Trial," *Nation* 108 (25 January 1919): 116-118.

BIOGRAPHIES, MONOGRAPHS AND HISTORIES

Bell, Daniel. *Marxian Socialism in the United States.* Princeton: Princeton University Press, 1967.

Brissenden, P. F. *The I.W.W.: A Study in American Syndicalism.* New York: Columbia University Press, 1919.

Carlson, Oliver. *Brisbane: A Candid Biography.* New York: Stackpole Sons, 1937.

Chafee, Zechariah, Jr. *Free Speech in the United States*. Cambridge: Harvard University Press, 1942.

Child, Clifton James. *The German-Americans in Politics*. Madison: University of Wisconsin Press, 1939.

Commons, John R., ed. *History of Labor in the United States*. Vol. 3: Don D. Lescohier, and Elizabeth Brandeis. *Working Conditions: Labor Legislation*. Vol. 4: Selig Perlman and Philip Taft. *Labor Movements, 1896-1932*. New York: Macmillan Co., 1935.

Conlin, Joseph R. *Bread and Roses Too: Studies of the Wobblies*. Westport: Greenwood Pub. Corp., 1969.

Cross, Ira B. *A History of the Labor Movement in California*. ("University of California Publications in Economics," 14) Berkeley: University of California Press, 1935.

Douglas, Paul H. *Real Wages in the United States, 1890-1926*. Boston: Houghton Mifflin Co., 1930.

Dowell, Eldridge Foster. *A History of Criminal Syndicalism Legislation in the United States*. Baltimore: Johns Hopkins University Press, 1939.

Draper, Theodore. *The Roots of American Communism*. New York: Viking Press, 1957.

Dubofsky, Melvyn. *We Shall Be All: A History of the I.W.W.* Chicago: Quadrangle Books, Inc., 1969.

Fainsod, Merle. *International Socialism and the World War*. Cambridge: Harvard University Press, 1935.

Fine, Nathan. *Labor and Farmer Parties in the United States, 1828-1928*. New York: Rand School of Social Science, 1928.

Ginger, Ray. *Eugene V. Debs: A Biography*. New York: Collier Books, 1962.

Hicks, Granville. *John Reed: The Making of a Revolutionary*. New York: Macmillan Co., 1936.

Hillquit, Nina. "Morris Hillquit, Pioneer of American Socialism." Typescript in Morris Hillquit Collection, State Historical Society of Wisconsin.

Hoan, Daniel W. *City Government: The Record of the Milwaukee Experiment*. New York: Harcourt, Brace and Co., 1936.

Hobsbawm, Eric J. *Primitive Rebels*. New York: W. W. Norton and Co., Inc., 1959.

Johnson, Donald. *The Challenge to American Freedoms: World War I and the Rise of the American Civil Liberties Union*. Louisville: University of Kentucky Press, 1963.

Kipnis, Ira. *The American Socialist Movement, 1897-1912*. New York: Columbia University Press, 1952.

Korman, Gerd. *Industrialization, Immigrants, and Americanizers: The View from Milwaukee, 1866-1921*. Madison: State Historical Society of Wisconsin, 1967.

Kreuter, Kent and Gretchen. *An American Dissenter: the Life of Algie Martin Simons*. Lexington: University of Kentucky Press, 1969.

Laslett, John. *Labor and the Left: A Study of Socialist and Radical Influences in the American Labor Movement, 1881-1924*. New York: Basic Books, 1970.

Leopold, Richard W. *The Growth of American Foreign Policy*. New York: Alfred A. Knopf, 1962.

Lewis, Oscar. *La Vida: a Puerto Rican Family in the Culture of Poverty—San Juan and New York*. New York: Random House, 1965.

Lorwin, Lewis L. *The American Federation of Labor: History, Policies and Prospects*. Washington: The Brookings Institute, 1933.

Margulies, Herbert F. *The Decline of the Progressive Movement in Wisconsin, 1890-1920*. Madison: State Historical Society of Wisconsin, 1968.

Maxwell, Robert S. *La Follette and the Rise of the Progressives in Wisconsin*. Madison: State Historical Society of Wisconsin, 1956.

Mock, James. *Censorship, 1917*. Princeton: Princeton University Press, 1941.

Moore, R. Laurence. *European Socialists and the American Promised Land*. New York: Oxford University Press, 1970.

Murray, Robert K. *Red Scare: A Study in National Hysteria, 1919-1920*. New York: McGraw-Hill Book Co., 1964.

Oneal, James, and G. A. Werner. *American Communism: A Critical Analysis of its Origins, Development and Programs*. New York: E. P. Dutton and Co., Inc., 1947.

Patterson, G. J. *Free Speech and Free Press*. Boston: Little, Brown and Co., 1939.

Paxson, Frederic Logan. *American Democracy and the World War*. Vol. 1. Boston: Houghton Mifflin Co., 1936.

Peterson, H. C. and Gilbert C. Fite. *Opponents of War, 1917-1918*. Madison: University of Wisconsin Press, 1957.

Quint, Howard H. *The Forging of American Socialism: Origins of the Modern Movement*. Columbia: University of South Carolina Press, 1953.

Renshaw, Patrick. *The Wobblies*. New York: Anchor Books, 1968.

Rogoff, Harry. *An East Side Epic: The Life and Work of Meyer London*. New York: Vanguard Press, 1930.

Still, Bayrd. *Milwaukee: the History of a City,* Madison: State Historical Society, 1948.

Shannon, David A. *The Socialist Party of America: A History*. New York: Macmillan Co., 1955.

Symes, Lillian, and Clement Travers. *Rebel America: The Story of Social Revolt in the United States*. New York: Harper and Bros., Pubs., 1934.

Taft, Philip. *The American Federation of Labor in the Time of Gompers*. New York: Harper and Bros., Pubs., 1957.

Wachman, Marvin. *The History of the Social-Democratic Party of Milwaukee, 1897-1910.* ("Illinois Studies in the Social Sciences," 28), Urbana: University of Illinois Press, 1945.

Weinstein, James. *The Decline of Socialism in America, 1912-1925*. New York: Monthly Review Press, 1967.

Weber, Max. *From Max Weber: Essays in Sociology,* H. H. Gerth and C. Wright Mills, eds. New York: Oxford University Press, 1946.

Wittke, Carl. *We Who Built America*. Rev. ed. Cleveland: Case Western Reserve Press, 1964.

SECONDARY ARTICLES

Caldwell, Louis. "Freedom of Speech and Radio Broadcasting," *Annals of American Academy of Political and Social Science* 177 (January 1935): 179-207.

Cantor, Milton. "The Radical Confrontation with Foreign Policy: War and Revolution, 1914-1920," in Alfred F. Young, ed., *Dissent: Explorations in the History of American Radicalism*. DeKalb: Northern Illinois University Press, 1968.

Cohn, Morris E. "The Censorship of Radical Materials by the Post Office," *St. Louis Law Review* 17 (February 1932): 95-119.

Currie, Harold W. "A Socialist Edits the Detroit Times," *Michigan History* 52 (Spring 1968): 1-11.

———. "Allan L. Benson, Salesman of Socialism, 1902-1916," *Labor History* 11 (Summer 1970): 285-303.

Deutsch, Eberhard P. "Freedom of the Press and the Mails," *Michigan Law Review* 36 (March 1938): 703-751.

Falk, Karen. "Public Opinion in Wisconsin during World War I," *Wisconsin Magazine of History* 25 (June 1942): 389-407.

Glaser, William A. "Algie M. Simons and Marxism in America," *Mississippi Valley Historical Review* 41 (December 1954): 419-434.

Hendrickson, Kenneth E., Jr. "The Pro-War Socialists and the Drive for Industrial Democracy, 1917-1920," *Labor History* 11 (Summer 1970): 304-322.

Korman, Gerd. "Political Loyalties, Immigrant Traditions, and Reform: the Wisconsin German-American Press and Progressivism, 1909-12," *Wisconsin Magazine of History* 40 (Spring 1957): 161-168.

Lerner, Max. "Victor L. Berger," *Dictionary of American Biography* 11, Supp. 1 (1944): 72-75.

McNaught, Kenneth. "American Progressives and the Great Society," *Journal of American History* 53 (December 1966): 504-520.

Miller, Sally M. "A Socialist Represents Milwaukee," *Historical Messenger* (Milwaukee) 22 (December 1966): 132-138.

———. "Socialist Party Decline and World War I," *Science and Society* 34 (Winter 1970): 398-411.

Muzik, Edward J. "Victor Berger's Early Career," *Historical Messenger* (Milwaukee) 17 (March 1961): 15-20.

———. Victor L. Berger: Congress and the Red Scare," *Wisconsin Magazine of History* 47 (Summer 1964): 309-318.

Nash, Roderick. "Victor L. Berger: Making Marx Respectable," *Wisconsin Magazine of History* 47 (Summer 1964): 301-308.

Olson, Frederick I. "Victor Berger: Socialist Congressman," *Wisconsin Academy of Sciences, Arts and Letters* 58 (1970): 27-38.

———. "The Socialist Party and the Unions in Milwaukee, 1900-1912," *Wisconsin Magazine of History* 64 (Winter 1960-61): 110-116.

Reinders, Robert C. "Daniel W. Hoan and the Milwaukee Socialist Party during the First World War," *Wisconsin Magazine of History* 36 (Autumn 1952): 48-55.

Saloutos, Theodore. "The Greeks of Milwaukee," *Wisconsin Magazine of History* 53 (Spring 1970): 175-193.

Shannon, David A. "The Socialist Party before the First World War:

An Analysis," *Mississippi Valley Historical Review* 38 (September 1951): 279-288.

Taft, Philip. "The Federal Trials of the I.W.W.," *Labor History* 3 (Winter 1962): 57-91.

Weinstein, James. "The Socialist Party: Its Roots and Strength, 1912-1919," *Studies on the Left* 1 (Winter 1960): 5-27.

CORRESPONDENCE

Lewis, Marx (Congressional Secretary to Victor L. Berger), 17 February 1965, 17 March 1965.

Thomas, Norman M., 15 December 1964.

Zeidler, Frank P. (Socialist Mayor of Milwaukee), 11 March 1961.

DISSERTATIONS

Anderson, Paul H. "The Attitude of the American Leftist Leaders toward the Russian Revolution." Ph.D. dissertation, University of Notre Dame, 1942.

Bedford, Henry F. "A Case Study in Hysteria: Victor L. Berger, 1917-1921." Master's thesis; University of Wisconsin, 1953.

Hingtgen, David V. "Victor L. Berger and *The Milwaukee Leader*." Master's thesis; Marquette University, 1962.

Iverson, Robert William. "Morris Hillquit: American Social Democrat." Abstract of Ph.D. dissertation. State University of Iowa, 1951.

Muzik, Edward John. "Victor L. Berger, a Biography." Ph.D. dissertation, Northwestern University, 1960.

Olson, Frederick I. "The Milwaukee Socialists, 1897-1941." Ph.D. dissertation. Harvard University, 1952.

Seyler, William C. "The Rise and Decline of the Socialist Party in the United States." Ph.D. dissertation, Duke University, 1952.

Smith, Harold Sherburn. "William James Ghent, Reformer and Historian." Ph.D. dissertation, University of Wisconsin, 1957.

Walden, Daniel. "W. J. Ghent: The Growth of an Intellectual Radical, 1892-1917." Ph.D. dissertation, New York University, 1964.

Index